UNDERSTANDING SPORTS COACHING

Sports coaching is as dependent on utilising good teaching and social practices as it is about expertise in sport skills and tactics.

Quality sports coaches commonly engage in practices usually associated with teaching such as reflection, feedback and instructional methods. However, many do so implicitly and without an explicit understanding of the complex interplay between coach, player, content and social context.

Understanding Sports Coaching provides an innovative introduction to the theory and practice of sports coaching, highlighting the social, cultural and pedagogical concepts underpinning good practice.

The book aims to deepen coaches' understanding of the coaching process in order to develop coaching programmes that are designed to get the very best out of athletes. It explores many aspects of coaching practice including:

- Athlete motivation
- Viewing the athlete as a learner
- Instructional methods
- Coaches' content knowledge
- Reflection
- Coaching philosophy and ethics

The book includes practical exercises to highlight issues faced by sports coaches. This book is essential reading for students of sports coaching and for professional coaches looking to develop their skills.

Tania Cassidy is a Lecturer in Pedagogy, at the University of Otago, New Zealand. **Robyn Jones** is a Reader in Sports Coaching (Department of Education), at the University of Bath, UK. **Paul Potrac** is a Lecturer in Sports Coaching, at the University of Otago, New Zealand.

UNDERSTANDING SPORTS COACHING

THE SOCIAL, CULTURAL AND PEDAGOGICAL FOUNDATIONS OF COACHING PRACTICE

Tania Cassidy, Robyn Jones
and Paul Potrac

Routledge
Taylor & Francis Group

LONDON AND NEW YORK

First published 2004
by Routledge
2 Park Square, Milton Park, Abingdon, Oxon OX14 4RN

Simultaneously published in the USA and Canada
by Routledge
270 Madison Ave, New York, NY 10016

Reprinted 2005(twice), 2006 (twice)

Routledge is an imprint of the Taylor & Francis group, an informa business

Typeset in Bell Gothic by Keystroke, Jacaranda Lodge, Wolverhampton
Printed and bound in Great Britain by TJ International Ltd, Padstow, Cornwall

British Library Cataloguing in Publication Data
A catalogue record for this book is available from the British Library

Library of Congress Cataloging in Publication Data
A catalog record for this book has been requested

ISBN10: 0–415–30739–2 (hbk)
ISBN10: 0–415–30740–6 (pbk)

ISBN13: 978–0–415–30739–0 (hbk)
ISBN13: 978–0–415–30740–6 (pbk)

In memory of our grandparents

Evelyn Cassidy
Jozef Potrac

TC: To my extended family, I owe you everything, your unwavering support and love is cherished in a way that is indescribable. To my friends, thanks for your understanding and patience – I can now come out to play. To the 'girlz' in the Acton flat, thanks for letting me 'doss', and use your kitchen table to write the first drafts

RJ: To Theresa, Savanna, Seren and Siân

PP: To Mum, Dad, Lisa, Nan, Nan and Grandad

▼ CONTENTS

Acknowledgements   xi

Introduction   1
Vignette: how it all started   2
The aims of the book   4
Why is the book needed?   5
Current practice and the value of reflection   6
Who is the book for?   8
How is the book organized?   9
Postscript   10

SECTION ONE: THE COACH   11

Chapter One
Reflection   13
Introduction   13
What is reflection?   15
Why is it useful to become a reflective coach?   17
Becoming a reflective coach: issues to consider   18
Concluding thoughts   24

Chapter Two
Coaching methods   26
Introduction   26
The relationship between coaching and teaching   27
An overview of methods   29
Taking a circumspect view of methods   33
Concluding thoughts   37

Chapter Three
Providing feedback to athletes   38
Introduction   38

Providing verbal feedback . . . it's not that straightforward   40
Intrinsic feedback   44
Concluding thoughts   44

Chapter Four
Quality in coaching   46
Introduction   46
A good coach   47
An effective coach   47
Quality in coaching   48
Why bother with the notion of quality?   50
Concluding thoughts   52

Chapter Five
Developing a coaching philosophy   53
Introduction   53
What is a coaching philosophy and why do coaches need to develop
   one?   55
Problematizing coaching philosophies   56
Developing functional, flexible philosophies   59
Concluding thoughts   62

End of Section One: Tasks   63

SECTION TWO: THE ATHLETES   **65**

Chapter Six
Understanding the learning process   67
Introduction   67
Vignette 1: coaching the U21s   69
Multiple orientations to learning   71
Vignette 2: unwinding after the training session   77
Consequences for the learner   78
Concluding thoughts   81

Chapter Seven
'Developing' athletes   82
Introduction   82
Developmentalism – what is it?   82
What does development do?   84
Doing development differently   88
Concluding thoughts   89

Chapter Eight
Understanding athletes' motivation 90
Introduction 90
What is motivation? 92
Theories of motivation 93
Exploring the social nature of athlete motivation 98
Concluding thoughts 104

Chapter Nine
Understanding athletes' identities 106
Introduction 106
What is identity? 107
Gendered identity 108
Sexualized identity 111
Ethnic identity 115
Concluding thoughts 117

End of Section Two: Task 118

SECTION THREE: COACHING CONTENT 121

Chapter Ten
Examining coaches' content knowledge 123
Introduction 123
What is content knowledge? 124
Additional things to consider when thinking about content knowledge 125
(Re)thinking coaches' knowledge 128
Concluding thoughts 129

Chapter Eleven
Assessing athletes' understanding 130
Introduction 130
The purposes of assessment (*Why?*) 132
Forms of assessment (*When?*) 132
Meaningful and authentic forms of assessment (*How?*) 134
Concluding thoughts 138

Chapter Twelve
Coaching athletes with a disability: exploring issues of content 139
Introduction 139
Viewing athletes with a disability 140
Integrating athletes with and without a disability 142
Concluding thoughts 145

End of Section Three: Tasks 146

Chapter Thirteen
The discourses of coaching   151
Introduction   151
What is discourse?   152
Why study discourse in the coaching context?   152
The dominant discourse of 'coaching science': performance,
   rationality and a hierarchical coach–athlete relationship   154
The effect of power-dominated discourse on athletes   156
An alternative coaching discourse   159
Concluding thoughts   160

Chapter Fourteen
Coaching ethics   162
Introduction   162
Ethical codes and ethical issues in coaching   164
Problematizing ethics: moving toward virtues-based conduct
   (McNamee 1998)   166
Personalizing coaches' ethical behaviour   170
Concluding thoughts   173

Chapter Fifteen
Coaching holistically: why do it and how can we frame it?   174
Introduction   174
The traditional model of multi-disciplinary coaching and coach
   education   175
The case for coaching holistically   177
Conceptualizing a holistic approach   179

Chapter Sixteen
Coaching holistically: a way forward for coach education   181
Introduction   181
A critical task-based approach   183
A narrative approach   184
A problem-based learning (PBL) strategy   186
A mentorship scheme   187
Concluding thoughts   189

End of Section Four: Tasks   190

Bibliography   193
Index   209

▼ ACKNOWLEDGEMENTS

Many people have knowingly, or not, contributed to the ideas presented in this book. We acknowledge the hundreds of undergraduate students who, over the years, have enrolled, willingly or not, in PHSE 201. They have been the catalysts for the book, as well as the 'guinea pigs' for the ideas in some of the chapters. We thank the representative coaches of the Otago Rugby Football Union who participated in the CoDe programme and, as a result, trialled some of the ideas discussed in this book. Their enthusiasm was infectious and their feedback on the ideas invaluable. A special thanks to Steve Martin for supporting the development of the CoDe programme. Also we acknowledge the assistance Ihi Heke and Cliff Mallett gave us when we were at an impasse, and Emma Neale when we were editing the chapters. Finally, we are grateful to our colleagues at the School of Physical Education, in particular Steve Jackson, Mike Sam, Olivia Maclaren, Rick Shuttleworth, Mark Falcous and Ken Hodge for agreeing to be the 'models', and to Chris Sullivan and Hamish Gould for their expertise in photography and graphics respectively.

INTRODUCTION

■ Vignette: how it all started   2

■ The aims of the book   4

■ Why is the book needed?   5

■ Current practice and the value of reflection   6

■ Who is the book for?   8

■ How is the book organized?   9

■ Postscript   10

VIGNETTE: HOW IT ALL STARTED

Tania

For five years I have been lecturing in a school of physical education (it could equally be described as a department of human movement, exercise science or kinesiology) where I teach a compulsory pedagogy course to approximately 220 undergraduates. The course has not been particularly popular with students, the most common objection being – 'I'm not going to be a teacher, so why do I have to do pedagogy?' Over the years I have tried different strategies in an effort to make the course more obviously relevant to students without compromising its educational content. Many times I've stressed that while the content focuses on educational and, to a lesser degree, sociological concepts, the course is relevant for human movement specialists in general, since the notions and ideas discussed govern much human behaviour. Until the fifth year of teaching the course I had, in the main, relied on the students themselves to make the links between the concepts examined and an area that particularly interested them if they were not considering becoming a teacher. It was clear from the student evaluations that this strategy was not successful.

In 2002, I decided to contextualize the content of the course in sports coaching. I based this decision on the assumption that most of the students would have had some experience of being coached or of being a coach, hence, could better relate to the subject and the linked conceptual matter. It was also much easier to engage with contemporary issues using a sports coaching context, given the coverage of sport by the media and its omnipresence in modern-day society. To hook the students in the first lecture, I asked them to list the characteristics of the person they considered to have been their best teacher. Then, I asked them to do the same for someone they considered to have been their best coach. When both lists were compiled and compared, it became obvious that they shared many similar characteristics. It was my intention that the students, through completing this task, would begin to see the connection between pedagogy and the wider world of sport.

In the second lecture, I introduced another exercise aimed at guiding the students to further recognize the apparent invisibility of critical sociological and educational ideas in the sports coaching context, and to see how this void may be detrimental to coaches and athletes. First, I provided the students with the following scenario: each was the coach of a team of elite athletes who could call upon unlimited resources. Despite being a very good team on paper, it was not performing very well. I asked the students to list the professionals/specialists they could call on in an effort to improve the team's performance. When collated, the final list contained a predominance of sport scientists such as physiotherapists, nutritionists, fitness trainers, biomechanists, motion analysts and exercise physiologists, and, when a social scientist was included, it was in the form of a sports psychologist. There was no mention of considering the coach as an educator, and therefore there was no

2

suggestion that a specialist could examine the educational and social practices of coaching. Plainly, the students' conception of the coaching role remained a narrow one, and, while their lack of recognition did not surprise me, it did get me thinking about why this might be so.

Robyn

When Tania and I shared a 'working coffee' one day, she told me of her intended strategy to hook students into pedagogy through the use of the sports coaching context. As a lecturer in coaching, she asked if I knew of any potential texts or readings that would be informative for the course and the slant it was taking. Unfortunately, I knew only too well that there was no published material that adopted a sociological and educational approach to coaching, although my developing work with a small group of others was beginning to theorize and provide empirical support for such a position. Not much earlier, I had begun to teach my sports coaching units using sociological and educational concepts, in addition to using the usual psychological and bio-scientific theories. I did this because I believed that, ultimately, coaching is a social endeavour, and while sport-specific, organizational, physiological and psychological tools are necessary, if the coaches lack the sensitivity to act appropriately within a dynamic social and educational environment, they can struggle to achieve their intentions of improving the quality of both performance and participation.

Additionally, it seemed to me, albeit principally from anecdotal evidence, that very few people who enrol in coach education or sport science programmes actually learn much about the messy reality of coaching and how best to deal with it. Nor do they learn much about educational and sociological theories. Despite the amount of information given about the various aspects of the process, during formal tertiary study its impact on subsequent practice appears to be minimal. Common rebutals we hear are 'That just wouldn't work for me', or 'It's OK in theory, but what if . . .?' Consequently, tried and trusted methods gleaned from experience have tended to override both the integration of academic knowledge into coaching practice, and the innovation that reflection upon such applied knowledge can produce. In short, many coaches, wary of stepping outside a comfort zone of given drills and discourse, tend to coach the way they were coached. For this reason, coaching has often come to characterize a repetitive one-dimensional circle, as opposed to a progressive three-dimensional spiral.

Paul

Having previously worked extensively with Robyn on a critical examination of the coaching process, I was more than happy to agree to become involved in the project. With academic roots in the sociology of sport, I needed no convincing of the relevance of 'social things' in the coaching context, and had often found the lack of theoretical and considered thought to support such a position frustrating. From my previous work with elite coaches, it seemed to me that they often did use sociological and educational concepts in their practice, but in a haphazard, almost accidental, way. If such strategies could be better formalized and acknowledged, I have no doubt that practice could be improved, with something akin to the mythical 'X' factor being achieved!

Working together

Our joint belief in the value of both sociological and educational ideas to the coaching process was the germ of this project. As the three of us talked further about how relevant the concepts are to the pedagogical process, we became convinced that a book outlining this stance was necessary, so that students could better develop a sociologically and educationally informed sense of what it means to be a coach. This book is our response to that perceived need.

THE AIMS OF THE BOOK

Recent empirical research (Jones *et al.* 2004; Potrac 2001) indicates that good coaches can evaluate and rationalize their actions. They think about, and are aware of, their practice before, during and after the event: reflecting in some depth about plans, actions and consequences. Taking our lead from such findings, we believe that if coaches are to understand why they are doing what they are doing and the consequences of their actions, and if they are to appreciate the limits and possibilities of their practice, it is useful for them to have some understanding of social, cultural and educational concepts. The principal aim of this book is to highlight some of these concepts and to link them directly to the practice of coaching, as we believe that they fundamentally inform it. Hence, a tentative framework is placed on a field which has been accused of theoretical imprecision, speculation and assumption (Saury and Durand, 1998).

We recognize that good coaches probably already use some educational and sociological concepts in their practice, which, in turn, wield considerable influence on their general coaching styles. However, the adoption of these concepts often occurs implicitly rather than explicitly and, as a consequence, leaves coaches unaware of the assumptions that inform their practices. By not questioning, and hence not engaging with these assumptions, practitioners make it difficult to systematically develop their programmes for the maximal benefit of their athletes; they also make it difficult for themselves to fully understand the ethical, moral and political consequences of their actions. Given that coaching does not occur in a social vacuum (Schempp 1998; Jones 2000), we also believe that the social and educational values that construct the person of the coach 'need careful and thoughtful [self] consideration if coaches are to act in enlightened effective ways' (Jones 2000: 39). Recognizing the constraints and possibilities for practice enables coaches to become aware of the suppressed culture of coaching rather than only of its visible, formal face (Grace 1998).

We recognize that building a purely theoretical case for the inclusion of sociological and educational concepts into coaching practice would, in all probability, have a limited impact on the practice of sports coaches. In an effort to give this book a wider application, we have provided practical exercises at the end of each section, to link the sociological and educational concepts to coaching practice. We hope that the exercises provided will resonate for coaches, as they are grounded in the messy reality of the coaching process itself. The aim of these exercises is to illustrate how the sociological and educational concepts discussed can be workably integrated into general practice and wider coach educational programmes, while also encouraging coaches to personally reflect on, and engage with, the technical, moral, ethical and political issues that occur in their own coaching contexts.

WHY IS THE BOOK NEEDED?

The principal rationale for writing this book comes from our difficulty as lecturers, researchers and coach educators to find coaching literature that is informed by sociological and educational perspectives. There is very little available literature that questions some of the taken-for-granted practices in coaching and acknowledges the complex reality within which coaches work (Côté et al. 1995). It has been argued that despite the recent increase in research on coaching, much of the work remains unproblematic and developmental in nature (Jones 2000; Jones et al. 2002; Jones and Cassidy 1999). As a result, the research often gives an 'oddly inhuman account of this most human of jobs' (Connell 1985: 4). However, this situation is being increasingly questioned (see Cross and Lyle 1999; Strean 1998; Jones 2000; Lyle 1999), with a call for coaching to be recognized as multivariate, interpersonal and dynamic; in effect this emphasizes the social within social cognition (Brustad and Weiss 1992). Such a stance implores us to avoid treating coaches as 'cardboard cut-outs' (Sparkes and Templin 1992: 118), and athletes as non-thinking pawns.

There is a small but growing number of coach educators and academics who currently engage with the sociology of coaching (see Jones and Armour 2000). Equally, there are a number who focus on the pedagogy of coaching (e.g. Kidman and Hanrahan 1997; Martens 1997). However, this latter group predominantly adopts a behaviourist teaching approach to the subject, and so concentrates on rather simplified 'how to' methods and effective coaching models. This differs from our interpretation of pedagogy, which we view as a problematic process that incorporates the interaction between how one learns, how one teaches, what is being taught (Lusted 1986) and the context in which it is being taught (Cassidy 2000). The key to adopting this view lies in making coaches aware of the social and educational dynamics which have created their identities and philosophies, and hence, their abilities to perform (Armour and Jones 2000). Developing such an awareness in coaches provides them with the ability to evaluate information from a range of sources, and the confidence and courage to take responsibility for decisions affecting their athletes.

We contend that a growing number of coaches want to develop athletes who can make decisions and adapt to changing situations on the field or the court (Kidman 2001). This trend implicitly supports the view that learning is less the reception of acts and facts, and more a social practice that implies the involvement of the whole person in relation not only to specific activities but also to social communities. In this respect, we agree that 'the study and education of the human is complex' (Zakus and Malloy 1996: 504) and it requires sensitivity, subtlety and subjectivity. If coaches want to produce decision-making athletes it is useful if they adopt coaching practices that take account of, and can facilitate, such a socially determined cognitive goal.

The significance of this book lies partly in response to Knudson and Morrison's (2002) call for a reality-based integrative approach to human movement. Such a stance is rooted in the belief that an interdisciplinary approach is imperative for understanding such a complex and dynamic activity as coaching, where, invariably, the whole is considerably greater than the sum of the constituent parts. Within this approach, the coach is viewed as a holistic problem-solver involved in the planning, prioritization, contextualization and orchestration of provision in an ever-changing environment. In this respect, it differs from the traditional approach to studying coaching from single and isolated sub-disciplinary perspectives.

Adopting such a framework means that our discussion can call on theoretical ideas from various disciplines as well as real-life sports coaching scenarios, as we seek to develop a holistic, credible view of the coaching process. However, despite our belief in the usefulness of an integrated approach to the coaching context, we cannot claim to wholly deliver it here. Rather, it is mentioned as a goal to which we aspire. Although a certain amount of integrating different disciplines is inherent in the book (i.e. the sociological and the educational), the principal aim here is to highlight the relevance of sociological and educational concepts to studying coaching, thus bringing different and previously lacking perspectives to the analytical table. Producing a truly integrated book, inclusive of all the disciplines that inform sports coaching, is another task for the future! We also acknowledge that the concepts selected for discussion in the book do not comprise all the related sociological or educational theory available, or all that could be applied to sports coaching. Rather we have selected concepts that reflect our preferences, and those that we consider could, even at the introductory level discussed here, directly assist coaching practitioners.

CURRENT PRACTICE AND THE VALUE OF REFLECTION

Recent empirical studies into coaches' knowledge has emphasized the importance of observing others, often respected mentors, in developing practice (Jones *et al*. 2004; Saury and Durand 1998; Côté *et al*. 1995). Although the expert coaches cited in these studies generally used observations as a foundation from which to develop their own philosophies and styles, the danger with an apprenticeship model lies in the production of robotic practitioners who accept without question the mode and manner of their mentors. Hence, there could be a tendency to adopt what Ziechner (1980) terms a 'utilitarian' teaching perspective, where the measure of good practice is the extent to which it solves the immediate problem at hand. It is merely a strategy that deals with the symptoms, that gets practitioners 'through the lesson' without major disruptions. The causes and consequences of behaviours, and whether understanding and consciousness develop, are barely considered, thus hindering fundamental progression in practice.

Recently one of us undertook a comparative review of two physical education texts authored by Tinning *et al*. (2001), and Siedentop and Tannehill (2000) respectively (Cassidy 2002). The review compared the paradigmatic positions of two prominent groups of scholars on teaching and learning physical education (see Kirk and Tinning 1990; McKay *et al*. 1990; O'Sullivan *et al*. 1992; Schempp 1987; Siedentop 1987). What was surprising when reviewing these two texts was that, despite the different leanings of the authors, a strong common theme emerged. Specifically, both used an idea advocated by Larry Locke, albeit interpreted slightly differently, as a basis from which to develop their positions. Tinning and co-authors attributed Locke with the belief that physical education was 'not so much bothered by poor teaching as it was by mindless teaching' (Tinning *et al*. 2001: 6). These scholars interpreted mindless teaching to mean unreflective teaching. Similarly, Siedentop and Tannehill's paraphrasing of Locke resulted in them claiming that '[i]t isn't bad teaching that plagues physical education so much as it is non-teaching' (2000: 3). Non-teaching in this context was taken to mean non-thinking teaching. Taking into account the differing paradigmatic starting points of these groups of scholars, the fact that they converged on this issue gives weight to the case that a basic barrier to achieving 'better' teaching, and corresponding learning, had been somewhat universally identified.

The concepts of 'mindless' teaching and 'non-thinking' teaching refer to the lack of consideration given to the teaching and learning process before beginning the act of teaching itself. The concepts attest to a lack of understanding of how students learn and why, of the micro and macro variables that impinge on this learning, and how teachers can best manage their complex and dynamic working environment to achieve desired results. Equally, coaches are guilty of giving little if any attention to understanding the teaching and learning process, what shapes it, and subsequently, how it can be done better.

Some recent coaching texts have included, and indeed emphasized, reflection as an element of good coaching practice (e.g. Kidman 2001; Kidman and Hanrahan 1997). However, such texts appear to hold that the reflective process begins and ends with the episodic act of coaching: for example, examining one's coaching style on a video, or thinking about which exercises worked well in a recent session. While we agree that reflection is an element of good coaching practice, we would argue that merely thinking about discrete events in coaching is not likely to lead to a deeper understanding of it. Reflection in coaching should comprise an in-depth examination of the complex pedagogical decisions that coaches are constantly faced with, as well as an engagement with the moral, social and political dimensions of coaching which inform how and why we coach as we do.

In a coaching world that is largely competency based, and where measurement takes precedence over process, coaches need to be encouraged to 'stand back and reflect upon the construction and application of their professional knowledge' (Hardy and Mawer 1999: 2). We hope this book will help coaches to achieve this; in other words, to understand why they coach as they do. We also hope that it will encourage and educate coaches to act in appropriate interpersonal ways, through addressing the twin fundamental questions of 'How do educational and sociological concepts inform my practice?' and 'What are the consequences of the way I coach?' Through addressing such questions, coaches expose their perceptions and beliefs to constructive criticism and evaluation, and they develop a heightened self-awareness which leads to a 'certain openness to new ideas [and] to alternatives to improvement' (Hellison and Templin 1991: 9).

WHO IS THE BOOK FOR?

The book is principally written for sports coaching students, whose numbers are rapidly rising as programmes related to coach education, sports science, kinesiology, and physical education proliferate in higher education institutions. It is also aimed at the teacher-education market, the students of which invariably become involved in coaching school sports teams. For undergraduate students of coaching, it can serve as an introductory manual to illustrate the social, cultural and educational nature of coaching, and how interacting educational and sociological philosophies can inform professional practice. Additionally, for beginning postgraduate students, the book may assist them to make links between theory and practice, and further develop their recognition that coaching can be a reflective endeavour. Since many sports science students are also working coaches, the book may give them greater awareness of the factors that influence their coaching, hopefully stimulating them to further evaluate their own practices, and where necessary consider alternatives.

We believe the book is applicable to both 'performance' and 'participation' coaches; a distinction underlined in the work of Lyle (2002). Although the use of such lines of demarcation could be viewed as simplifying a complex process, we believe that the concepts discussed within the book are relevant to any coach who wishes to maximize the sporting experience for his or her charges, whatever the aims of the context might be. This is precisely because coaching, in whatever guise it is packaged, is essentially a social and learning enterprise. It is social in that it involves human interaction, and learning in that it extends from learning to have fun and to work together (re)creatively, to knowing about the minute intricacies of body adjustment and tactical awareness so necessary for success in elite sport.

Finally, there is a potential market for this book in established, and developing, official coach-education programmes, some of whose co-ordinators are presently evaluating the content of their courses to see how they can better equip coaches to deal with the complex social and educational nature of their work.

HOW IS THE BOOK ORGANIZED?

The framework of this book is informed by our understanding of the term pedagogy. We accept that there are conceptually diverse interpretations of pedagogy, as it is a culture-bound discipline (Crum 1996). Yet, for our purposes here, we explicitly define pedagogy as a social and educational practice that recognizes the interconnections between the teacher, learner and content (Lusted 1986); we also acknowledge the importance of the context within which the practice occurs (Cassidy 2000). This interpretation of pedagogy also coheres with our view of coaching, which is that to fully understand (and achieve quality practice), we need to take account of individual coach biographies, their socialization and their personal interpretations of quality practice. Hence, the book is divided into four sections, namely the coach, the athlete(s), the content and the context. Each section contains a number of chapters relevant to it, with each section concluding with an exercise that encourages readers to critically reflect upon their own, and others', practice.

Specifically, Section One explores the coach in relation to concepts of reflection (Chapter 1), coaching methods (Chapter 2), feedback (Chapter 3), quality in coaching (Chapter 4), and developing a coaching philosophy (Chapter 5). Section Two deals with the athlete(s). Here, we discuss understanding the learning process (Chapter 6), and the development of young athletes (Chapter 7): this latter chapter is written by Dr Lisette Burrows, from the University of Otago. Dr Burrows is respected for her knowledge of developmental issues in the physical education context and we thought her insights would be useful for sport coaches, especially those working with children and young people. Also included in Section Two are chapters relating to the motivation of athletes (Chapter 8), and athletes' identities (Chapter 9). Section Three focuses on coaching content, and includes chapters on coaches' content knowledge (Chapter 10), assessing athletes' understanding (Chapter 11), and coaching athletes with a disability (Chapter 12). Finally, Section Four explores the context in which coaching occurs and comprises a discussion on coaching discourses (Chapter 13), ethical issues associated with coaching (Chapter 14), and taking a holistic approach to coaching and coach education (Chapters 15 and 16 respectively).

Although the analysis has been presented in a linear format, many of the concepts discussed have cross-chapter relevancy, highlighting the inter-disciplinary nature of the subject matter. At relevant points, to assist readers in making the interconnections between the coach, athlete(s), content and context, we will direct the reader to go to complementary discussion in other chapters.

POSTSCRIPT

We began the project of writing this book united in the belief that linking sociological and educational concepts to the coaching practice would assist coaches to
make some sense of the messy realities of the coaching process. We also agreed
to problematize taken-for-granted practices in coaching and advocate for more
recognition to be given to the social aspect of the coaching process. What we did
not foresee was that the practice of writing about the coaching process was just
as messy and complicated as the coaching process itself.

We all came to the project with different experiences of coaching, writing and
life. For example, Robyn had experience of being a performance-orientated coach,
while Tania had experience of being a participation-orientated coach. Robyn had
written a number of books, while Tania had not written any, and Paul was somewhere in between. Also the context in which the ideas were being conceived, and
tried, were different. Some of us were working with undergraduate students who
were specializing in coaching science, whilst others were working with students
who were enrolled in more general human movement type degree programmes.
Paul and Tania were also trying some of the ideas with representative coaches.
Added to the mix was the tyranny of distance. The project had been conceived over
a coffee with a colleague a few doors away in the same building but was developed
by colleagues who were literally half a world away. The social aspect of the project
very quickly became a distant memory. Finally, although not surprisingly, even our
different cultures influenced the writing process.

The influence of these contextual factors on the project became very evident
the first time we swapped our 'draft' chapters with each other. Suffice to say, it
did not look as if we were singing from the same song book. Over time, and with
the help of each other and other colleagues, the ideas became more harmonious
again, although our different experiences are still reflected in the various chapters.
The reason we share this experience is to highlight that even with the best of
intentions, and a reasonable level of theoretical and practical understanding,
collective compromise and consideration, in addition to individual determination,
are required to realize one's goals.

SECTION ONE
THE COACH

1 Reflection   13
2 Coaching methods   26
3 Providing feedback to athletes   38
4 Quality in coaching   46
5 Developing a coaching philosophy   53

CHAPTER 1

▼ REFLECTION

■ Introduction   13
■ What is reflection?   15
■ Why is it useful to become a reflective coach?   17
■ Becoming a reflective coach: issues to consider   18
■ Concluding thoughts   24

INTRODUCTION

In the past two decades the focus on reflection, or on being/becoming a reflective practitioner, has gained popularity in a wide range of contexts that include education (Smyth 1991), graphic design (Poynor 1994), art (Roberts 2001), engineering (Adams *et al.* 2003), and medicine (Middlethon and Aggleton 2001). The resurgence of interest in the notion of reflection can largely be attributed to the work of Schön (1983) who discussed reflection in relation to architecture, town planning, engineering and management. Reflection is a term that has multiple interpretations that include: 'turning a subject over in the mind and giving it serious and consecutive consideration' (Dewey 1910: 3); having 'a capacity for autonomous professional self-development through systematic self-study' (Stenhouse 1975: 144); the study of other professionals; and the testing of ideas in practice (Stenhouse 1975).

In a coaching context, Kidman (2001: 50) discusses reflection in terms of self-reflection which she argues is a 'particularly significant part of empowerment, whereby coaches themselves take ownership of their learning and decision making'. She draws on what Fairs (1987) calls the *Coaching Process – A Five-Step Model for Self-Reflection*. This model encourages coaches to reflect on their coaching skills (Kidman 2001). Gilbert and Trudel (2001) use reflection as a conceptual framework to understand how coaches draw on experience when learning to coach. While there are numerous interpretations of reflection, in and out of the coaching context, Smyth (1991) cautions us to be aware that there are consequences of reflection becoming so commonplace. One is that it has the potential to lose its intended meaning because it can be interpreted in so many different ways. Second, is that the popularity of the term has created what has been described as a 'paradoxical situation' where reflection is used in 'an unreflected manner' (Bengtsson 1995: 24).

When attempting to gain an understanding of the complexities associated with reflection, it is useful to consider Tinning's (1995: 50) point that 'if becoming reflective were simply a rational process then it would be easy to train . . . teachers [read coaches] to be reflective'. He argues it is not easy to 'train' people to become reflective practitioners because 'many of the issues' on which practitioners 'should reflect are not merely a matter of rational argument', rather they 'have a large measure of emotion and subjectivity embedded within them' (Tinning 1995: 50). Many coaches learn how to coach as a consequence of being an apprentice to another coach, often a coach they admire, and base their own practices on those of their mentor. Not surprisingly, reflecting on, and possibly critiquing, taken-for-granted practices that are associated with valued memories, that may also have become integral to a sense of self, can be challenging.

While there are people who support the increasing emphasis being placed on coaches becoming reflective practitioners (see Fairs 1987; Gilbert and Trudel 2001; Kidman 2001), Crum (1995) questions if being a reflective practitioner should become standardized practice, in other words should it become the 'norm'? While he debates this question in the physical education context, the debate has relevancy for sports coaches. According to Crum, the answer depends on the definition of physical education, or coaching, that is held. If a practitioner holds a 'training-of-the-physical' view of coaching and believes his or her role is only to improve fitness and adopt a technical/utilitarian approach, then becoming a coach who reflects in depth is not going to be paramount. In contrast, if a coach holds a view that coaching is 'a teaching-learning process', does 'not focus on the body-machine . . . but on humans moving' and views coaching as a process that is 'socially constructed and historically situated' then he or she is required to reflect in depth on a wide range of issues (Crum 1995: 15). Despite agreeing with Crum that it may not always be necessary for some coaches to reflect in depth, we contend that it is still useful for all coaches to engage in some degree of reflection, even if it is only at the technical level (we will discuss the various levels later in this chapter). As we said in the introductory chapter, by reflecting on practice a coach may expose his or her perceptions and beliefs to evaluation, creating a heightened sense of self-awareness, which in turn may lead to a 'certain openness to new ideas' (Hellison and Templin 1991: 9).

The aims of this chapter are three-fold, and it is around the aims that the discussion is structured. The first aim is to introduce some of the ways in which reflection has been interpreted and discussed in the literature, in particular Schön's (1983) concept of 'reflection-in-action'. The second is to suggest possible reasons why it may be useful to become a reflective coach. Building on this, the final aim is to provide a discussion of some of the issues to consider when attempting to become a reflective coach in the modern sporting context.

WHAT IS REFLECTION?

Many consider John Dewey to be the 'founder' of reflection. He contrasts routine behaviour with reflective thought, defining the latter as the '[a]ctive, persistent, and careful consideration of any belief or supposed form of knowledge in the light of the grounds that support it, and the further conclusions to which it tends' (Dewey 1910: 6). According to Dewey (1966), those who adopt a reflective pose investigate the assumptions that inform their behaviour and accept responsibility for their actions. Dewey (1916) suggests that before an individual can engage in reflective thinking, three personal attitudes need to be present – open-mindedness, whole-heartedness and responsibility. These attributes are defined as follows:

- Open-mindedness is 'an active desire to listen to more sides than one; to give heed to facts from whatever source they come; to give full attention to alternative possibilities; to recognise the possibility of error even in the beliefs that are dearest to us' (Dewey 1916: 224).
- Whole-heartedness, as the name suggests, refers to being 'absorbed' and/or 'thoroughly interested' in a particular subject.
- Responsibility refers to when the consequences of actions are not only considered, but also accepted, thereby securing integrity in one's beliefs.

Over eighty years later these attributes still appear to be relevant to contemporary coaches as evidenced by Wayne Smith's (assistant All Black rugby union coach) description of the attributes needed to be a quality coach. In his own words:

> the key thing I think is the openness to learning. I think coaches need to look at things on merit and understand that just because they've played the game, they don't know everything about it. . . . Having a passion to improve is important. Knowing that you are a part of the problem means that you can also be part of the solution.
>
> (Wayne Smith in Kidman 2001: 43)

Despite Dewey being considered the 'founder' of reflection, the increased interest in the term in the past two decades has been attributed to the work of Schön (1983, 1987) and Zeichner (1983, 1987) (Crum 1995). In contrast with Dewey's view of reflection, whose focus is 'outside the action' and on 'future action rather than current action' (Eraut 1995: 9), Schön's (1983) interpretation of reflection takes into account practice. While Schön provides examples of practice from professions such as town planning and architecture, Zeichner provides examples from teaching and teacher education (Crum 1995) and, as such, we consider the work of the two former authors to be particularly useful when discussing reflection in a coaching context.

In discussing the concept of reflection, Schön (1983: 50) introduces the notion of reflection-in-action, which, as the name suggests, describes what professional and lay people alike do in practice, namely 'think about what they are doing, sometimes even while doing it'. For example, a big-league baseball pitcher describes the process of reflecting-in-action by explaining how in the midst of playing the game '[You get] a special feel for the ball, a kind of command that lets you repeat the exact same thing you did before that proved successful' (1983: 54). Further, Schön stresses that phrases such as 'keeping your wits about you', 'thinking on your feet' and 'learning by doing' highlight 'not only that we can think about doing but that we can think about doing something while doing it' (Schön 1983: 54). Schön (1983: 50) identified three general patterns prevalent in reflection-in-action. First, is that reflection is often initiated when a practitioner is 'stimulated by surprise'. Here, in the process of dealing with the unexpected phenomenon, the practitioner reflects on his or her understandings that are implicit in the action and then critiques, restructures and embodies the practice in future action. In other words, when something unexpected happens 'they turn thought back on action' (1983: 50) and then try and deal with it.

The second pattern prevalent in reflection-in-action is what Schön (1983: 268) calls a 'reflective conversation with the situation'. What he means by this is that while an 'inquiry begins with an effort to solve a problem . . . [t]he inquirer remains open to the discovery of phenomena' (1983: 268). It may come to pass that in the process of attempting to solve the initial problem, a discovery is made that is incongruous with the initial efforts to solve the problem. If this happens, the inquirer then 'reframes' what is considered to be 'the problem' (1983: 268). Schön argues that one of the consequences of having such a reflective conversation with a situation is that it is possible for practitioners to achieve some degree of professional growth by reflecting-in, and reflecting-on, practice. The third pattern in reflection-in-action is what Schön (1983: 62) calls the 'action-present'. He describes this as the 'zone of time in which action can still make a difference to the situation' (1983: 62). While all processes of reflection have an 'action-present' it 'may stretch over minutes, hours, days, or even weeks or months, depending on the pace of activity and the situational boundaries that are characteristic of the practice' (1983: 62). For example, in the middle of a verbal exchange with an athlete, a coach's reflection-in-action may occur in a matter of seconds, but when the context is a season, the reflection-in-action may occur over several months. As the example illustrates, the duration and pace of when reflection occurs will vary depending on the duration and pace of the context. Arguably, the way one interprets the 'action-present' will dictate whether the more generic reflection-in-action term is utilized or whether reflection-on-action or retrospective reflection-on-action (Gilbert and Trudel 2001) is used in describing the reflection process.

As illustrated above, reflection-in-action enables practitioners (athletes and coaches) to engage in 'on-the-spot' experimentation (Eraut 1995). Yet, not only are they reflecting-in-action but they are also reflecting-on-action. While it appears Schön (1983) views reflection-on-action to be integral to reflection-in-action, others such as Gilbert and Trudel (2001) view it as a separate type of reflection. What is more, the latter argue that reflection-on-action can be further broken down and, as a consequence, suggest that there is a third type of reflection which they call 'retrospective reflection-on-action'. They describe this type of reflection as 'that [which] occurs outside the action-present (e.g. after the season or after a coach's reflection can no longer affect the situation)' (Gilbert and Trudel 2001: 30). In addition, Gilbert and Trudel (2001: 30) argue that reflection-on-action is reflection that 'still occurs within the action-present, but not in the midst of activity'. For example, a coach reflecting on an issue in between practice sessions. Another who also views reflection-on-action as separate from reflection-in-action is Bengtsson (1995), who suggests that the former type of reflection can also occur before the action and when the problems arise. In this chapter we follow the lead of Schön (1983) by considering reflection-on-action to be integral to reflection-in-action.

WHY IS IT USEFUL TO BECOME A REFLECTIVE COACH?

There are a number of parallels between the way many teachers were trained at the end of the nineteenth century and how many coaches are still being trained today, namely via the apprenticeship system that emphasizes the technical skills and the 'expert'. The following example, albeit from the physical education context, has many parallels to the current debates within the coaching community regarding coach education. Also the example highlights the way an increasing awareness of the limitations of a technical approach to practice has resulted in the promotion of a more reflective pose.

Traditional practices in physical education teacher education have been generically classified under the nomenclature of 'craft' pedagogies (Tom 1984), a notion that stems from 'teacher education's roots in the apprenticeship system' (Kirk 1986: 158). Within the craft perspective, teacher-education students are often placed in schools for lengthy terms of 'teaching practice'. One consequence of this practice is that little value is placed on theory and the emphasis is on the technical teaching skills and the 'expert' teacher. According to Hoffman (1971: 100) the hallmark and rationale of craft pedagogies 'has its basis not in science or even theory, but in the unglamorous realities of life'. There continues to be plenty of support for 'on the job' teaching practice experience 'by school and college or university supervisors. The school practice is also supported by courses in '"methods" which attempt to provide students with '"how to teach" skills' (Kirk 1986:158), or what Lawson (1993: 155) calls a 'methods-and-materials orientation'. Despite the continued support by some physical education teacher educators for the craft perspective, others have turned to the natural science paradigm in reaction to perceived shortcomings within it (Kirk 1986) and in an attempt to gain credibility in the education community. The primacy of the natural science paradigm means it has become acceptable to privilege rational thought and scientific logic, and compartmentalize the teaching act into 'a discrete series of skills that could be isolated, practised, and applied in a systematic manner' (Tinning 1991: 7). Yet Lawson (1993: 154) observes that, while 'scientific-technological discourses dominate the research literature, this does not guarantee their domination of actual practices in PETE [physical education teacher education] and school programs'. As pointed out in Chapter 13 the dominant discourse of modern sport is embedded in performance pedagogy and technical rationality that is based on scientific functionalism (Johns and Johns 2000). So if we accept Schön's (1983) argument that the notion of reflection-in-action has emerged as a consequence of the limits of technical rationality what are some of the issues for the coaching community to consider?

BECOMING A REFLECTIVE COACH: ISSUES TO CONSIDER

Drawing on the work of Tinning *et al.* (2001), we argue that there are numerous benefits of a coach reflecting on his or her practice. Specifically, a coach may become more sensitive to the backgrounds, needs and interests of the athletes and may develop practice sessions that are more meaningful for all concerned. Also a coach may become more aware of the values and beliefs that shape their practices which may result in better and more inclusive coaching, leading to enhanced athlete learning and therefore performance. We recognize that reflecting on one's practice is not an easy or quick exercise and that there are many traditions, rituals, and so-called norms associated with the sport culture that act as constraints on one's willingness to experiment with becoming a reflective coach. In the following section we explore some issues that both constrain and enable coaches to become reflective practitioners.

Expertise and professionalism

Drawing on anecdotal accounts, Lyle (2002: 245) contends that many coaches in professional sport are 'recruited almost exclusively from the performer base' with 'high value' being 'placed on lengthy experience, sport-specific skills and technical insight, to the exclusion of other knowledge and skills'. But it is not only those who select coaches who value technical expertise. Not surprisingly, coaches also value this knowledge as evidenced by the following quote from Ian McGeechan (ex-Scotland rugby union coach)

> I don't think that you can coach at this level without a reasonable technical knowledge, because a lot of the things that you do are technical, in that you have to see when something is right, or wrong, you have to put something in place, or be part of a conversation or discussion which can put something in place. Now if you cannot be a full part of that, you would lose respect from the players.
>
> (Jones *et al.* 2004: 61)

What is more, Lyle (2002: 200) suggests that there is a widespread public perception that a 'key factor in coaching appointments is previous "playing" experience rather than education, training and apprenticeship'.

Yet, emphasizing sport-specific technical expertise over other attributes does little to assist those who wish to promote sports coaching as a profession. We are not suggesting that technical expertise is not important for a coach to possess. It is, but if the sports coaching community desires to be viewed as a profession[1] then the community needs to recognize that the technical expertise of a professional is that which a lay person does not possess and which is developed over an extended period of education where the emphasis is on the development of cognitive skills (Lyle 1998). When judging sports coaching against numerous criteria of professionalism, Lyle (2002: 310) argues that 'the realisation of the professionalisation of sports coaching is yet some way off'. Having said that, he did note that sports coaching had recently been classed as an 'associated profession' (2002: 200) in the Standard Occupational Classification index. Some of the things Lyle (2002) suggests need to occur within the sport coaching community before it can be considered a profession include more emphasis being placed on the 'interpersonal dimension' of coaching as well as on the 'process elements of the job'. He goes on to say that while technical knowledge is a given, 'we need to build on the co-ordinating, managing, planning, decision-taking role, with appropriate levels of delivery expertise' (2002: 308).

While sports coaching *per se* may not yet be formally considered a profession, some coaches do act professionally. It is the association, and at times tension, that exists between professionalism and technical expertise that constrain coaches who aim to become reflective practitioners (Schön 1983). For example, when a coach has become extremely skilful at the techniques associated with coaching, and view themselves as 'technical experts', surprises do not often occur; therefore, the knowledge or expertise of the coach is preserved. If, over time, the coach begins to value unproblematic knowledge preservation, then uncertainties become a threat or an admission of weakness, and therefore something to be avoided. By avoiding coaching situations that may solicit surprises or uncertainties a coach may miss the opportunity to reflect on his or her practice.

'Thinking interferes with doing'

Another possible constraint on one's willingness to experiment with becoming a reflective coach is associated with a commonly held belief that 'thinking interferes with doing' (Schön 1983: 276). Schön describes at least three specific ways thinking is supposed to interfere with doing. First, there is no time to reflect when in the middle of the action. We recognize that sometimes in a sporting context it

---

[1] Evidence of this is the title of the proceedings of the VII Commonwealth and international conference on sport, physical education, dance, recreation and health, held in Edinburgh in 1986. The proceedings were entitled Coach Education: Preparation for a Profession. Over the years this desire has only intensified as a consequence of improved career opportunities in coaching, improved coach education and access to coaching studies in tertiary institutions, greater resources and media attention to some performance sports (Lyle 2002).

REFLECTION

is 'dangerous to stop and think' (Schön 1983: 278). For example, it would be dangerous for a scrum-half in rugby union to stop and think of all the options when he or she was holding on to the ball at the back of the scrum. But as Schön (1983: 278) reminds us, 'not all practice situations are of this sort'. It is unlikely that a coach would find him or herself in a 'dangerous' position if he or she chose to stop and think when in the middle of a coaching session. As such the argument that 'thinking interferes with doing' is less convincing when applied to coaching practices. Having said that, Jones *et al.* (2004) point out that the 'front' coaches put up is important in maintaining credibility. Therefore, it is possible that if a coach often visibly 'stopped and thought' it would interfere with his or her persona of being a credible coach.

A second way that thinking is supposed to interfere with doing is the perception that when we think about an action we over analyse it and, consequently, lose the flow of the action. We acknowledge that it is possible, if there is an extended action-present period, that excess thought can interrupt the flow of the action. However, coaches and athletes can be taught to provide information about action and think about their actions respectively in a very short period of time. For example, in tennis, a coach can teach a skilled athlete to take a moment to plan the next shot. If the athlete correctly gauges the time for reflection and integrates the outcome of the reflection into the action then it is likely that the performance is enhanced. Not only can a coach teach the athlete to 'take a moment', but a coach who is committed to becoming a reflective coach can also use the same strategies to integrate reflection into their own coaching action.

A third way that thinking is supposed to interfere with doing is that when we begin to reflect it is possible that 'we may trigger an infinite regress of reflection on action, then on our reflection on action, and so on ad infinitum' (Schön 1983: 277). Schön contends that this fear of regressing into a state of continual reflection is derived 'from an unexamined dichotomy of thought and action' (1983: 280). To break down the dichotomy Schön has constructed the notion of reflection-in-action in such a way that 'doing and thinking are complementary' (1983: 280). Not only are they complementary but '[e]ach feeds the other, and each sets boundaries for the other. It is the surprising result of action that triggers reflection, and it is the production of a satisfactory move that brings reflection temporarily to a close' (1983: 280) until new issues trigger further reflection. For example, a coach has observed that, despite providing explanations and demonstrations, an athlete on the team continually fails to comprehend new drills or plays as quickly as other athletes. This surprises the coach because the athlete is an engaging, bright and articulate individual, and once the drills or plays have been practised a few times the athlete does not forget them. In an attempt to find out why this athlete is slow to respond to the explanations and demonstrations, the coach discusses the observations with colleagues, and in the process, reflects on how he or she is presenting the material and what learning media is being privileged. As a consequence of the discussions, the coach recognizes that athletes who are aural and visual learners are initially advantaged when the material is presented compared to those athletes who learn via their kinesthetic senses. In subsequent training sessions, the coach introduces the drills and plays via aural, visual and kinesthetic media and finds that the athlete who was initially slow to comprehend now understands what is expected as quickly as the others.

As illustrated above, thinking does not have to interfere with the flow of the action, yet this is not always the case. Sometimes thinking does interfere, albeit temporarily, with action. For example, a golf coach may suggest that an athlete change the grip on the club. In this situation, it is reasonable to expect that there would be a loss of flow until the athlete becomes accustomed to the new grip. Similarly, if a coach changes his or her coaching methods by including, for example, some problem-solving tasks in practice sessions that have previously been dominated by an authoritarian approach, then it is reasonable to expect that there would be a loss of flow in the practice until the coach and athletes become accustomed to the expectations, rights and responsibilities associated with the problem-solving method.

Whether or not coaches are prepared to pay the price of a loss of flow depends on their ability to construct a 'low-risk' environment in which to practise, and the value they place on 'incurring a temporary loss of spontaneity' (Schön 1983: 280). We contend that, more often than not, the price is worth paying since reflection-in-action is often initiated when a performance is unsatisfactory. As such, we agree with Schön (1983: 279) who asserts that the question then becomes 'not so much *whether* to reflect as *what kind* of reflection is most likely to help us get unstuck'. We have interpreted 'kinds' of reflection to mean levels of reflection, a topic that we discuss in more detail below.

Reflection is an insular process

While the scope for reflection is great, one of the concerns that we, and others, have with reflection is that the focus is largely 'inwards' on the practitioners' own practice 'without sufficient attention to the social conditions that frame and influence that practice' (Zeichner and Liston 1996: 19). One way of moving away from thinking of reflection as only an internally focused process is to think of reflection as occurring on a number of different levels. Drawing on the work of those sociologists associated with the Frankfurt School, Van Manen (1977) argued that there are three levels of reflection: a) technical; b) practical; and c) critical. It must be pointed out that while Van Manen identified three levels of reflection, he did not position one level as necessarily being better than another.

According to Van Manen (1977), a *technical* level of reflection can occur when a coach focuses on achieving objectives and on the effective and efficient application of knowledge (Van Manen 1977; Zeichner and Liston 1987). Some questions a coach could ask at this level of reflection include:

- How can I make sure all the athletes hear me?
- What resources could I utilize to improve the teaching of this task?
- Did I achieve the goals I set for this session?

- How can I fix this problem?
- What part of the training could I change so the training finishes on time?
- What is wrong with the athletes? Why do they not want to do this drill?
- How can I better structure this drill?

Alternatively, a *practical* level of reflection occurs when a coach is aware of, and analyses, the athletes as people, and the assumptions that he or she and the athletes bring to the coaching environment. It also occurs when the coach acknowledges the culture of the sport, is approachable and flexible and recognizes the practical and educational implications of an action (Van Manen 1977, 1995; Zeichner and Liston 1987, 1996). Some questions a coach could ask that illustrate a practical level of reflection include:

- What is it about the way I have structured the session that does not appear to suit the athletes?
- What other ways can I get my message across?
- What messages are being portrayed by my posture(s) and what I am wearing?
- How are my experiences of being coached influencing what I do and my expectations?
- How does my behaviour reinforce stereotypes?
- Who gets performance feedback and who gets behavioural feedback?
- What effect does each type of feedback have on what the athletes learn?
- What am I doing as a coach to include all learning media?

Finally, a *critical* level of reflection occurs when a coach focuses on the political, moral and ethical meaning of knowledge and the domination of various forms of authority. It occurs when the coach questions the worth of knowledge, works towards justice and equality, and problematizes the context in which the activity occurs (Van Manen 1977; Zeichner and Liston 1987). Some questions a coach could ask that illustrate a critical level of reflection include:

- Whose knowledge, and whose point of view, is represented in the knowledge being (re)produced in the training session?
- What do I do if one of the athletes is only 80% fit but he or she is the best on the team? Do I play him or her when the team is up against the leaders in the competition?
- What do I do about those practices that are inequitable or unjust but are part of the team or club traditions?
- Why is there a difference between the type of feedback I give to the more skilled and less skilled members of the team?

We recognize that many conscientious coaches already ask themselves these sorts of searching questions but, as we highlight throughout this book, it is not always easy to answer them rigorously and systematically due to multiple contextual pressures and constraints.

Another way of moving away from thinking of reflection as only as internally focused process is by incorporating some form of collegiality into the process. We

THE COACH

recognize that in a sporting context it may be difficult for coaches who wish to be reflective practitioners to be part of a like-minded group, given the varied aspects of the sport culture that act as constraints in this regard. Yet, the like-minded group does not need to be made up of co- or assistant coaches, it could be administrators, friends, parents, and/or academics. Discussing ideas with like-minded people does not imply accountability, rather the process of verbally articulating an observation or judgement to a group can generate insight and provide another perspective on the situation, thereby facilitating the reflective conversation with the situation. One tool that can be used to support coaches to have a reflective conversation with their situation and with colleagues is action research. Despite incorporating the term research, action research was not devised for academics, rather it was promoted as:

> a form of *collective* self-reflective enquiry undertaken by participants in social situations in order to improve the rationality and justice of their own social or educational practices, as well as their understanding of these practices and the situations in which these practices are carried out.
> (Kemmis and McTaggart 1992: 5, *emphasis added*)

The action research process is made up of four phases (planning, acting, observing and reflecting) that are repeated, thereby forming a spiral. The *plan* must be orientated around some future action and be flexible enough to cope with unforeseen circumstances. The plan should also assist the coach to realize new potential for action. The *action* is a carefully planned, and critically informed, variation of practice and is acknowledged as a 'platform for the further development of later action' (Kemmis and McTaggart 1992: 12). Yet, it is also recognized that 'plans for action must always have a tentative and provisional quality; they must be flexible and open to change in the light of circumstances' (1992: 12). As a consequence, action is considered to be dynamic 'requiring instant decisions about what is to be done, and the exercise of practical judgement' (1992: 12). The role of *observation* in the action research process is to document the effects of the action and to provide data upon which to reflect in the next stage of the process. Not only is the overt action observed but so are 'the effects of action (intended and unintended), the circumstances of and constraints on action, [and] the way circumstances and constraints limit or channel the planned action and its effects' (1992: 13). *Reflection* is based upon the data that is collected and is usually fostered by discussion with others (hence the collective character of action research). 'Reflection has an evaluative aspect — it asks action researchers to weigh their experience — to judge whether effects (and issues which arose) were desirable, and suggest ways of proceeding' (1992: 13). The above four steps may well be steps that all conscientious coaches go through. However, Kemmis and McTaggart (1992: 10) argue that when a practitioner is informed by action research these steps occur 'more systematically, and more rigorously' and we would argue that it also incorporates a sense of community by encouraging coaches to discuss the situation with colleagues.

Aspiring reflective coaches cannot solely rely on observations of actions that are over in a blink of an eye. In order to reflect-on-action there is a requirement that some sort of systematic data-collection occurs. It is possible that one reason why many practitioners do not reflect on their practices (other than maybe at a technical level, e.g. can the athletes hear me?) is that they do not have reliable data upon which to reflect. To reflect at a practical and critical level (e.g. is there any difference between the type of feedback I give to the more skilled and less skilled members of the team? If so, why?), coaches need to reflect on data collected on their practice.

While data-collection strategies that are planned in advance do have limitations, such as not being able to document unplanned action, and only being able to record observable action, it is nonetheless useful for the coach to be aware of some data-collection strategies. Possibly the most obvious way of recording practices for future analysis is to record them on video, or audio-tape. Once this has been done, the coach then has the possibility of analysing the same footage repeatedly, each time looking and listening for different things and reflecting on different levels. While video and audio-tape may be the ideal ways to collect data, there are less technologically advanced methods which require little more than pen and paper and an extra set of eyes, which could belong to an assistant coach, manager, injured athlete, a parent or such like. There have been many data-gathering strategies, or systematic observational strategies developed for assessing teacher effectiveness (for examples see Siedentop and Tannehill 2000) that can be adapted and used to collect data on coaches' practices. Despite the limitations of systematic observational strategies they are still a useful entrée into the process of collecting data on coaching practice and can still be used to support reflection at a critical level by observing for example, language used that reinforces sexist, gender or ethnic stereotypes.

CONCLUDING THOUGHTS

We began the chapter by stating that the notion of reflection has gained incredible popularity over the past two decades, thanks largely to the work of Schön (1983). This book is but one example of how that popularity has been manifested in the sports coaching community. However, it is useful to recognize that despite the rhetoric about the proposed benefits of reflection, some environments are more supportive of practitioners becoming reflective than others. Schön claims that reflection is more likely to occur in an environment that prioritizes flexibility, acknowledges that there are multiple views on issues, appreciates the complexity of issues and is non-hierarchical. This does not sound like your typical coaching environment. Combine this with George and Kirk's (1988) claim (albeit sixteen years ago) that within the sport culture there exists a degree of anti-intellectualism then it does not augur well for coaches to become reflective practitioners. Even if the anti-intellectualism is a thing of the past, in some sports coaching communities disdain still exists for anything that has been informed by research other than bio-physical research, and this continues to pose a challenge for those who propose the development of reflective coaches.

But it is not all 'doom and gloom' for those advocating the benefits of sports coaches becoming reflective practitioners. As the sports coaching community strives to become recognized as a profession, practices will change and questions will be asked of some traditional practices and sentiments. These questions may come from coaches who have graduated with tertiary qualifications in coaching science (or the equivalent) and who have had the opportunity and the time to combine theory and practice. Time will tell, but one thing is sure, coaching practice will change. The challenge is to make sure that the change is engaged with an open mind and with integrity (which just happen to be two attributes of a reflective pose).

CHAPTER 2

▼   **COACHING METHODS**

■ Introduction   26
■ The relationship between coaching and teaching   27
■ An overview of methods   29
■ Taking a circumspect view of methods   33
■ Concluding thoughts   37

INTRODUCTION

Many terms have been used to describe what it is that the coaches actually do. Two terms that are often incorrectly used interchangeably are 'styles' and 'methods'. When Lyle (2002: 156) discusses coaching styles he is referring to 'the distinctive aggregations of behaviours that characterize coaching practice' although he does recognize that they are 'not simply about instructional behaviour'. Others refer to styles as 'a manner of self-expression peculiar to the individual teacher [read coach]' (Tinning *et al.* 1993: 118). Similarly, Siedentop and Tannehill (2000: 281) contend that style 'refers to the instructional and managerial climate for learning; and is often most easily seen through the teacher's [read coach's] interactions'. In this chapter we do not focus on styles, rather we explore coaching methods, which Tinning *et al.* (1993: 118) call 'principles in action', to illustrate some of the practices that coaches could adopt, and examine the consequences of adopting particular methods.

Those who have participated in sports, either as a coach, athlete or spectator, will have witnessed, and/or experienced, a variety of coaching methods. As such, many people are knowledgeable about coaching methods and have opinions about what methods are successful and what are not. Despite the variety of coaching methods that coaches could demonstrate, anecdotal evidence suggests that the majority of the methods adopted by coaches can be broadly classified as authoritarian. What we mean by this is that many coaches still position themselves, and are positioned by others, as the 'boss' or 'expert' of the coaching and game sessions. Arguably, this positioning of coaches, and the consequences it has on coaching practice, may be part of the reason why some young people drop out of sport. If increasing the number of people participating in sport, reducing drop-out rates, enabling people to gain more enjoyment and success from playing sport and improve sporting performance is considered important, then maybe it is time to scrutinize the taken-for-granted coaching methods and explore other possibilities.

In this chapter we introduce the historical and contemporary links that exist between education and coaching and (re)acquaint the reader with a framework we consider to be useful for thinking about coaching methods. The purpose of this chapter is not only to introduce Mosston's (1966) framework, rather it is to explore some of the consequences the methods adopted by coaches have on athletes as learners. We also recognize the limitations of Mosston's framework, and spend the final third of the chapter taking a circumspect view of coaching methods.

THE RELATIONSHIP BETWEEN COACHING AND TEACHING

It is generally acknowledged that historically there has been a strong relationship between teaching and the coaching of games. In the USA, in the early part of the twentieth century, the teaching of physical education and athletics (read games and sports) merged (Figone 2001). One consequence of this merger was that those who valued the educational aspect of school physical education were marginalized compared to those who placed importance on the interscholastic athletics programme and those who coached at the varsity level (Templin et al. 1994). As coaching became the preferred role for many employers (Chu 1984), it also became the preferred role for many teachers (Figone 2001). In the UK, and in Commonwealth countries such as Australia and New Zealand, the relationship between teaching and coaching did not manifest itself the same way as it did in North America. The team games, that originated in the English public (read private) schools, were introduced to the masses in the UK, and the colonies, at the end of the nineteenth century as a way of 'civilising the bodies of the children of the working classes' (Kirk 1998: 89). Maybe it was due to the amateur ethic and values supposedly associated with team games that many teachers in schools, in New Zealand at least, volunteered, and continue to volunteer, to coach games and sports outside of school hours in conjunction with a full teaching load.

The common history of teaching and coaching may help explain why, when Gilbert (2002) grouped 611 coaching science articles into five categories, the three most popular categories had a strong connection to education: namely behaviour, cognition and measurement. This connection was further highlighted when Gilbert coded articles within each category. For example, under the behaviour category he coded articles under topics such as feedback, communication, effectiveness, and instruction, which are all topics that have been, and continue to be, discussed in the educational literature. Despite teaching and coaching sharing a common history, in recent years a number of articles have been written on the theme of coach–teacher differences (for examples see Lyle 2002). It appears that there is some effort, especially by those in sports circles, to stress the differences between coaching and teaching arguably because of the 'higher value placed on sport as opposed to education in our society' (Bergmann Drewe 2000: 79). Despite the attempts to emphasize the differences between coaching and teaching, Lyle (2002) claims that on the whole this has not been very successful due to

> the extensive reliance in the literature on dual role teacher-coaches in North America . . . the emphasis on episodic/sessional interpretations of the coaching role . . . and the use of 'teaching' tasks in coaching research.
>
> (Lyle 2002: 37)

In examining the relationship between coaching and teaching, Bergmann Drewe (2000: 80) discusses the education/training dichotomy, specifically, the hypothesis that training is the 'development of competence in a limited skill or mode of thought whereas "educated" suggests a linkage with a wider system of beliefs'. One consequence of the coach being positioned as someone who develops competence in a limited range of skills and/or finds more effective ways to hit the ball for example, is that coaching tends to be associated with training. However, Bergmann Drewe (2000), in arguing against applying the education/training dichotomy to coaching, suggests it would be 'helpful' if coaches, and others, viewed what they did as teaching. Viewing it this way may mean it would be possible for them to be in a better position to educate the whole person, since teachers are expected to develop the cognitive (thinking), affective (feeling) and psychomotor (physical) domains. Arguably, educating the athletes in the three domains may lead to improved performance in terms of athletes' understanding and the working climate established with the coach. To date, many coaches typically focus on the psychomotor domain, with some recognition given to the cognitive domain, while giving relatively little acknowledgement to the affective domain. This is despite many of them working with relatively small numbers of athletes, spending a considerable amount of time with them and working with them in a social environment. We discuss in more detail coaching as a holistic practice in Chapter 15, and in Chapter 16 we discuss coach education in the same way.

Bergmann Drewe (2000: 82) goes on to describe the benefits of 'shifting coaches' mindsets from training to educating'. We totally support her position, because focusing on educating, and education, may encourage coaches to engage with the discussions that are occurring in the broader educational literature. By focusing on concepts such as reflection (see Chapter 1) and ethics and philosophy (see Chapters 14 and 5 respectively) coaches are less likely to restrict themselves to the literature that focuses on the more observable, technical skills (that have been identified in systematic observation systems), associated with teaching. Finally, Bergmann Drewe (2000) contends that shifting coaches' focus from training to education could also have positive results in relation to the instructional methods adopted by coaches. If coaches consider coaching to be a holistic practice that develops the cognitive, affective and psychomotor domains of the athlete they may be less likely to adopt (for the majority of the time at least) an authoritarian method of coaching. Instead, they are more likely to treat the athletes as knowledgeable and creative beings who are able to think for themselves. Adopting an instructional method, that recognizes the athletes as knowledgeable, requires coaches to refrain from positioning themselves as the experts who know it all, and instead reposition themselves as someone who can help athletes assume a degree of responsibility, and be available to assist them when they identify the need. By positioning themselves this way, coaches increase the likelihood that the athletes will become less dependent on the coach (Martens 1988). We discuss in more detail below the various instructional methods and the consequences of adopting each method.

We recognize that it will not be possible to convince all coaches and administrators of the benefits of being an educator. Many coaches face the pressure to win, and Bergmann Drewe (2000: 83) even argues that 'it may be justifiable in the professional sports domain to tie coaches' jobs to their performance'. Yet, it must be remembered that most coaches do not work in the professional sports domain. Nonetheless, if coaches are to successfully position themselves as educators they need to be able to 'offset the powerful pro model, withstand unreasonable outside pressures, and understand that their athletes are not full-time athletes. They must reinforce . . . the *long-standing, uncommercial* reward of sports' (Lindholm in Bergmann Drewe 2000: 83, *emphasis added*) such as playing for the love of the game.

AN OVERVIEW OF METHODS

In the physical education community, the work of Musska Mosston is most commonly cited when the discussion turns to methods (even if he discusses his work in terms of styles). Mosston (1966) designed a spectrum of teaching styles in an attempt to create some cohesiveness around teaching behaviour. The popularity of Mosston's work may help explain why the terms 'methods' and 'styles' have been used interchangeably. Mosston (1972) claims he did not design the spectrum with the intention of prescribing specific teaching practices, rather he designed it to be a prompt for teachers to reflect on their teaching. Further, he considers that the 'beauty of the spectrum is the ability to awaken teachers to their potential for reaching more students than is possible with a less comprehensive approach to teaching' (Mosston 1972: 6).

In 1966, Mosston designed a continuum, which encompassed 11 teaching styles (read methods). Some of these methods were only marginally different from the neighbouring method. Thirty years later, Kirk *et al.* (1996) synthesized the spectrum in an attempt to make it more 'user-friendly'. They did this by grouping some of the related styles together and reducing the number of methods on the continuum to five: direct, task, reciprocal, guided discovery and problem-solving. Illustrating the continuum on a graph, Kirk *et al.* (1996) highlight the relationship between the methods and learner-centred practices. For example, there is a strong relationship between learner-centred practices and the guided discovery and problem-solving methods. We contend that understanding the teaching/learning relationship may assist coaches to further understand the complexities associated with the coaching process (see Chapter 6 for a more detailed discussion on learning).

Before discussing the consequences of the methods, we preface it with an overview of some of the characteristics of the methods. Our rationale for doing this is that some readers of this book may not be familiar with some of the methods and how they could be used in a sports coaching context. Not being familiar with the range of methods would make it difficult to question current practice and make choices about the appropriateness of adopting particular method(s). We recognize that quality coaching requires more than the ability to reproduce the technical strategies associated with each method but, as we discuss in Chapter 4, having competence in the technical aspects of coaching is part of what makes a quality coach.

The characteristics of a *direct* method involve the coach:

- providing the information and direction to the group/individual;
- controlling the flow of information;
- privileging the demonstration, (it can be given by the coach or the athlete, or be on video) (Kirk *et al.* 1996);
- giving little recognition to the diverse needs of the athletes;
- behaving in ways that can be categorized as managerial and organizational;
- setting goals that are specific and criterion based.

A coach adopting a direct method is a very common sight, possibly more so with junior or less experienced athletes, where the coach is positioned, and positions her- or himself as the knowledgeable one. An example of this in a basketball context is where the coach wants to teach the players how to dribble the basketball. After identifying five key elements of dribbling and demonstrating the skill, the coach outlines a drill that requires the players to practise dribbling in various poses, changing their pose on the sound of the whistle.

The characteristics of a *task* method include many of the characteristics of the direct method but also include the coach:

- designing the learning environment so that it has several different tasks (e.g. stations/circuits);
- designing the session so that the tasks are performed simultaneously, not sequentially;
- organizing the content of the stations so that they are slightly shifted towards recognizing the needs of the athletes;
- designing the sessions so that the players can, at times, work independently from the coach (Kirk *et al.* 1996).

This method could be adopted in a soccer context where the aim of the coach is to improve the players' ball dexterity. To achieve this aim the coach organizes the session so that there are a number of stations positioned around the field. The instructions at each station require the players to perform a different task. While the tasks are different (e.g. dribbling around cones, juggling the ball), they all reflect the aim of the coaching session. The players have five minutes at each station before they change (on the coach's commands) to work at another station. When they are at the stations they work by themselves, or with team mates, and the coach wanders around the various stations providing specific feedback or answering questions.

The characteristics of the *reciprocal* method reflect some of the characteristics of the above two methods in that the coach is still responsible for selecting and sequencing the content. However, where the reciprocal method differs from the previous two methods is that the coach:

■ requires the athletes to work with each other;
■ designs the content of the session to suit the athletes' abilities and needs;
■ requires an athlete's peer (ideally one who is more skilled and knowledgeable) to become responsible for demonstration and feedback;
■ encourages the athlete to develop feedback and social skills (Kirk *et al.* 1996).

Many semi-professional or professional teams have squads which are made up of the 'first-string' and the 'off-the-bench' athletes. This type of arrangement enables a coach to easily adopt a reciprocal approach to coaching. For example, a rugby union coach who wants to improve the ability of his players to throw the ball into the line-out could use a reciprocal coaching method by using the two hookers (the players who throw the ball into the field of play) to work together with the locks (generally those who catch the ball). While it could be expected that the more experienced players would provide the majority of the feedback, each athlete could take turns to provide performance-related feedback, as well as develop new, or adapt existing throwing options to suit their respective strengths. This method supports the tuakana/teina view of learning (Tangaere 1997), a view that is discussed in more detail in Chapter 6.

The characteristics of the *guided discovery* method include the coach:

■ incorporating activities that require the athletes to become more independent;
■ requiring the athletes to move through a series of tasks, in response to a number of questions, with the goal of discovering a predetermined solution;
■ asking in-depth, challenging questions to guide the athlete to a predetermined end (Kirk *et al.* 1996).

A guided discovery method can be seen in tennis when a player comes to the side of the court having completed the first set. At this point the coach, who wants to improve the percentage of winning shots, asks the player some specific open-ended questions. For example, 'What action could you take if your opponent lobbed the return to the middle of the court? Why?' Or 'Can you tell me where you would place the ball if your opponent was standing on the base line covering her back hand? Why?' Or 'What happens when your opponent returns the ball to your back hand? How can you make the situation better?' While the coach knows the answer to the question, she encourages a response from the player, believing that the process of answering the questions will enhance the latter's understanding of the situation.

The characteristics of the *problem-solving* method are similar to the guided discovery method except that they include the coach:

■ establishing the problem, which may come from a situation the team/athlete has experienced;
■ accepting that outcomes may be more varied;
■ accepting that there is not necessarily one 'right' solution to the problem;
■ encouraging the athletes to be responsible for the process of finding solutions;
■ enabling work to be individualized or performed in groups;
■ recognizing the athletes' background knowledge and preferred pace of learning, and the media through which they prefer to learn;
■ recognizing that problem solving demands tasks that require more cognitive processes (Kirk *et al.* 1996);
■ having a 'debrief' at the end of the problem-solving scenario so that the athletes can review what has been learned.

A coach can adopt a problem-solving method when he or she wants the athletes to apply their understanding to a game-like scenario. For example, a netball coach may design a scenario along the following lines: the defensive players in the team are required to play the defensive pattern of the forthcoming opposition. The attacking team has the centre pass off and they are told that there are 15 seconds left on the clock until the final whistle sounds and the score is tied. The problem to be solved is: develop three options of breaking the defence and score a goal within 15 seconds. The coach tells the team that they have 10 minutes to come up with some solutions. At the end of 10 minutes the coach brings the group back together and proceeds to ask the team questions about what happened, what worked, what did not work and what are the options they could try in the forthcoming match and why.

The success of the latter two methods hinges, to a large extent, on the coach's ability to ask meaningful and probing questions and to use questions to extend the players' knowledge. While many coaches do ask questions, the questions are often rhetorical, for example 'What do you think you are doing?', or closed questions that only require a 'yes' or 'no' response. When a coach adopts guided discovery and problem-solving methods of coaching she or he is required to ask questions in a different way from those that have traditionally been asked by coaches. If coaches want to develop athletes who can make decisions, and adapt to changing situations as they occur (Kidman 2001), then it is desirable to challenge athletes' cognitive capacities. In drawing on an empirical study that compared the types of questions coaches asked when adopting guided discovery type methods and when adopting the direct method, Butler (1997) found that those coaches adopting the former methods asked not only more questions but also a wider range of questions. The range of questions went from memory-level questions, which involved little cognitive involvement, to the analytical and synthesis-level questions that required considerable cognitive involvement.

TAKING A CIRCUMSPECT VIEW OF METHODS

Many coaches never make a conscious decision regarding the coaching method(s) they adopt, or could adopt. Often coaches adopt methods they experienced as athletes, or as a consequence of watching other coaches, maybe as a spectator, or as an assistant coach. This approach to learning how to coach is often called the apprentice model because the learning occurs 'on the job' and at the side of a more experienced coach. This model may work well if the exemplar coach is a quality coach and has the time to spend with the apprentice coach, but many times this is not the case and the result is that undesirable coaching practices continue to be reproduced.

Drawing on the work of Tinning *et al.* (1993) we are reminded against slipping into the belief that methods exist separately from the coach, and that they can be simply implemented unproblematically by the coach. As discussed in our introductory chapter, coaching is a social practice, and this implies the involvement of the whole person, in relation to specific activities as well as social communities. Therefore, methods can be viewed not as a

> set of strategies which can be successfully or unsuccessfully implemented by a teacher [read coach], they are more like a set of beliefs about the way certain types of learning can best be achieved. They are as much statements about valued forms of knowledge as they are about procedures for action.
>
> (Tinning *et al.* 1993: 123)

If we accept that methods are as much about 'statements about valued forms of knowledge' as they are about 'procedures for action' (Tinning *et al.* 1993: 123) then we need to accept that there are consequences associated with adopting each method.

The consequences of the various methods for coaching practice

Most often coaches do not rely totally on one method, rather they draw on various methods to suit their objectives. Some coaches may draw on the direct and task methods while others may combine direct and guided discovery methods. This has to be kept in mind when considering the following discussion on the consequences of the various methods.

A consequence of a coach adopting a direct method is that the athletes are not perceived to be active learners. Rather they are expected to memorise and regurgitate information provided to them by the coach instead of developing an understanding of the nuances of the game or activity (Kidman 2001). Also, because the coach controls the flow of information there is little new knowledge produced, rather the whole experience reproduces existing knowledge. Coaches often adopt the direct method when they are teaching young and/or inexperienced athletes. The rationale often given for doing so is that the athletes do not have the knowledge or skills to play the game. It is interesting to note that much of a youngster's learning prior to the age of five (or when they go to school) does not occur via a direct method but rather through guided discovery or problem-solving methods. One possible consequence of predominantly adopting a direct method with youngsters is that their problem-solving and creative abilities are not encouraged.

Since common characteristics exist between the direct and task methods they also share the consequences of adopting the particular methods. Two consequences more specific to adopting the task method are that a coach begins to recognize that the athletes are capable of some degree of self management, and hence provides the opportunity for athletes to work in the various stations away from his or her direct gaze. This freedom, albeit rather limited, also provides an opportunity for the athletes to assess the requirements of the task and modify them, if need be, to their own specific needs, thereby developing new understandings or knowledge. However, because the coach determines the content of the stations the practices still, to a large extent, reproduce existing knowledge.

The direct and task methods provide little opportunity to develop a social dimension to the coaching process. Some of the consequences of adopting a reciprocal method relate more to developing the social aspect of team dynamics. Having the athletes work together, and provide feedback to each other, can improve their physical skills as well as their social and cognitive abilities. The latter abilities are enhanced because the athletes work closely with each other, and they have to develop movement analysis skills, as well as communication skills, if they are to provide concise and meaningful feedback to their peers. Because the coach sets the content of the session, adopting a reciprocal method can continue to reproduce existing knowledge. Nonetheless, because of the interaction between the athletes it is possible that new knowledge can be produced.

Developing the cognitive abilities of athletes is also a consequence of adopting a guided discovery method. For athletes to be actively involved in their learning the coach is required to construct the practice sessions in ways that enable the athletes to gain an understanding of why they are doing what they are doing. Although the coach does ask the athletes questions in an effort to get to a predetermined solution, the athletes do have an opportunity to answer the questions in ways that are unique to them and their situation. As such there is the possibility that athletes will arrive at new knowledge. However, because the coach asks the athletes questions about what they think is happening, and what could happen, the coach does not establish him- or herself as the 'expert'. One consequence of this is that some athletes, especially those who have been successful under a more orthodox approach to coaching, may challenge the coach's ability.

The consequences of adopting the problem-solving method are similar to those associated with the guided discovery approach, in that the coach recognizes the athletes as active learners and that setting problems for them to solve assists in the production of new knowledge. Using this method may also mean that the ability of the coach will be questioned, especially if he or she sets irrelevant problems and accepts all solutions. But, adopting a problem-solving method does not mean that the coach abdicates all responsibility to the athletes. On the contrary, setting up relevant problem-solving scenarios, and expertly debriefing the scenarios at the completion of the exercise, requires knowledge of the content and context as well as considerable communication and interpersonal skills.

Choosing what method(s) to adopt is not like selecting a recipe

Choosing a method is not a straightforward exercise, especially if methods are viewed as a 'set of beliefs' (Tinning *et al.* 1993: 123). A coach's belief about decision making can determine what methods are adopted in the training session. The coach, in an effort to ascertain his or her beliefs about decision making, can ask him- or herself specific questions, such as: 'Who makes the decisions in the pre-training, during the training, and after the training?' 'How are they made?' 'In what circumstances are they made?' 'For what purpose are they made?' If a coach believes that it is her or his role to dominate the decision-making process then it is likely that she or he will adopt *direct* and/or *task* methods which tend to *reproduce* existing knowledge and will view the athletes as passive learners. If a coach believes it is possible to share the decision-making process with the athletes then he or she may adopt a *reciprocal* method that can *reproduce* existing knowledge as well as potentially inviting the *production* of new knowledge. If a coach shares the decision-making process more fully with the athletes, then he or she may adopt *guided discovery* and *problem-solving* methods and this is likely to invite understanding of existing knowledge as well as the *production* of new knowledge (Mosston 1992). These last two methods help the athletes to become knowledgeable decision makers. While not specifically viewing methods as a set of beliefs, Siedentop and Tannehill (2000) argue that it may be useful for teachers, and we would argue coaches, to consider their own preferences and skills when choosing what methods to adopt. The rationale they give for doing so is that a coach needs to believe in what they are doing.

Another factor that is useful for coaches to be aware of when choosing methods is the characteristics of the athletes with whom they are working, since experienced athletes are more likely to require different methods than novice athletes. Moreover, the type of content being taught in the sessions may also dictate what method(s) coaches employ. For example teaching the swan dive (which will ultimately be performed off a 10-metre platform) will more than likely require the use of different method(s) than when encouraging experienced athletes to develop a defensive strategy for a particular opponent. Finally, the context in which the practice session occurs may also influence what method is adopted. For example a tennis coach, who is responsible for a large group of tennis players and had the use of eight courts, may be more inclined to choose between task, reciprocal or problem-solving methods rather than a direct method because the latter method could waste time if the players were bought back together every time the coach wanted to explain and demonstrate a skill.

Not only do we consider it unwise for coaches to view the selection of methods as being synonymous with the selection of a recipe, we also think it is undesirable because it is useful for coaches to consider:

- who is being advantaged and disadvantaged by adopting a particular coaching method?
- what are the consequences of adopting a particular coaching method?

When coaches ask themselves these questions it helps them to consider the methods in relation to their own coaching situation rather than as a set of pre-described set of strategies for coaching. The process of choosing a method is 'loaded with taken-for-granted assumptions' so if a coach is interested in creating the best learning experiences for his or her athletes then the methods 'must be exposed and open to scrutiny and challenge' (Tinning *et al.* 1993: 124).

One way of opening up the methods to scrutiny and challenge is to consider the hidden meanings or implicit learnings associated with the methods (we discuss the hidden curriculum in more detail in Chapter 10). All methods have hidden meanings, so it is not possible to simply choose a method that does not have them. As such, coaches need to make judgements as to the 'appropriateness' of the methods (Tinning *et al.* 1993: 124) in relation to the bigger picture of a practice session and the season. Consider a situation where a coach, who adopts a pre-dominantly direct method, asks the most skilful athlete in the team to demonstrate a desired skill, and then after the team has had some time practising it, asks the other athletes to display their attempts to the whole group. What meanings could the athletes infer from this practice? What do the athletes learn when they listen to the explanation of the task? What do the athletes learn when the most skilful is picked to perform the demonstration? What do the athletes learn when they are asked to perform the skill in front of their peers? It is possible that the athletes learn that there is only one way to perform the skill; they could also learn that they are not considered skilful at the task. Moreover, they could learn that it is somewhat embarrassing to perform the task, out of context, in front of their peers. Another situation, informed by the problem-solving method, produces other meanings. Consider a situation where a coach sets the athletes a number of problems to work on. After a period of time the coach calls the athletes in for a debrief and proceeds to question them about the various solutions they had discovered. What meanings could result from this practice? The athletes could learn that the problems set by the coach have no interest to them as they have no bearing on the actual game situation, or they could find that the supposed problems are not really problems at all and do not challenge them physically or cognitively.

Moreover, the athletes could learn that the coach will accept any solution regardless of practicality.

CONCLUDING THOUGHTS

We are well aware that there are plenty of reasons why some coaches find it difficult to embrace a variety of methods. Coaches will not necessarily adopt a new method of coaching based on a convincing rational argument. This reluctance to change is due, in part, to the culture associated with the sport or activity. It is possible that coaches may be reluctant to challenge taken-for-granted practices of a sporting culture, especially if they have been a successful participant in that culture. Even if coaches are prepared to challenge some of the taken-for-granted practices, maybe as a consequence of enrolling in tertiary study or professional development, it is possible that the athletes they are coaching, or the administrators of the sport, may not wish the practices to be challenged. To overcome the barriers put in place by the athletes and administrators, coaches may have to 'prove' themselves to be adept at using the more orthodox methods associated with the culture of the sport or activity. By working adeptly within the orthodoxy the coaches may gain the credibility to enable them to experiment with so-called 'alternative' methods. However, gaining this credibility may take some time. Even when coaches feel that the athletes and administrators may be open to some experimentation in relation to methods it is still wise to tread slowly and carefully as the latter two groups have been socialized into what it means to be a coach and therefore have certain expectations. If expectations are challenged 'overnight', it is possible that coaches could experience a degree of resistance. To reduce the possibility of resistance occurring it is useful for coaches to explain why they doing what they are doing. It is also good practice to introduce the 'new' method in only one activity at a time, to allow athletes and administrators the opportunity to become used to the different expectations placed upon them, and to feel comfortable about having different expectations of the coach.

CHAPTER 3

▼ PROVIDING FEEDBACK TO ATHLETES

- Introduction   38
- Providing verbal feedback . . . it's not that straightforward   40
- Intrinsic feedback   44
- Concluding thoughts   44

INTRODUCTION

Feedback comes in a range of forms, via various media, at different times, delivered for a variety of reasons, by different people and with disparate consequences. According to Gilbert (2002) only 7 per cent of the sports coaching science articles written in the past thirty-two years have focused on feedback. In contrast, Solomon *et al.* (1998: 300) claim that the research that has examined feedback in the coaching context is 'extensive'. One possible explanation for the discrepancy between Solomon *et al.* and Gilbert is that discussion on feedback in coaching science has occurred under many different guises, such as coach–athlete relationships, leadership style, communication, or motivational climate. While Gilbert (2002) and Solomon *et al.* (1998) differed on the amount of research that has focused on feedback, they did agree that much of the research was undertaken in the 1980s when effectiveness research was very fashionable. An aim of the coaching effectiveness research was to 'identify specific behaviors exhibited by coaches and to determine their influence on various achievement and psychological outcomes' (Amorose and Weiss 1998: 396). One behaviour that received attention was the feedback, in particular the verbal feedback, a coach provided to athletes. In other words, the discussion has largely focused on feedback as a form of coach intervention strategy (Knudson and Morrison 2002). This may have been a consequence of Schmidt's (1982) claim that feedback is one of the more important variables to affect the learning of motor skills.

Coaches spend a considerable amount of time conveying a range of verbal information to athletes. They provide technical advice, knowledge of performance, knowledge of results, praise or scold an athlete and use verbal feedback to target learning preferences. Further, coaches use verbal feedback to provide encouragement, guide athletes' explorations, introduce strategic concepts, and educate athletes as to where, and on what, to place their attention. To provide this diverse range of information to athletes it is useful for coaches to have some pedagogical and sociological understanding of feedback and the consequences verbal feedback can have on athletes. Verbal feedback is one example of augmented feedback, which is defined as 'information provided to a learner from an external source that describes the *outcome* of a performance and/or the *quality* of the performance' (Rose 1997: 265, *emphasis added*). In the motor control and learning communities the former is known as knowledge of results (KR) while the latter is known as knowledge of performance (KP). Athletes can also receive feedback another way, via their sensory receptors, for example through their muscles or their eyes. This type of feedback is known as intrinsic feedback (Rose 1997). In this chapter we focus predominantly on augmented feedback, specifically verbal feedback, since this is the most common form of feedback provided by a coach. This reflects the primary purpose of this chapter, which is to debunk the notion that verbal feedback simply relates to a coach providing technical instruction, encouragement and reinforcement, and to highlight the complexities associated with providing verbal feedback. In particular, how the amount, timing and kinds of feedback affects learning, how perception of ability influences what feedback is provided and how it is received, and how verbal feedback can influence social realities. The secondary purpose of the chapter is to challenge coaches to encourage athletes to reflect on their own learning by recognizing the feedback they receive from internal sources, also known as intrinsic feedback. In the final section of the chapter we suggest some strategies that assist coaches to facilitate athletes' reception of intrinsic feedback.

One of the consequences of effectiveness research being fashionable in the 1980s is that numerous systematic observation systems such as the Coaching Analysis Instrument (CAI), the Coaching Behavior Assessment System (CBAS) and the Computerized Coaching Analysis System (CCAS) were developed to analyse coach behaviour such as verbal feedback (More *et al.* 1996). Over time, some of these systems, such as the CBAS, have become more refined and are now able to focus on specific categories of verbal feedback (Amorose and Weiss 1998). As such, it is now possible to identify 'coaches who provide higher frequencies of positive reinforcement following performance successes, and encouragement and technical instruction following mistakes' (Amorose and Weiss 1998: 397).

Despite the interest in verbal communication, Allen and Howe (1998) found that there has been a lack of attention given to non-verbal forms of communication such as body language, facial expressions and gestures. They found this surprising, given that by their estimates, 'over 70% of communication is non-verbal' (1998: 283). Drawing on the work of Crocker, Allen and Howe (1998: 284) note that athletes' 'perception of the content of a verbal message' depends upon the accompanying facial expression. For example, if a coach gave positive feedback but at the same time had 'a negative facial expression (e.g. anger, disgust)' the feedback is distorted in a negative direction (1998: 284). These findings highlight the need for coaches to be aware of their non-verbal expressions since they can provide valuable intrinsic feedback to an athlete via the latter's visual sensory receptors, in other words, through their eyes. Also the findings highlight the need for coaches and researchers to consider the social consequences of verbal feedback. In the following section we explain some of the limitations of viewing verbal feedback as an objective independent act. We contend that coaches and athletes may benefit by viewing verbal feedback as a socially constructed practice that can be used to legitimate the interests of some, at the expense of others. According to Kirk (1992: 42) hidden agendas exist 'in the realm of communication, meaning making, in a symbol world of action, gesture, word, intonation and sound'.

PROVIDING VERBAL FEEDBACK . . . IT'S NOT THAT STRAIGHTFORWARD

Quality verbal feedback is not as simple as a coach providing positive rein-forcement, being encouraging and supplying technical instruction. One of the complexities associated with providing verbal feedback is that 'the kind, amount, and timing of augmented feedback may have differentiating effects on the acquisition and learning of motor skills' (Markland and Martinek 1988: 290). This is illustrated in the following anecdote of a coach who knows from experience not to give one of her athletes corrective feedback three days prior to competition. If she does, the athlete will interpret the feedback as a personal attack and will sulk and play below her capabilities on game day. The coach also knows that this athlete never responds well to feedback given to her in public (even if it is positive feedback). Consequently the coach provides feedback to this athlete one-on-one and away from the public gaze. If the coach does not take the time to do this, she knows it will take considerable effort to win back the trust and loyalty of the athlete. What this anecdote highlights is the need for coaches to be aware that they have to balance group feedback with individual feedback. To do this the coach needs to know his or her athletes as people in order to tailor feedback in ways that are appropriate to them.

Another complexity associated with providing verbal feedback is the relationship between feedback and perceived ability. This relationship can be viewed in two ways. The first relates to the way a coach's perception of an athlete's ability influences the type of verbal feedback the coach gives. The second is the way that the athlete's interpretation of the verbal feedback from the coach can influence his or her perception of competence. In relation to the first view, researchers have identified that the feedback a coach provides an athlete is based on the coach's evaluation of the athlete's abilities (Sinclair and Vealey 1989; Solomon and Kosmitzki 1996). Solomon et al. (1996) identify that coaches primarily attend to those athletes that they perceived to be high-ability athletes and provide these athletes with mistake-contingent feedback. In relation to the second view, Allen and Howe (1998) identify what appear to be some contradictions in the research.

They found that 'more frequent encouragement and corrective coaching behaviors for skill errors were related to lower perceptions of competence' (Allen and Howe 1998: 294). This finding was contrary to some other research that found that 'greater contingent encouragement and corrective information and lower criticism following an undesirable performance were associated with higher perceived competence' (1998: 294).

In offering explanations for the contradictions, Allen and Howe (1998: 294) suggest it is possible that adolescent female athletes (who were the focus of their study) are more 'sensitive to corrective information from coaches than previously recognized'. They hypothesized that when a coach provides adolescent female athletes with a high amount of corrective feedback following a mistake, 'even when it includes encouragement', some may perceive the feedback to be an indicator that they have failed, thus resulting 'in feelings of lower perceived ability' (Allen and Howe 1998: 294). The second explanation they provide focuses on the importance that adolescents place on peers. They suggest that 'it is likely that adolescents are aware of differences between the content as well as the frequency of feedback they receive and the feedback their peers receive for a similar performance' (Allen and Howe 1998: 295). Further, they illustrate their explanations using a vignette in which they highlight possible responses of two female adolescent athletes who, upon performing similarly, receive different types of feedback. One athlete receives praise for the performance while the other athlete receives encouragement and technical information.

> The athlete receiving praise may interpret this feedback to indicate that she has performed well. However, knowing that another athlete received encouragement plus information on how to improve, she may interpret the feedback as indicating the coach thinks her level of performance was the best she could do (hence the praise), while the coach expects superior performances from her teammate. In the same example, the athlete who received the encouragement plus information may infer she made a mistake and failed, while the athlete receiving praise did not fail, leading her to think she is not as good as the first athlete. The interpretations of this example are speculative, however, and highlight the potential influence coach feedback can have on athletes and how it may be interpreted differently by children and adolescents.
>
> (Allen and Howe 1998: 296)

What the vignette demonstrates is that providing quality verbal feedback is not as simple as some may have us believe. What is more, Allen and Howe's (1998) research demonstrates the way the gender and age of athletes adds to the complexities associated with providing verbal feedback.

Not only does the kind and timing of verbal feedback have differentiating effects on the learning of motor skills, verbal feedback can also influence the social reality of athletes. Sport has played, and continues to play, an important role in the construction of masculinity and femininity. When children begin to play an organized and/or competitive sport or activity they are not just learning how to play a game, they are entering an organized institution, and with that goes learning how to be a woman or man. This is cleverly illustrated in a comical five-minute video called *Kick to Kick* (Australian Film Institute Distribution Ltd year unknown) where a father attempts to provide feedback to his son on how to use his body when playing Australian Rules Football. The feedback that the father provides his son is laced with information about needing to show 'some heart', 'g & d' (guts and determination) and courage and to have the expectation of being hurt and inflicting hurt on others when playing 'footy'. Not only does this video highlight the way feedback can influence the social reality of athletes but also the way non-verbal feedback (such as a raised eyebrow or ignoring a situation) can change the meaning of the verbal feedback.

Continuing the line of thought that verbal feedback is not an objective independent act but rather is socially constructed leads us to introduce some research from the physical education context that has highlighted various gendered patterns in verbal feedback. Arguably similar verbal feedback patterns can be identified in coaching, and for that reason we draw on this research to highlight some of the consequences that verbal feedback has on the (re)construction of athletes' social reality. Twenty years ago, Griffin (1983) noted that feedback given to boys is often performance-orientated (e.g. 'keep your elbow high') while the feedback given to girls is more behaviour-, or participation-orientated (e.g. 'keep going', 'good girl'). Given that many sports at the junior level are co-educational (at least in New Zealand and Australia) it is useful for coaches to be aware of this research in an effort to eliminate the often unconscious gender bias present in their verbal feedback. What is more, if it is the aim of the coach to improve the skills of the boys *and* the girls then providing girls verbal feedback that focuses predominantly on behaviour or participation, does little to help them improve their performance (Griffin 1983).

More recently, Wright (1997a) observed verbal exchanges between a) male physical education teachers and male students, b) female physical education teachers and female students and, c) male physical education teachers and female students, and analysed the language patterns (which included feedback patterns) of the teachers. She demonstrates that not only does the gender of those receiving the feedback add to the complexity of providing verbal feedback but so does the gender of the person giving the feedback. In other words, language is gendered not only by *who* said it, but *what* is said and the *way* it is said. It is useful to remember that feedback can be gendered even when the team or group is made up of a single-sex grouping. For example, anecdotal evidence suggests that it is still common for coaches in all-male settings to tell the males that they are playing 'like a girl' or suchlike. Giving such feedback is not only derogatory to females, but the use of such language by the coach creates a particular social reality, not only for the receiver of the feedback, but also for the larger team community. Not only can feedback (re)produce societal sex-stereotypes and reinforce social inequities, but Wright (1997a) argues that understanding the way language is used can provide insight into issues of power in the relationship between teacher and pupil, and, we would argue, between coach and athlete. Given the increasing interest in the coach–athlete relationship we believe that Wright's (1997a) findings could be useful to sports coaches and researchers alike. In the following section we have summarized some of the findings of Wright's (1997a) work that may be of interest to those working in a sports coaching context.

When comparing the feedback patterns of two gymnastic teachers, (a female teacher teaching females and a male teacher teaching males), Wright (1997a) notes that the exchange between the male teacher and male students was likely to be one way, with the teacher constructing himself as expert, asking few questions except to clarify organizational arrangements or to regulate athlete behaviour. Moreover, the male teacher constructed the male athletes as having sufficient intellectual and physical resources to participate in a skill-orientated session. In contrast, the exchange between the female teacher and the female students comprised of the teacher giving lengthy explanations, using sentences joined by 'if', 'when', and 'because' (thereby contextualizing the tasks) and identifying with the students and their assumed reticence by using terms such as 'we'. Wright (1997a) also observed that the use of language and feedback patterns of the same male teacher changed somewhat when he taught volleyball skills to female students compared to when he taught baseball skills to male students. When he taught the male students his language structure was characterized by 'a series of statements' which established what had 'to be done and how' and then the students were given the freedom to get on and perform the skills (Wright 1997a: 66). In contrast, when he taught a skill-orientated volleyball session to female students his language structure was more comparable to the female teacher teaching the female students since his explanations were lengthy and he provided reasons for why he was asking the students to perform the skills.

One consequence of Wright's (1997a) findings for the coaching community is that verbal feedback provided to female athletes (from both male and female coaches) can position them as being reluctant and less competent than their male counterparts. This positioning maintains the expectations and perceptions of difference in male and female behaviour, thereby reinforcing dominant notions of masculinity and femininity. Another consequence relates to the way verbal feedback provided by the coach enables and constrains athletes to become problem solvers and decision makers. For example, a male coach, working with male athletes, adopting a position where he asks few questions and establishes himself as the expert, may restrict the male athletes' ability to become competent decision makers and/or problem solvers. In contrast, when male and female coaches work with female athletes they are more likely to take into account the athletes' expectations, subjectivities, reactions and experiences, thereby assisting the female athletes to have a more meaningful learning experience and possibly become competent decision makers and/or problem solvers.

INTRINSIC FEEDBACK

Intrinsic feedback is information that is immediately available to athletes via the sensory receptors (Rose 1997). It is not easy for a coach to identify what intrinsic feedback the athletes are receiving, because unlike augmented feedback, intrinsic feedback cannot be identified using systematic observation systems. It is possibly for this reason there has been little focus on intrinsic feedback in the sports coaching literature. In the following section we outline a number of strategies that coaches can adopt that encourage athletes to utilize intrinsic feedback. One strategy that coaches can use is video footage of the athletes, since this enables athletes to receive feedback from their visual and possibly aural senses. Another way coaches can enhance the possibility of athletes utilizing intrinsic feedback is by explicitly designing activities and providing opportunities for athletes to focus on their kinesthetic sense. For example, if a coach provides opportunities for athletes to feel a desirable movement, and replicate the feel, it is possible that the athlete may be able to replicate the desirable movement without the need for augmented feedback. Coaches can encourage athletes to utilize their sensory receptors by using words to cue athletes into targeting the various receptors. By using words such as 'feel', 'experience', 'simulate', 'sense', 'perform', 'demonstrate', 'move' and 'do' the coach encourages the athletes to draw on their kinesthetic receptors. Using words such as 'see', 'look', 'watch', 'observe', 'view' target the visual senses, while words such as 'detect', 'listen', 'rhythm', tempo', 'pace' and 'flow' emphasize the aural senses. To further support athletes utilizing intrinsic feedback coaches could adopt a movement-analysis framework designed by Rudolf Laban (1948) that focused on the elements of time, space, weight, and flow. One coach educator (Rod Thorpe) has incorporated some of Laban's ideas into his coach-education practices. For an example of how this works in practice see the *Game Sense* resources (Thorpe 1997).

In Chapter 1 we discussed the notion of the reflective practitioner in relation to the coach, but it is also possible for a coach to encourage athletes to become reflective. If coaches wanted to encourage athletes to reflect in, and on, their action they would be required to provide athletes with the opportunities to gather data upon which to reflect. Some ways a coach could do this would be to supply the athletes with a video-recording of the games and practices or to encourage them to keep diaries of their experiences, thoughts and feelings associated with the training sessions and games.

CONCLUDING THOUGHTS

There is more to providing verbal feedback than meets the eye (or should that be ear?). The verbal feedback that a coach provides to athletes reflects the assumptions upon which he or she draws. What does this mean? If a coach assumes 'behaviours are strengthened when they are rewarded and weakened when they are unrewarded or punished' (Sinclair and Vealey 1989: 78) then he or she will provide verbal feedback in an effort to shape desirable behaviour in their athletes.

If however, the coach also assumes that learning occurs in a social context then it is possible that he or she will recognize that providing verbal feedback is not an independent, objective act. Rather it is replete with complexity as illustrated in this chapter. Also if a coach views the athletes as active constructors of meaning then his or her role becomes one of facilitator, which has implications for the type of feedback provided to the athletes. In the latter situation a coach may encourage the athletes to develop confidence in the feedback provided by their own sensory receptors, thereby enabling the athletes to become more self-reliant. It is our hope that coaches, as a result of exploring some of the complexities that surround verbal feedback that were discussed in this chapter, may begin to think about the consequences the words that come out of their mouths have on their athletes.

CHAPTER 4

▼ QUALITY IN COACHING

- Introduction   46
- A good coach   47
- An effective coach   47
- Quality in coaching   48
- Why bother with the notion of quality?   50
- Concluding thoughts   52

INTRODUCTION

During the course of a season various people make judgements of a coach. Athletes, parents, club members, employers, sponsors, owners of the club and supporters judge the coach based on issues such as enjoyment, safety, win/loss record, and cost. The decisions people make, in turn, form the basis of a judgement as to whether a coach is a *good* and/or *effective* coach. Contrary to popular belief these terms should not be used interchangeably since each term is based on quite different assumptions. In the past few decades the notion of the effective coach has been prevalent in the literature and rhetoric associated with sports coaching. The reason Lyle (2002) gave for this situation is that many coaches are pragmatists. However, pragmatism can be used as an excuse for maintaining the status quo, or at least maintaining the focus on the technical and practical issues. As we illustrate in this chapter, the notion of the effective coach is increasingly being challenged, not only in the literature (see Lyle 2002) but also by some successful (performance-orientated) coaches (see Jones *et al.* 2004).

The purpose of this chapter is to introduce a framework (informed by the concept of quality) that we consider generative for judging the practices of coaches. Before we describe this framework it is necessary to discuss how concepts of good and effective have been previously, and at times continue to be, used, with mixed success, to judge the performances of coaches. In the second half of the chapter we explain the characteristics of the quality framework and conclude by outlining why we think it is useful for judging the practices of coaches.

A GOOD COACH

More often than not, when someone inquires about a coach, one of the first questions is framed along the lines of: 'is she or he a good coach?' When 200 undergraduate students were asked to compile a list of characteristics that described a good coach they came up with the following:

Patient	Flexible
Experienced	Organized
A good communicator	Not just a dictator
Knowledgeable about skills	Open-minded
Motivator	Has the ability to teach
Has a sense of humour	Punctual
A people manager	Has a loud voice
Adventurous	Uses time wisely

In compiling the list it became apparent that the students had a 'common-sense' understanding of what 'good' meant. Their understanding reflected a dictionary definition of 'good' – namely having 'admirable, pleasing, superior or positive qualities' (Collins 1992: 549). It is not only undergraduate students who have an understanding of, and interest in, what makes a 'good' coach. The lay population also has an understanding, and interest, in this notion as evidenced by the large number of coach biographies and autobiographies that are purchased every year. These biographies are popular, not because they provide a detailed outline of the coaching sessions but because they tell a more subjective story of coaching, with descriptions of what happened inside the changing rooms, and away from the gymnasium or field.

This popular, or lay, notion of the 'good' coach implicitly recognizes objective, measurable characteristics such as punctuality and organization, as well as subjective, less easily measured characteristics such as a sense of humour and flexibility. However, judging coaches on whether they are 'good' or not has largely disappeared from formal coach evaluation. Since the 1970s there has been a push towards coaches becoming accountable not only to the athletes, and the families of athletes, but increasingly to a board of directors and sponsors. In many cases the characteristics on which coaches are judged are those that are easily objectified and measured rather than subjective characteristics that are less easily measured. The push for accountability and the use of objective measures has utilized the language of effectiveness.

AN EFFECTIVE COACH

Despite the push for effectiveness becoming more prevalent since the 1970s there has been a focus, albeit limited, on effectiveness in the coaching literature, at least as far back as the 1950s when Friedrichsen (1956) studied the effectiveness of loop films as instructional aids in coaching gymnastics. Since then grids have been developed to increase the effectiveness of coaching games (Bean 1976), coaching effectiveness programmes have been designed (Bump 1987), and guides written that have focused on helping coaches to know 'how to' teach sport skills (Christina and Corcos 1988). In an effort to provide some 'conceptual clarity' regarding coaching effectiveness and the effective coach, Lyle (2002) undertook a comprehensive review of the literature that focused on these notions. In the process of reviewing the literature, one of the observations he made was that it was clearly evident that educational literature had influenced the research in coaching effectiveness and effective coaching. This was due in part to the development, and use of systematic observational tools like Academic Learning Time–Physical Education (ALT–PE) (Metzler 1979, 1989) which, in the1980s, became a very popular measure of teacher effectiveness. In the area of effectiveness, the educational literature has had a strong influence on the coaching literature because of 'the use of North American high-school/collegiate samples, the participation coaching emphasis, the borrowing of hypotheses from educational practice and a focus on the direct intervention role' (Lyle 2002: 261). One consequence of Lyle's review was that a valiant attempt was made to answer the question: are effective coaching and the effective coach the same concept? While he did not come up with a specific answer to this question, Lyle (2002: 259) did recognize that the 'apparent certainty' that some have when answering the question, 'continues to mask some important questions'. He went on to suggest that because of the lack of conceptual clarity that surrounds the terms 'coaching effectiveness' and 'effective coaching' it is necessary to consider alternative ways of judging coaching and coaches. While he identified and discussed a number of approaches such as process competence, value adding, and data-led goal setting, we consider the notion of quality to be another useful framework for judging coaches and coaching.

QUALITY IN COACHING

At first glance, the concept of quality in coaching may appear better suited to those coaches who have a participatory orientation rather than those coaches who have an elite performance orientation. Yet this was not supported by the commentaries of eight successful elite coaches (Steve Harrison, Hope Powell and Graham Taylor from association football (soccer), Ian McGeechan and Bob Dwyer from rugby union, Di Bass from swimming, Lois Muir from netball, and Peter Stanley from athletics) (Jones *et al.* 2004). When the coaches reflected upon their careers in coaching, their responses suggested that they believed coaching to be *more than* 'a process of passive instruction or training' (Carr 1989: 3). Drawing on the coaches' stories, Jones *et al.* (2004) claim that the coaches were well aware that they must, among other things, understand the athletes, care for them inside and outside the sporting environment and possess a set of technical and tactical ideals that they can clearly implement in a competitive situation. These reflective (and successful) coaches not only appeared to focus on the observable, practical, technical and measureable characteristics of coaching but also recognized the value of the subjective, social and cultural processes associated with coaching.

In other words they focused on the *instrumental* and *intrinsic* characteristics of coaching, which Carr (1989) considered to be a sign of being a quality practitioner (we discuss the characteristics in more detail below).

Quality can be defined in two ways: a) 'characteristic trait' and b) as a way of indicating a 'degree of excellence' (Carr 1989: 2). Quality can also be considered to be an amalgam of both definitions. It is this amalgamated definition that we draw on in this chapter. Consequently, quality in coaching requires the identification of those characteristic traits that constitute coaching excellence.

Instrumental characteristics

We define instrumental characteristics as those that focus on the practical and technical issues relating to coaching. If we return to the list at the beginning of the chapter where the undergraduate students identified what they thought were characteristics of a good coach, we can see that they did identify a number of instrumental characteristics. For example, they identified that a 'good' coach was required to have a loud voice, be punctual, be organized and be able to communicate ideas to the athletes. We contend that it is important for coaches to possess instrumental characteristics especially if they want athletes to be engaged in meaningful physical activity in the training sessions. Research in the physical education context has demonstrated that in many physical activity settings students spend (approximately): 25 per cent of their time participating in physical activity, 20 per cent being managed, 20 per cent receiving information and 28 per cent waiting for something to happen. While teachers spend (approximately): 20 per cent of their time managing, 30 per cent instructing and 20–40 per cent monitoring (Tinning *et al.* 1993). Arguably, similar findings could be found in many coaching contexts. Developing competency in various practical and technical strategies and the other instrumental characteristics of coaching may assist coaches to increase the amount of time athletes are engaged in physical activity and decrease the time spent waiting around, receiving information and being managed (Siedentop and Tannehill 2000). However, it must be stressed that there is no point in increasing the amount of physical activity in a session unless the activity is meaningful to the athletes. For example, a coach could easily increase the amount of time an athlete is physically active by simply increasing the number of laps of the field they do in the warm up. While that would increase the percentages it would hardly be very meaningful to the athlete unless the coach had a specific aim of increasing cardiovascular fitness.

While it is important that coaches do posses instrumental characteristics, there are limitations in solely focusing on these characteristics. As we have mentioned throughout this book, we value the ability of the coach to be reflective, not only at the technical and practical levels but also at the critical level. If a coach solely relies on instrumental characteristics then it is likely that there will be an over-emphasis on technical and practical issues and less emphasis on the subjective (social) aspects of the coaching process. One consequence of this may be that coaches would not consider how their actions might impact on the morale of the athletes as well as their ability to learn.

Intrinsic characteristics

Identifying quality in coaching requires the identification of those characteristic traits that constitute coaching excellence. We define intrinsic characteristics as those that focus on the subjective (social) issues related to coaching. If we revisit the list of characteristics which undergraduate students identified as those that made a 'good' coach, we can see that they identified characteristics such as a sense of humour, open-mindedness, patience and the ability to be a good motivator. We contend that it is important for coaches to possess intrinsic characteristics if they wish to develop a positive working relationship with the athletes. For example, Bob Dwyer (ex-Australian rugby union coach) talks about the importance of a coach having a sense of humour.

> The players I think get enjoyment out of being able to mimic the [silly] things I do and say, so I leave them in my repertoire. I know they think some of the expressions are right funny, but I'm happy about that because I think they'll remember it and it gives them a laugh. It's all part of the psychology of coaching.
>
> (Jones *et al.* 2004: 50)

While it is important for coaches to posses intrinsic characteristics, there are limitations in solely focusing on intrinsic characteristics. Being the athletes' 'best mate' will not be enough to improve performance or even guarantee continued participation. The following quote from an English premier league soccer coach highlights his belief that a coach would have 'trouble' if he relied solely on intrinsic characteristics.

> Footballers will test you . . . they will test you to see if you know. They usually pump you with questions . . . if I can't say why I want it done that way, if I can't give a good reason, then I've got trouble. You can't afford to lose players. So, you've got to know your subject . . . if you don't know your subject then you have real problems.
>
> (Potrac *et al.* 2002: 192)

WHY BOTHER WITH THE NOTION OF QUALITY?

We acknowledge that some coaches will continue to be judged on instrumental characteristics because they are easy to measure. But if there is a genuine desire to ascertain how 'good' a coach really is, then it may be worthwhile for coaches and administrators to consider using the notion of quality as a framework to judge coaches and coaching. Adopting this framework may not be as difficult as it may initially appear, given that elite coaches can often negotiate their contract conditions, and many other coaches have participatory motives and/or are involved in age-group and developmental teams. We have pragmatic and philosophical reasons why we believe a focus on quality in coaching is preferable to focusing on effective coaching or the effective coach. From a purely pragmatic point of view, quality in coaching encompasses intrinsic and instrumental characteristics, and as such it can be considered to be much more amenable to a holistic approach to coaching. Adopting a holistic approach to coaching enables the coach to consider the athlete as a human being not just as a mechanical body or a commodity to do with as he or she pleases. (For more detailed discussion on using a holistic approach to coaching and coach education see Chapters 15 and 16 respectively). If the athletes feel valued then they are more likely to want to train hard and play well for the coach. The following two quotes from Graham Taylor (an ex-England soccer coach) and Bob Dwyer (an ex-Australian rugby union coach) respectively highlight the way these coaches valued the intrinsic as well as the instrumental characteristics of coaching.

> Unless people are willing to listen to you, unless you are prepared to listen to them and understand them as people, the best coaching book in the world isn't going to help you. It all comes back to the relationships that you have with your players and the trust that exists between you. That's just life.
>
> (Jones *et al.* 2004: 28)

> The total environment is essential, and the total environment is affected by as much what you do off the pitch as what you do on it. It's about developing a sense of confidence, self-worth, and well-being in the players, which can have a real effect on the players and their performances.
>
> (Jones *et al.* 2004: 107–108)

Another pragmatic reason for focusing on quality in coaching is that it is a term that is already associated with judgement, as, for example in quality management and quality control. Adopting it in a coaching context gives legitimacy to the judgement that a notion like 'good' can no longer provide. However on a more philosophical point of view Tinning *et al.* (2001: 303) remind us that the notion of 'quality' is not the 'end point but a process', what is more, it is a 'reflective process'. This means that when focusing on quality, two questions are placed in the foreground: what are the implications for what I coach? and what are the implications for the way I coach? Tinning *et al.* (2001: 304) argue that a focus on quality requires practitioners to explore ways in which their practice can be 'more meaningful, purposeful, just and enjoyable'. Not only that, but they suggest that practitioners need to make a conscious effort to search for contradictions in their practice. Discovering the difference between what coaches think they are doing and what they are actually doing, in other words, discovering the difference between hope and happening, can highlight the contradictions. While it may be unrealistic to expect all contradictions to be eliminated in coaching practice

– after all it is a social process – at least acknowledging the contradictions that do exist may assist in the development of quality in coaching.

CONCLUDING THOUGHTS

Hopefully, most of us will have experienced at least one quality coach or teacher. If one can be remembered, it may also be possible to recount why this particular individual was a quality practitioner. Possibly one reason why they were valued was because they made a connection between us as the learner and them as the coach or teacher. While the connection could have been made because they possessed exceptional instrumental *or* intrinsic characteristics, anecdotal evidence suggests that the connection was made because they possessed exceptional characteristics from both categories. In contrast, many of us have knowledge of a coach who had tremendous technical ability (maybe as a consequence of being an elite athlete some years earlier), but who was not well received by the athletes whom he or she was coaching. Possessing the technical and even possibly the practical knowledge and having been an elite performer did not automatically make this individual a quality coach. We believe the anecdotal evidence supports our position that the concept of quality, as described in this chapter, would be a worthwhile framework for judging the practices of coaches.

CHAPTER 5

▼ **DEVELOPING A COACHING PHILOSOPHY**

- Introduction   53
- What is a coaching philosophy and why do coaches need to
  develop one?   55
- Problematizing coaching philosophies   56
- Developing functional, flexible philosophies   59
- Concluding thoughts   62

INTRODUCTION

It is widely accepted that what coaches do in their practice, and how they do it, tends to be shaped by their personal principles and values: attributes that are thought to comprise their coaching 'philosophy'. It is also believed that clearly articulating one's philosophy is a pre-requisite to good practice, as it provides direction and focus in relation to how one goes about doing the job of coaching. Indeed, a sub-section and/or an accompanying 'reflective' exercise aimed at developing a coaching philosophy can be found in almost every related coach education publication or course. Despite this official recognition that a philosophy has a direct impact on behaviour, many coaches consistently fail to adequately engage with the philosophic concept, not really grasping its relevance and accompanying influence over practical problems. It appears that they just can not see how investing in the process of developing and defining a clear philosophy can really have an impact on their daily problems at work. Hence, the negative mantras of 'it'll never work in the real world' or 'we've never done it like that here before' continue to block tentative philosophic routes of inquiry. It is a situation reflective of coach educators and coaches situated at opposing theoretical and practical positions 'talking past one another', or even of coaches not talking (in terms of philosophizing) about coaching much at all (Green 2000). This lack of engagement appears to have been aggravated by the comparative lack of research done into the motives that drive coaches' actions (Wilcox and Trudel 1998), which has led to rather superficial and simplistic assumptions about the value of establishing and locating definitive philosophies within the overall coaching process.

The principal aim of this chapter is first to conceptualize what is commonly referred to as a 'coaching philosophy', before making the case for and 'sign-posting' how coaches can develop a clear and credible one. It therefore invites coaches to 'hike along a philosophic trail' (Kretchmar 1994: xiii) in order to hone their related skills before determining their own functional philosophy. The development of such skills is important, as coaches frequently encounter novel situations that require clear thinking and analysis. Similarly, a definitive personal philosophy is valuable as it can provide practitioners with both 'cause and compass' on which to base action (Kretchmar 1994: xiii). However, in line with the book's theme, we emphasize that developing a philosophy, far from being a straightforward exercise, is quite problematic. It is a course of action fraught with ethical and moral questions, as the coaching process itself is grounded in various and complex interpersonal dimensions and driven by multiple goals (Lyle 2002) (see our Chapter 14 on coaching ethics for a fuller discussion of this issue). Consequently, we do not suggest that all coaches should possess one ideal philosophy and operate in a similar way, as there is no 'right' coaching philosophy. In this respect, we agree with Lyle (1999a), who stated that when developing a philosophy, care must be taken that it does not turn into an insincere tidy wish-list or model for coaching practice full of 'pat answers' that is perhaps at odds with underlying beliefs (Kretchmar 1994). We also recognize that, while based on principles, if a philosophy is to be deemed a credible and useful one, it should be flexible enough to take account of contextual factors. The objective then is to raise awareness of the problematic nature of a philosophy and the need to engage in-depth with that complexity, thus providing a framework to better develop one's own system of beliefs and practice. It is also to challenge coaches to examine and re-think personal biases and assumptions about the nature of coaching, and how they behave as coaches.

Following a section on the nature of a coaching philosophy and the need to create and clarify one, a discussion of the current literature and its shortcomings as it relates to developing a personal coaching philosophy is undertaken. This, in turn, is followed by suggestions of ways to cultivate more realistic coaching philosophies, which take into account the complex and contradictory social world within which coaches operate. In this respect, we are aware of the need to strike a balance between practicality and idealism; of the need to develop philosophies that both promote dreaming and speculating, whilst being able to play an active role in solving real, everyday problems (Kretchmar 1994). Lyle's (1999a, 2002) work provides a general framework for this discussion, as he is one of the few scholars to have problematically engaged with developing and defining a functional coaching philosophy.

WHAT IS A COACHING PHILOSOPHY AND WHY DO COACHES NEED TO DEVELOP ONE?

We begin our answer to these twin questions by addressing another asked by many coaches in this context: 'what's the point of spending time on my coaching philosophy, when what I really need are practical coaching tips?' The answer lies in accepting the role of philosophy as the precursor of action, because every element of coaching (i.e. the what, why and how of it) is affected by personal beliefs. An interesting analogy is to view one's philosophy as a pair of glasses, created by personal opinions, experiences and values, through which a particular perception of reality is filtered. It has, therefore, a direct bearing on how we understand the world, what actions we take, and why we take them. This definition of a philosophy appears to be common ground for many coaching scholars. For example:

> Coaching philosophy is defined as a set of values and behaviours that serve to guide the actions of a coach.
>
> (Wilcox and Trudel 1998: 41)

> A coaching philosophy is a personal statement that is based on the values and beliefs that direct one's coaching.
>
> (Kidman and Hanrahan 1997: 32)

> A coaching philosophy is a comprehensive statement about the beliefs that . . . characterize a coach's practice.
>
> (Lyle 1999a: 30)

A coaching philosophy, then, can be considered to be a set of principles that guide an individual's practice. Consequently, an examination of it delves into the heart of coaches' actions, investigating why they coach as they do. Indeed, according to Lyle (1999a), such an exploration should not be viewed as an 'optional extra' if we are to better understand coaching practice, as it provides a framework within which its delivery can be understood.

The value of developing a philosophy is to allow both coach and athletes a base from which to build and learn according to a consistent, coherent way of thinking. More specifically, it can help coaches clarify motives and provide direction to their coaching, whilst addressing what uniquely valuable contributions they might make as coaches (Kretchmar 1994). Without a definitive philosophy, behaviour can become too situation-specific, too reactive. A philosophy provides boundaries within which the coach–athlete relationship can be located. Writing one also has the potential to develop fresh ideas by encouraging us to think creatively and imaginatively about what we do as coaches and why we make these choices. For the individual then, thinking through actions to determine their root cause can become an enlightening process, as the value systems that guide a person's coaching need to be understood if we are to equally comprehend his or her actions. Additionally, as coaching has the potential to be power dominated and harmful to athletes (Kidman and Hanrahan 1997), clarifying and adhering to a coaching philosophy can assist in reminding ourselves of why we coach, thus guarding against the excesses that circumstances may drive us to (Lyle 1999a). This is not to dispute that the coach–athlete relationship in many instances should be hierarchical and thus characterized by power, but to ensure that that power be used in a sincere, meaningful and progressive way (Kidman and Hanrahan 1997).

We agree with many others in believing that, as a part of their training, coaches should become aware of their beliefs about coaching and how those deep-seated values influence their practice. Where we differ from most texts in this regard is to take issue with the largely unquestioned assumption that stated value-frameworks or philosophies unproblematically guide a coach's actions. Alternatively, we are realistic about the range of behaviours open to coaches; a range that is often constrained by operating within a particular cultural tradition. Indeed, although a coach's behaviour will often reflect deep-seated values and beliefs, sometimes opposite pressures are also present which complicate the decision-making process.

PROBLEMATIZING COACHING PHILOSOPHIES

Although we often assume that a philosophy is observable in behaviour, or that it should be, from empirical examinations of coaching behaviour we can see that the connection is not as straightforward as much of the current coaching literature would have us believe (Lyle 1999a). This is because little account is taken of contextual pressures and constraints when writing philosophies. Consequently, when produced, they lack the flexibility and credibility they would need to be truly functional. For example, in a situation where a coach holds a developmental philosophy, does the less skilled child in the group, who is low on self-confidence and needs special attention, *really* receive the required time investment in relation to others? Usually not. On the other hand, even if the child did receive such attention, are his/her needs being unfairly prioritized over more talented children who equally deserve to have their abilities further developed and fulfilled? Not addressing such 'real' issues as the multiplicity of goals inherent in coaching only leads to a superficial adoption of stated values, which are then perceived as of no practical use to coaches. In this respect, 'philosophic statements often seem easy to make but hard to keep' (Lyle 1999a: 28). Subsequently, coaches appear to have little confidence in the validity of the philosophic process and the practical application of the resulting product. Despite being frequently committed to paper then, philosophies are often discarded, or at best only paid lip service to, with coaches retreating into aspects of the process they can actually see or feel (Kretchmar 1994). This tendency was most recently found in a study by McCallister *et al.* (2000), where coaches, although able to clearly verbalize their philosophies, struggled both to articulate how they attempted to teach youngsters the stated outcomes and to demonstrate actual implementation of them. Such a finding is consistent with Stewart's (1993) belief that most coaches are effective at 'talking' rather than 'walking' a good philosophy.

Lyle (1999a) is one of the few scholars who has critically examined the assumption that coaching behaviour reflects philosophy, a notion that underpins much current coach education literature. He criticizes the view that the coach is free to allow any value framework to influence his or her behaviour, emphasizing that coaching practice can never be so objective. Rather, he contends that coaching is a social construction, developed from a personal set of views, which, in turn, are derived from such sources as experience, observations and education programmes, among others. Although such beliefs are framed reasonably early in life, they remain susceptible to alteration as influencing networks and forces become ever more complex and compelling (Green 2002). Consequently, they are constantly pressured by many external factors, which compete with one's ability to implement a stated philosophy in influencing coaching behaviour (Stewart 1993). Such factors include the particular ethos of the organization or club where the coach is employed, a definitive coaching sub-culture, athlete expectations, and the pressures associated with getting results. A coach may feel the need to adhere to some or all of these expectations, or alternatively to fight against and subvert them within his or her practice. As a result, there could be various reasons that underlie coaching behaviour, ranging from an adherence to personal ethics, to a desire to fit in with the coaching culture, to meeting the needs of athletes and the employing organization. Here then lies the potential for conflict between stated beliefs, personal values and actual practice (Lyle 1999a). Little wonder that pedagogical philosophies, as well as practices, represent something of a compromise (Green 2002). To further complicate the issue, Lyle (1999a) noted that probably not all standards are applied in all aspects of coaching practice. For example, while coaches could appear willing to 'tow the party line' with respect to some policies, others are not treated with such reverence, particularly where the result has far-reaching consequences. It is a tension between operational and fundamental ideology, which more than often leads to some modification of the latter (Evans 1992). It is also a tension which many in coaching, particularly at the performance level, are very aware of, although it remains largely unaddressed and, therefore, unresolved.

Unfortunately, with the exception of the work of McCallister *et al.* (2000), the link between coaches' beliefs and their actions has rarely been examined through field studies (Wilcox and Trudel 1998; Jones *et al.* 2003). Additionally, the research that has been carried out has been based on the assumption that coaching behaviour is easily changeable, and thus has failed to deal adequately with the subtlety and scope of philosophies and their influence over practice (Lyle 1999a). At present then there is little evidence 'on which to evaluate the contribution of a coach's value system against other environmental factors' in relation to practice and its basic resistance to deep-rooted change (Lyle 1999a: 28). Indeed, according to Lyle (2002) there is no proof that coaching style (read methods), as influenced by any particular philosophy, bears any influence over performance. What has further hindered our understanding of practice in this regard is the simplistic aggregation of coaching 'styles' (methods) into the autocratic–democratic dichotomy. This model leaves little room for the fact that a coach may be more democratic in one area of practice while being more autocratic in another. The complexity here has been 'simplified for the sake of a "cleaner" research design', which may well mask important variations (Lyle 1999a: 29). Such a sentiment was echoed by the recent findings of Wilcox and Trudel (1998), who discovered that overly simplistic accounts of coaches' convictions, opinions or views may well be inaccurate, as they are likely to abide by different beliefs and principles in different situations. Hence, depending on the situation, coaches may favour one option over another, or look for a balance between them. They concluded by calling for future investigations to avoid over-simplifying coaches' convictions and beliefs, and highlighted the need to help coaches develop philosophies that both reflect and leave room for these complexities.

The inadequacy of current thinking in relation to coaching philosophy also appears to be a result of the unquestioned focus given to both increased athlete involvement in the decision-making process, and to their leadership preference. Although athletes may pronounce themselves to be more motivated as a consequence of such participation and perceptions, the optimum coaching environment is more complex than the need to merely make athletes happy. Lyle (1999a) also believes that current research could well have been influenced by popular perceptions of ethical standards when discussing the development of coaching philosophies. Hence, coaches, particularly if such philosophies are meant for public consumption, may feel pressure to cite more politically correct value statements in them than might actually be observed in their practice. Indeed, coaches' notions of their philosophies appear more ideological than philosophical; that is to say, they are made up of seemingly mythical ideas of how they perceive they are supposed to act under a vague umbrella of 'good sportsmanship' or 'fair play'. The end result is the same: a simplified, sanitized list of statements, which is not sufficiently refined to apply in the subtle, contradictory world of coaching.

Let us now examine, in a little more depth, some of the difficulties inherent in applying a definitive coaching philosophy to practice. Such a philosophy is usually given in the form of a declaration about an aspect of practice. For example, a statement regarding sincerity could be presented as 'I will be open and honest with my athletes' (Lyle 1999a). The values proclaimed are clear, but the circumstances in which they will be evident are not specified, giving the assumption that a sincere coach will *always* be honest and open with athletes. The problem with such a declaration comes not with its worthy intent, but with its practicality and appropriateness in all circumstances. It does not address the thorny issue of *should* a coach always be honest with athletes, for instance, in terms of selection, opinions on performance, and the like. This, in turn, begs the question of are there certain situations where being less than honest is in the best interests of athletes or 'for the greater good'? (Lyle 1999a). A principal problem here then is that the statement of intent is too far removed from the ambiguous and complex reality to have much effect.

Giving credence to Lyle's (1999a) considerations, recent research by Jones *et al.* (2004) found that, although acknowledging the value of honesty and trust in the coach–athlete relationship, elite coaches were not averse to using 'white lies' when they judged it to be in the best interests of the athlete and/or team. The point to be made here is not that the coaches cited were unprincipled, but that they had found a way to be flexible within the confines of their respective philosophies. Consequently, they believed that what could be construed as a behavioural contradiction was in fact entirely consistent with overriding aims. These philosophies then, although sincere and believed, were primarily functional ones, which gave the necessary degree of credibility to be of use in guiding action. Perhaps this then is one way forward.

DEVELOPING FUNCTIONAL, FLEXIBLE PHILOSOPHIES

In order to generate more realistic and functional coaching philosophies, the first step is to acknowledge that they are very complex and complicated. Hence, they cannot be realistically created in a thirty-minute workshop or through a 'quickie' self-reflective exercise since, to make them credible, they need careful and realistic consideration. Similarly, there is a need to move away from bland, generic statements written as if they were meant as ideals to aspire towards (Lyle 1999a), or reflections that are too abstract for addressing actual coaching needs in practice. Alternatively, philosophies should be highly individualized, grounded in reality and be based on personal objectives founded on experiences (Kidman 2001; Kidman and Hanrahan 1997). Indeed, the diversity of knowledge allied to personal idiosyncrasy means that coaches' practice will invariably differ; a creative individualism that should be encouraged. Whilst acknowledging that there may be many means to the same end and that coaches will act according to their perception of the context, the clarification of purposes and guidelines encapsulated in a philosophy is still valuable as it leads to informed choices and better priorities. Such boundary definition is also beneficial as it lays the foundations for consistency (Kidman and Hanrahan 1997). Within this process, Lyle (2002) points to the need to consider and link issues of philosophy and behaviour. Hence, not only do we need to differentiate between delivery style and core purpose, but also to sketch outlines of appropriate practice in relation to both. The important point here is that the objective is not to tie the coach down 'to a prearranged act, but to definitively guide action while maintaining the required flexibility to be contextual' (Lyle 1999a: 37).

Recent research into elite coaches' philosophies (Saury and Durand 1998; Jones *et al.* 2003) indicates an awareness of the need to remain flexible in practice, thus maintaining the ability to adapt to changing circumstances. It includes a belief that definitive standards cannot be applied outright, as they often conflict with other constraints inherent in the coaching situation (Saury and Durand 1998). However, and echoing the point made earlier, this does not mean that such coaches acted without principle. In explaining this apparent contradiction, Raffel (1998) draws a distinction between the 'principled' and the 'rule-guided' actor. Whilst the latter would view practice as a set of prescriptions with which he or she is obligated to comply, the principled actor believes in the rightness of his or her actions, with practice clearly reflecting values. Consequently, there is room to explore and manoeuvre within a principled commitment to stated values. Of importance is that principled individuals view their practice as something that is intrinsically worth doing; as something to actively further and not merely to comply with (Jones *et al.* 2004). In this sense, they 'live' their own training sessions vicariously and emotionally, as they invest much of themselves in their practice (Saury and Durand 1998; Jones *et al.* 2004). It is the difference between being competent in relation to a philosophy and being *committed* to it.

Allowing flexible adherence within philosophical boundaries goes some way to explain expert coaches' actions and their belief in applying sensitivity to unexpected and problematic tasks (Saury and Durand 1998; Côté *et al.* 1995). Indeed, according to Saury and Durand (1998: 264), the practice of such experts is 'very flexible and based on continuous step-by-step tuning to the context', albeit embedded in a deep knowledge of sport and a commitment to an established framework of behaviour. In this respect, the coaching process and coaching practice can be considered as 'regulated improvisation' (Bourdieu 1977: 79), which takes into account the particular challenges and tensions that are unique to it. Here, the particular is malleable within stated guidelines. Such practice was clearly evident in the accounts of expert coaches researched by Jones *et al.* (2004). For example, clear value statements were relatively readily applied to the purpose of coaching, while flexibility was acknowledged as vital to 'test the edges' of philosophy as it manifests itself in contextual practice (Lyle 2002). It appears then that top-level coaches are able to manage well the inevitable dilemmas between philosophy and practice, in that they are realistic and practical about their goals while retaining a strong personal set of values and standards (Lyle 2002).

How should one go about developing such a functional, yet sincere personal philosophy? As stated in the introduction to this chapter, the aim here is not to provide 'correct' prescriptive thinking for all, but rather to assist coaches through a process by which they can arrive at their own individualized, personalized guides for action. A good place to start however is to utilize higher thinking skills in addressing fundamental questions about one's own personal involvement in coaching, whilst allowing more detailed reflective questions to emerge once the conceptual issues have been clarified. An important point to remember is that this process should be carried out in a systematic, careful, and rigorous way, so as to give the findings definitive meaning. Here, Kretchmar (1994) suggests that we should use inductive, intuitive and/or deductive reasoning in developing philosophy, thus creating it from experience and reflection. This would give us a degree of security and confidence in its personal applicability. First then, the following questions could be addressed:

- What is coaching, and why do I think that?
- Why am I a coach?

- Have my coaching motives changed? How? Why?
- Is there another way?
- Why are these athletes participating?
- Why did a particular coach have such a meaningful impact on me?
- What are my future hopes both for the athletes I coach and for myself as a coach?
- Are they 'my' athletes or am I 'their' coach?
- Who holds the power in a coach–athlete relationship?
- What is my role as a coach and why do I think that?

Although lists of similar questions appear in current coaching workshops, the superficiality with which they are engaged, makes the exercise of little value. To create a worthwhile functional philosophy such questions need to be carefully and sincerely addressed. For example, in examining the last question cited above ('what is my role as a coach?'), instead of merely brainstorming potential functions, we would implore coaches to address such issues related to role as, how do I 'play' the role of the coach? Whose expectations am I fulfilling? Why? Is there a case for me to expand and explore the boundaries of the traditional coaching role? Do I want to, and what are the implications of doing so? How can I allow my own personality to emerge through the coaching role? Am I fulfilling myself within the coaching role? Through addressing these and other such carefully crafted questions to address both meaning and purpose, a deeper sense of a coaching philosophy and identity can emerge: one that is grounded in personal reality.

Once a philosophical framework has been established, or perhaps in tandem with it, more practical questions should also be addressed so that the philosophy maintains a working credibility and usefulness for coaches. Such questions here could include:

- Is my approach educationally sound?
- Do the drills I use best serve the purpose for which they are intended (i.e. the objective of the session)? Why and how?
- Is the approach appropriate for the athletes?
- Is there a better way of doing what I'm doing?
- Can I explain and justify my coaching actions and decisions?
- How do I ensure that I follow my coaching philosophy?
- What happens if my coaching philosophy is challenged?
- How will I deal with the different values of other people? (Kidman and Hanrahan 1997)
- What is key about the inter-personal relationships I have with athletes?
- Are there situational compromises in the application of my stated values? (Lyle 2002)

Such reflective questions could be applied to all aspects of the coaching process, from pedagogical and motivational issues to those of planning, monitoring and organizing, to ensure that the developed philosophy is realized through behaviour. In many ways, it is important to commit the philosophy to paper for all to see, because a written document easily reminds everyone of the ethos of the sporting experience undertaken. It also forces the writer to organize his or her ideas and to defend a position. It allows them to see if they have really clarified their thoughts. Of more importance however, is the need to regularly re-examine and re-evaluate the philosophy, as our experiences constantly shape and evolve our thoughts. The philosophy should therefore be written in pencil not in ink! (Kretchmar 1994).

CONCLUDING THOUGHTS

Writing a personal coaching philosophy gives coaches the opportunity to identify and clarify what is important to them at the personal level. It is a chance to consider both the most appropriate destination for each of us, and to decide on the best route to get there (Kretchmar 1994). What needs to be avoided, however, when developing a philosophy, is the superficial adoption of public statements of intent, which have little bearing on day-to-day practice. We advocate an in-depth engagement with the philosophic process, which can help us become aware of why certain decisions are made and actions taken. Indeed, the process is perhaps more important than the outcome, as involvement in it develops the clarity of thinking skills required for such a dynamic activity as coaching. To make a philosophy functional it should also take into account the external constraints on coaches' actions, thus appreciating the contextual complexity within which they work. Furthermore, perhaps we should pay close attention to the elite practitioners interviewed in the work of Jones *et al.* (2004) who not only believed in the value of clarifying philosophies as flexible guides to action but sincerely tried to live their coaching lives through them. In conclusion, we believe that the time it takes to evaluate, understand, choose and develop a functional yet sincere philosophy will be time very well spent, with the result being better guided, more thoughtful and imaginative coaches (Kretchmar 1994).

▼ END OF SECTION ONE: TASKS

To complete Tasks 1 and 2 you are required to select one, sometimes two, coaches to observe. To make the tasks more meaningful it would be useful if the coach was involved in a sport or activity in which you are involved. Preferably the coach will be working with more than one athlete. You MUST ask their permission to observe them.

TASK 1

1   Using your knowledge of the characteristics of various coaching methods, describe what methods the coach adopts in the coaching session. Provide examples and discuss the consequences for the athletes of the coach adopting these methods.
2   Discuss what methods, if any, the coach does not use, or does not use frequently. Explain why you think this might be the case.

TASK 2

Ideally the following questions will be asked when observing a coach working in a single-sex context and again when observing a coach working in a co-educational setting. (Take note, even in a single-sex setting, athletes can be positioned along gendered lines. For example, if a male athlete is not working hard enough he may be called a 'girl' which calls into question his masculinity and sexuality as well as being demeaning to females.) When answering the following questions you may wish to seek some assistance from a friend to assist with the data collection.

1   How many occasions (n = ?) did the coach provide behavioural feed-back? Provide some examples of who received the feedback and under what circumstances.
2   How many occasions (n = ?) did the coach provide performance feed-back? Provide some examples of who received the feedback and under what circumstances.

3   Describe any examples of feedback you witnessed that either reinforced or challenged gender, sex, ethnic or ability stereotypes.

4   Describe the forms of nonverbal feedback that the athletes may have received in the coaching session. Discuss some possible consequences of this feedback.

TASK 3

Recently you have been appointed to coach a team in the premier competition in your local area. The contract you have been asked to sign states that you will be evaluated at the completion of your first season. Before signing the contract, you ask the governing body to identify the criteria upon which you will be evaluated. They supply you with some performance indicators that you recognize as being very instrumental. You explain to them that you are aiming to be a quality coach and want to be judged accordingly. For this to happen you wish to draw up your own criteria which will include some of their instrumental criteria but will also include intrinsic criteria.

Prepare criteria upon which you (as a quality coach), would be prepared to be judged. Alongside each criterion identify what evidence will need to be presented to demonstrate whether or not you have met the criteria.

SECTION TWO
THE ATHLETES

6   Understanding the learning process   67
7   'Developing' athletes   82
8   Understanding athletes' motivation   90
9   Understanding athletes' identities   106

CHAPTER 6

▼   **UNDERSTANDING THE
LEARNING PROCESS**

- Introduction   67
- Vignette 1: coaching the U21's   69
- Multiple orientations to learning   71
- Vignette 2: consequences for the learner   77
- Consequences for the learner   78
- Concluding thoughts   81

INTRODUCTION

We are all knowledgeable, albeit to varying degrees, about the learning process. This knowledge has been acquired not only as a consequence of being a participant, willing or not, in formal education systems but also as a result of being a member of humanity. However, being knowledgeable about the learning process does not mean that an individual can verbally articulate his or her knowledge. Much of the knowledge required to 'go on' in everyday life is practical in character (Giddens 1984) and has been defined as practical consciousness or tacit knowledge (Giddens 1979). It is this knowledge that enables us simply to 'do' things while concentrating on activities that require conscious effort (Giddens 1984), such as manually chang-ing the gears whilst driving a car. We contend that many coaches' knowledge of the learning process is tacit, thereby enabling them to concentrate on other aspects of the coaching process such as instruction or management. The design of a coaching session, and understanding what a coach considers to be 'common sense' provides insights into what theories of learning inform the coach. Even when individuals are able to verbally articulate their understanding of the learning process, it is still often implicitly informed by the research that has stemmed from the discipline of psychology, and the sub-discipline of educational psychology.

When Gilbert (2002) coded his comprehensive annotated bibliography of coaching science by theme, cognition (a common topic of study in psychology) was the second most common theme. Yet, when Gilbert further coded the cognition articles by keywords, the articles were grouped around issues such as: attitudes; anxiety; beliefs; decision making; efficacy; goal orientation; knowledge; perceptions; and values. What is interesting, especially in light of the arguments we made in the introductory chapter of this book, is that that there were no articles identified as focusing on the learning process, or the athlete as learner. This should not have come as a surprise. Even the physical education literature, which is explicitly connected to education, has paid little attention to the learner or the learning process (Hunter *et al.* 1999; Rovegno and Kirk 1995; Smith 1991), although this is slowly changing (see Kirk and Macdonald 1998; Rovegno and Bandhauer 1997).

The purpose of this chapter is to make explicit connections between some of the learning theories that have been informed by psychology and educational psychology, and existing coaching practices and the consequences the various learning theories have on the learning process of the athlete. But we must point out that this chapter is not a detailed overview of learning theories, as plenty of psychology and educational psychology texts exist, should more detail be required. Nor do we champion one learning theory over another since we recognize that each theory has different learning outcomes and therefore will be suitable for different contexts. Nonetheless, we did argue in the introductory chapter for learning to be viewed less as the reception of acts and facts, and more of a social practice. The latter position is supported by those theorists who developed learning theories that are located under the constructivist banner.

Deciding on the organization of this chapter was not straightforward due to history not being a linear process, and factors such as fashion, politics and language barriers influencing when learning theories became widely known and accepted. As such we have written two vignettes in an attempt to have students of sports coaching become aware that what are often considered 'common-sense' practices are in fact informed by particular learning theories and these have consequences on the athlete as a learner. The first vignette illustrates a coaching situation where two coaches, who have quite different views of the learning process, are appointed to co-coach a team. After we have presented the vignette we discuss some aspects of three generally accepted orientations to learning. The focus is mainly on two of these orientations, namely behaviourism and constructivism. We have chosen these two orientations because there has been an ongoing debate in education between the constructivist and behaviourist views of learning (Diessner and Simmons 2000). However, there are difficulties associated with organizing the chapter around these two positions because not every theory, or theorist, fits neatly into the respective camps. Some theorists such as Bandura have developed theories that integrate concepts that have 'traditionally been associated with separate positions' (Lefrançois 2000: 328). As such we conclude our discussion on the learning theories by focusing on an integrated orientation to learning. At the completion of the discussion on learning theories we introduce another vignette in which the athletes provide their views on the practices of the coaches illustrated in the first vignette. In the second vignette the athletes provide insights into the consequences that the practices of the coaches have on them as learners. After we

have presented this vignette we discuss what the literature says about the consequences each learning theory has on learners.

VIGNETTE 1: COACHING THE U21'S

Earlier in the year Alex and Denis had been appointed to coach a rugby union
Under 21 representative team. This was the third year Alex had been appointed
as coach but it was Denis's first appointment at the representative level. Alex's
expertise was in coaching the forward pack while Denis had been appointed to
coach the back line. It was widely known that the administrators were trying
to find a coaching combination at the U21 level that would develop athletes
who could, in time, successfully make the transition to the senior teams. In placing
Alex and Denis together, the administrators were gambling that the skills and
attributes they brought to their coaching would complement each other.

Alex and Denis did not know each other very well, although Denis knew Alex by
reputation since he was 25 years his senior and had played for the national team
for five years. Denis had also played for the national team but only three games.
Alex had been involved in the game for 40 years and he had learnt how to be a coach
from watching other coaches, as an athlete and novice coach, and from trial and
error. He had attended some coaching clinics as a requirement of his employment
with the rugby union. In contrast, Denis had only been coaching for five years and
most of this had been in age-group school teams as a consequence of being a
teacher of physical education in a local secondary school. While both coaches were
excited at their appointment and were looking forward to the challenge, they
were wary of each other with Alex thinking that Denis was a bit 'green' and Denis
thinking Alex was a bit 'old fashioned'.

The athletes in the U21 team were a diverse bunch. Some were university students,
others were tradesmen, and the remainder had temporary jobs so they could concentrate on playing rugby. The squad had an equal number of athletes identifying
as Māori, Samoan, and Pakeha (non-Māori/European). Some of the athletes had
been in the U21 squad the previous year and had already experienced Alex's
coaching regime. Of the players who were new to the squad, some had come through
the representative age-group teams, while others had no experience of being in a
representative team.

In deciding upon a routine for their coaching sessions Alex and Denis agreed that,
after the trainer had completed the warm up and fitness session, they would take
the forward pack and back line respectively to opposite ends of the field to begin
position-specific training. In planning for his session Alex made sure each aspect
of the session had a designated time to begin and end. He prided himself on the
fact that there was very little time spent standing around in his sessions. Over the
years he had developed a set of standard instructions that were clear and concise.
He mirrored his method of coaching on what he remembered his favourite
coach doing with him in the 1980s. The method comprised of verbally describing

the drill and then getting experienced members of the squad to demonstrate it. As far as Alex was concerned the only time the method did not appear to work was when the athletes did not listen, or pay attention. For the most part, when athletes did not pay attention and were off task, Alex ignored them and turned his attention to those athletes who were on task. He adopted this strategy because he had heard somewhere that the reason athletes did not stay on task was because they wanted to get his attention or the attention of the other athletes.

The 'pick and go' drill was Alex's favourite. The drill focused on improving the athletes' ability to pick the ball up off the ground quickly, make some territory and then, when tackled, lay the ball on the ground away from their body so that team mates could gain easy access to the ball, thereby carrying on forward momentum. Before running the drill with all the athletes Alex would break it down into parts. For example, he would require the athletes to pick a ball off the ground, take three steps and then place the ball down on the ground, repeating the drill until they got to the end of the field. If an athlete fumbled the ball because he did not get down low enough to pick the ball up off the ground Alex would require the athlete to do ten press-ups (to remind him what the ground looked like). If an athlete continued to perform badly throughout the session Alex would inform him that he would not be making the starting line up for the next game. In contrast, when an athlete completed the drills speedily and skilfully Alex would smile and praise his ability and efforts or excuse him from having to do some of the chores associated with training, such as picking up the cones at the completion of the session.

Before Alex ran the complete 'pick and go' drill he would stress the need to lay the ball away from the body when tackled because this would provide team mates easy access to the ball and reduce the chance of the ball carrier being stood on. When the athletes practised the drill Alex did not reprimand those athletes who stood on the ball carrier. He believed that being stood on would remind the ball carrier, the next time he had the ball, to place it on the ground away from his body.

While Alex worked with the forward pack at one end of the field, Denis was at the other working with the back line. He had a plan of what he wanted to do with the backs but he was not too prescriptive because he thought that would stifle the talent and flair he knew the athletes possessed. In the time between selecting the team and the first coaching session Denis had met and talked with the athletes in an effort to get a sense of their background, inside and outside of the rugby union context, and what they wanted to achieve playing in the U21's. He also had gained some understanding of the athletes' rugby background from the files the rugby union kept on the athletes.

In his coaching plan Denis identified learning outcomes he wanted to achieve and various ways of achieving these. One of Denis's favourite strategies was to pose the athletes a problem and get them to work in groups to solve it, before bringing them back together to discuss the various solutions. Denis knew from experience that at the beginning of the season he would have to contribute quite significantly to the problem-solving exercise, but over the course of the season the athletes would gain confidence in their ability to solve problems and would require less input from him. Some times the problem required the involvement of the entire back line while other problems required smaller units (such as the scrum half, fly half and inside centre or the centre, wings and fullback) to work together. To pose a problem that was meaningful to the athletes required Denis to do plenty of homework such as researching the forthcoming opposition. Having done the research Denis could then present the back line with problems that were opposition-specific and therefore meaningful to the athletes. Denis encouraged the athletes to use a range of media when reporting their solution to the problem back to the group, e.g. diagrams on a whiteboard, verbal explanations, models, walking the group through the move, etc. While a group was explaining a solution, Denis would take notes. After the coaching session he would compile the notes in some sort of order and give them back to the athletes at the beginning of the following session. Once the athletes had explained the solutions to their peers Denis would set up a situation where the athletes could physically practise the solutions. Denis recognized that learning occurred over time and that it did not occur in an uninterrupted, upward trajectory. As such, his intention was to increase the athletes' understanding over the season, not necessarily over the duration of one practice session, and it was for that reason that, as a rule, Denis never punished the athletes for getting things wrong, especially if they were genuinely trying. Instead, he would take the athlete who was having trouble aside, and use a range of communication strategies, in an attempt to increase his understanding of what was happening.

MULTIPLE ORIENTATIONS TO LEARNING

Alex and Denis may not have been able to verbally articulate the characteristics of the learning theories that informed their practices. Nonetheless, as we illustrate in the following section, they had tacit knowledge of behaviourist and constructivist learning theories and these were visible in their practices.

Behaviourist orientations to learning

Notable contributors to the growth of behavioural psychology were Russian physiologist Pavlov and Americans Watson and Skinner (Carlson and Buskist 1997). Pavlov's experiments with a salivating dog, and the subsequent formulation of the theory of classical conditioning, were valuable insights for behaviourism. Watson's book, *Psychology from the Standpoint of a Behaviorist*, formalized behaviourism as a 'school of psychology', while Skinner became 'one of the most influential psychologists of the twentieth century' (Carlson and Buskist 1997: 16). Lefrançois (2000: 67) contends that Skinner was significantly influenced by the work of Thorndike, with the latter 'almost single-handedly' defining and establishing educational psychology. Under the mentorship of Thorndike, educational research became a science 'dedicated to control rather than making sense of the forms and processes of schooling and teaching' (Doyle 1992: 489). Thus, the focus of the research was 'behavioral, experimental, and atomistic' with the aim of defining 'precisely what teachers must do in order to cause student learning' (1992: 489).

Over his career Thorndike developed a number of laws to explain learning. One of the most important was the Law of Effect. Carlson and Buskist (1997) explain that this law

> specifies a relation between behavior and its consequences. If a stimulus that follows a response makes that response become more likely, we say that the response was reinforced. If the stimulus makes the response become less likely, we say that it was punished. The reinforcing or punishing stimulus must follow the behavior almost immediately if it is to be effective.
>
> (Carlson and Buskist 1997: 145)

The influence of the Law of Effect, and the notion of reinforcement, has been significant as evidenced by it informing the development of other learning theories and day-to-day practice (Lefrançois 2000). The Law of Effect can be seen in Alex's practices with the forward pack in the above vignette. When Alex was running the various forms of the 'pick and go' drill his smile and praise could be viewed as a stimulus that followed an athlete's speedy and efficient completion of the drill (the response). Since the athletes valued receiving Alex's praise and his smile, their behaviour of performing the drill speedily and efficiently was reinforced and therefore they would try to repeat the behaviour. In contrast, his request that an athlete perform ten press-ups as a consequence of fumbling the ball could be viewed as a stimulus that makes fumbling the ball (the response) less likely to reoccur. In other words, the press-ups were the punishing stimulus.

Thorndike also developed the Law of Exercise which explains the 'bonds between stimuli and responses' (Lefrançois 2000: 67). This law 'did a great deal to encourage the repetitive "drill" approaches to learning that became increasingly popular in the 1930s and 1940s' (Lefrançois 2000: 67) and we would argue are still popular in sport coaching to this present day. As illustrated in the vignette, apart from some instruction and demonstration, Alex's practice session comprised solely of drills such as the 'pick and go'.

A contribution Skinner made to our understanding of learning was through his definition and subsequent research on what he called operant or instrumental conditioning. Conditioning is a term used by behaviourists to mean 'the process of training or changing behaviour by association and reinforcement' (Jary and Jary 1991: 110). Skinner describes two types of reinforcement – positive and negative (Lefrançois 2000). The former is a reward such as Alex providing the athletes with praise and smiling at them. The latter form of reinforcement is relief from an annoying situation, like when Alex excuses the athletes who performed the drill speedily and efficiently from doing chores associated with coaching such as picking up the cones at the end of the session.

Skinner also contends that punishment, like reinforcement, affects behaviour. However, unlike reinforcement, the aim of punishment is not to strengthen a behaviour but rather suppress it (Lefrançois 2000). There are two types of punishment – presentation and removal. The former is when an individual is castigated or reprimanded for a behaviour (Lefrançois 2000), such as when Alex requests an athlete to perform ten press-ups as a consequence of fumbling the ball in the 'pick and go' drill. The latter is when something pleasant is removed from the individual (Lefrançois 2000), which is what Alex did when he told an athlete he was dropped from the starting line up as a consequence of performing badly throughout the training session.

A popular term to describe the systematic use of Skinner's operant conditioning is behaviour modification. It is commonly known in the professional and lay population that 'positive reinforcement and punishment can be highly effective for modifying behavior' (Lefrançois 2000: 127). Another practice associated with behaviour modification is extinction. This is often used by practitioners who want to stop unwanted behaviour but do not want to punish the perpetrator of the behaviour. According to Skinner's notion of extinction, individuals can 'often be made to stop engaging in some unwanted form of behavior by removing their source of reinforcement' (Lefrançois 2000: 128). An example of this is when Alex ignored the behaviour of the athletes who were off task, with the aim that they would return to being on task once the reinforcement (his attention) was removed. The way Alex conducts his coaching sessions can be viewed as an example of a behaviour-modification programme at work, since he systematically uses rewards and punishments to modify the behaviour of the athletes in the forward pack.

Constructivist orientations to learning

Over the twentieth century, educational trends and fashions have changed, and this has resulted in advocates of cognitive and constructivist orientations of learning beginning to receive more favourable attention. Vygotsky, with his socio-cultural perspective of learning, and Piaget's cognitive perspective, as well as theorists such as Dewey and Bruner have been grouped under the banner of constructivism (Buck 2003). Constructivism is the theory behind the principle that 'human beings do not find or discover knowledge so much as construct or make it. We invent concepts, models and schemes to make sense of experience and we continually test and modify these constructions in light of new experience' (Schwandt in Buck 2003: 47). Despite there being similarities between the cognitive and socio-cultural perspectives, differences still exist. For example, Piaget argues that learning occurs as a consequence of the 'unfolding of internal capacities' which he refers to as 'cognitive development' (Morss 1991: 27). In contrast, Vygotsky argues that learning occurs in 'collaboration with others, some of whom are relative experts on the task in hand (and some of whom may be relative novices)' as well 'as a result of the "taking in" of the culture by which the child [read learner] is surrounded' (1991: 27).

One theorist who is often grouped under the constructivist banner is Dewey, who viewed science as a way of understanding the 'social complexities of education in its concrete forms' (Doyle 1992: 489). To achieve this, Dewey saw experimentation as a 'collaborative process' between researchers and teachers with the aim of understanding ways of bringing the curriculum and the student together in 'natural settings' (Doyle 1992). Dewey adopted 'ecological' metaphors, and as a consequence rejected

> the narrow stimulus-response conceptions of behavioural psychology and found much greater affiliation with sociological and anthropological formulations of the day.
>
> (Doyle 1992: 489)

Denis's practice of researching the opposition and setting problems for the athletes that were specific to the forthcoming opposition reflects Dewey's view that experimentation is collaborative, and that learning is a complex process that is enhanced when it is located within a 'natural setting'.

Vygotsky also valued the idea that learning occurs in a social context, although he is quick to point out that the social context is different for each learner (McMillan 1991). An important idea proposed by Vygotsky is that development, and consequently learning, is a 'continual progress but with periodic crises and revolutions' (McMillan 1991: 33). A useful metaphor for understanding Vygotsky's theory of learning and development is a staircase. According to Vygotsky, learning

> gives rise to a variety of internal developmental processes that are able to operate when the child is interacting with people in a given situation. Once these processes are 'internalised' or understood, they become part of the child's independent development of achievement.
>
> (Tangaere 1997: 48–49)

When related to the staircase metaphor, the learner's independent development of achievement can be conceived as the stair on which the learner is standing, having successfully climbed up the lower stairs.

One hypothesis in Vygotsky's theory for learning and development is that there is a 'zone of proximal development' which is the zone between what can be achieved by the learner alone and what he or she is able to achieve with assistance (Tangaere 1997). In terms of the metaphor of the staircase, the zone of proximal development can be viewed as the vertical distance between the stair on which the learner is standing and the next highest stair. To reach the higher stair the learner has to internalize the learning and no longer require assistance to perform the activity. Once the higher stair has been reached the zone of proximal development becomes the vertical distance to the next stair, and so on (Tangaere 1997). An illustration of how athletes' zone of proximal development can be recognized is highlighted by the way Denis knew at the beginning of the season he would have to significantly contribute to solving the problems he set the athletes but, over time, the athletes would internalize how to solve problems without his assistance. By the end of the season the knowledge of how to solve Denis's problems would have become part of the athletes' independent development of achievement.

Another contributor to our understanding of learning is Bruner, who advocated for the recognition to be given to the cultural and social context of the learner (Diessner and Simmons 2000). Bruner, along with constructivists such as Vygotsky, draw on the metaphor of a scaffold to describe a system to support learning (Tangaere 1997). Scaffolding assists 'learners to solve a problem that they would otherwise be unable to solve themselves' (Tangaere 1997: 51). The learner draws on the expertise of another, with the latter providing clues to enable the learner to solve the problem. Each time the learner acquires new skills or information (gained either from the learner's own perception or from the expert), it complements existing knowledge and advances the learner towards solving the problem. What is more, the scaffolding supports the development of a relationship between the learner and the more skilful individual, and enables the former to test out what has been learned in a safe environment. Once the learner is comfortable with the task, the support can be slowly withdrawn, thereby assisting the learner to become more independent. An example of scaffolding is the way Denis supports the athletes to solve the problems he sets by providing clues, but also gradually withdrawing his support throughout the season as the athletes become more confident of their abilities to solve the problems.

The relationship between the learner and the so-called expert is not one way, rather it can be viewed as reciprocal. Often in the process of teaching, or answering questions posed by a learner, the more experienced member in the relationship also learns (Tangaere 1997). This relationship is known by Māori as 'tuakana/teina' with tuakana meaning 'older sibling (brother to a boy or sister to a girl), and teina a younger sibling (brother to a boy or sister to a girl)' (Tangaere 1997: 50). Since the tuakana/teina concept is related to both teaching and learning 'it is an acceptable practice for the learner [read athlete] to shift roles and become the teacher [read coach] or for the teacher to become the learner' (1997: 50). One way of incorporating the tuakana/teina concept into coaching is to encourage the more knowledgeable (although not necessarily the more senior) athlete to become the tuakana on, as well as off, the field to the less knowledgeable athletes (teina). An example of this was provided by Daniel Carter (a 21-year-old Canterbury Crusaders fly half) who was interviewed about his meteoric rise, which saw him become the starting fly half for the team. In the interview he talked about the way Andrew Mehrtens, (the then incumbent All Black fly half and All Black record holder for number of points scored in test matches), had assisted him in training sessions by being his partner in drills and providing him with insights into the game (TV3 2003). From the interview, it was unclear whether the tuakana/teina relationship had been formally mandated by the coach, or whether it had been informally arranged by the athletes themselves. Either way, from the perspective of the teina, it was a useful arrangement. Many of the features of tuakana/teina were also reflected in the notions of peer teaching or reciprocal teaching (Mosston 1966) that were discussed in Chapter 2.

The practice of the rugby union appointing Alex and Denis as co-coaches can also be viewed as reflecting the tuakana/teina relationship, with Alex the tuakana, and Denis the teina. The rugby union was gambling that the relationship would not be a hierarchical arrangement of head coach and assistant coach. Rather, it would be a relationship where the flow of knowledge would go both ways between Denis and Alex, with the former passing on knowledge that he had gained in his tertiary education, and with the latter sharing what he had learned by experience. Denis also used the tuakana/teina concept in his practices, for example when he required various groups of athletes in the back line to teach moves to their team mates.

Bruner, in his cognitive theory of learning, emphasizes the 'formation of coding systems' and hypothesizes that the coding systems 'facilitate transfer, improve retention, and increase problem-solving ability and motivation' (Lefrançois 2000: 209). This view of learning resulted in him advocating a discovery-orientated approach to learning which requires practitioners to use methods by which the learner is encouraged to 'discover facts and relationships themselves' (Lefrançois 2000: 209). The way Denis set problems that were specifically orientated towards the forthcoming opposition and required the athletes to discover solutions to a problem are examples of a discovery-orientated approach to learning.

Integrated orientations to learning

In an attempt to explain human behaviour, such as learning, behaviourists focus on 'the external environment through reinforcement' while constructivists place an emphasis on the 'internal world' and the way learners construct their own knowledge (Diessner and Simmons 2000: ii). Bandura is one theorist who 'maintains that it is impossible to explain human behaviour solely by reference to either internal or external stimulus events; both are inevitably involved in most human behavior' (Lefrançois 2000: 329).

Not surprisingly, given the influence of Skinner, Bandura's early work was informed by behaviourism, in particular the model of operant conditioning. However, over time Bandura's work became more 'socially orientated', focusing on 'how people influence each other' and 'how social behaviors are acquired through imitation' (Lefrançois 2000: 305). Bandura also became interested in the cognitive aspect of behaviour, 'assigning an increasingly important role to the human ability to anticipate the consequences of behavior' (Lefrançois 2000: 305). Bandura claims that one example of an operant was imitation, also called observational learning, which occurs as a consequence of observing some form of model. He argues that 'important aspects of social learning (that is, learning of socially appropriate behavior) cannot easily be explained using simple learning principles without considering imitation' (Lefrançois 2000: 123). Modelling and imitating was an aspect of Alex's *and* Denis's coaching practice. Alex used demonstration and explanation prior to commencing any drill, using experienced members of the forward pack as the model. Denis did not set up a modelling situation as explicitly as Alex, but when some members of the back line taught their team mates a move they often demonstrated what they required the others to do.

VIGNETTE 2: UNWINDING AFTER THE TRAINING SESSION

After the training session a number of the athletes would congregate in one of the sponsor's establishments to unwind. In this environment, away from the gaze of the coaches, the athletes could relax and talk freely amongst themselves. Not surprisingly, since they had just finished training, Alex and Denis were often the topic of conversation. Within the squad there were mixed opinions about the methods adopted by the coaches. Mark and Andrew (the two locks in the forward pack) constantly sang Alex's praises. They loved the way he used the same drills he had participated in when he was in the national squad, as it made them feel as if one day they too could play for their country. For a similar reason, they liked it when Alex used the experienced members of the squad to demonstrate some of the drills because a number of their experienced team mates had already played for the national U21 squad. They appreciated the way Alex maintained a similar routine to all the practices as this enabled them to just concentrate on doing what they were told to do. Mark and Andrew agreed with many of their team mates that Alex was a hard task-master. But on the whole they did not mind because it maintained their fitness levels, there was never any confusion about who was the boss, and they did not get cold at training hanging around chatting, unlike the prima donnas in the back line.

However, not all the forwards shared Mark and Andrew's feelings towards Alex. Toby and Jakob respected Alex because he had been a legend of an athlete, but they did not like the way he treated them like kids and did not acknowledge that they were knowledgeable about the game. They would have liked to have been able to have some input into what they did in practice, as they had worked for different coaches over the years, and as a consequence, knew a number of enjoyable and creative drills. Toby and Jakob found Alex's training sessions boring because it was always exactly the same. This was exacerbated because Alex required the drills to be practised in isolation. Also, they could see that practising the drills in isolation meant that there was a tendency for them to break down in a game when the opposition did something that had not been planned for in practice. While they appreciated Alex working them hard because it meant they did not get cold, and it maintained their fitness levels, at times they would have liked to be able to ask questions regarding the appropriateness of some drills in certain situations.

The back line athletes talked about Denis quite differently to the way the forwards talked about Alex. While the athletes knew he had played some games for the national team, his playing ability did not afford him the same respect as Alex. Also they were conscious that he was not much older than they were. On the one hand this was considered to be a bonus since it enabled the athletes to relate to him more easily and vice versa. However, some athletes did not respect Denis, or consider him to be very knowledgeable, because he was not a very experienced athlete. Tama and Victor were two athletes who really enjoyed working with Denis, because he created an environment that supported them to be creative and develop moves that would challenge the opposition. Providing input into designing new moves, and showing what they could do to their peers, made them feel good about themselves. Also because they had some sort of ownership of the moves they were easy to remember. Sometimes, Denis encouraged the members of the back line who had played for the national U21 and 'Sevens' teams to share some of the moves the national coaches had taught them. This always put a spring in the step of the back line. At times Denis made the practice sessions feel like a game of 'pick up' with family and friends in the park. Tama and Victor believed the camaraderie that this strategy engendered helped in game situations when they needed to improvise because they knew they could depend on someone to be there in support. What most of the back line appreciated was the way Denis did not punish them for not always understanding straightaway what was required of them when a new move was being taught. They welcomed the way he was very patient, and how he would often take aside an athlete who was struggling and talk, or walk, him through the move, or draw it on the miniature whiteboard that was never far from his side.

But not all the athletes in the back line were as satisfied with Denis's coaching style as Tama and Victor. George and Merv thought that Denis was too uncertain about things and it really annoyed them that he rarely told them what was the right move to adopt, and when was the right time to adopt it. They joked that his favourite saying was 'it all depends'. Also when they compared Denis's training sessions to the one Alex ran at the opposite end of the field, theirs always appeared to be unstructured, with Denis spending a lot of time on talking and not enough on running through drills.

CONSEQUENCES FOR THE LEARNER

The primacy of behaviourism has meant it has become acceptable to privilege rational thought and scientific logic, and separate the teaching and coaching acts into 'discrete series of skills that could be isolated, practised, and applied in a systematic manner' (Tinning 1991: 7). Some of the consequences of skills being broken down and taught in isolation are that the drills become boring, as highlighted by Toby and Jakob, and they also do not prepare athletes for the complexities that arise when playing the game in a competitive environment.

It has been argued that when learning is framed by behaviourism the learner can be dismembered (Smith 1991). One way that this dismembering can occur is by practitioners focusing on keeping the learner 'busy, happy, and good' (Placek 1983: 49). Another way is when the practitioner adopts a pedagogy that is under-pinned by necessity. According to Tinning (1988: 82) a 'pedagogy of necessity' is 'characterized by an emphasis on "going with what works" (Zeichner, 1980) . . .

and by what Dewey has called "'routine action'". Further, it occurs when the actions of the practitioner are 'guided primarily by tradition, circumstance, and external authority' (1988: 82). The consequences of dismembering are numerous. Athletes such as Toby and Jakob feel undervalued due to the lack of opportunity to share their ideas, experience, and enthusiasm with the other members of the forward pack. A possible repercussion of feeling undervalued and bored, is that the athletes stop anticipating what is coming next and just do as they are told, when they are told to do it, thereby becoming robotic in their approach to the game.

When a coach's practices are informed by behaviourism it is highly probable that the psychomotor learning domain will be prioritized at the expense of the cognitive and affective learning domains. The psychomotor domain focuses on the development of physical skills and abilities, whereas the cognitive domain focuses on the intellectual ability to think, recall, conceptualize and solve problems. The affective domain focuses on inner feelings, attitudes and socially acceptable behaviour in a given setting (Metzler 2000). Prioritizing the psychomotor domain does little to assist in the development of decision makers, problem solvers or creative athletes. One outcome of the psychomotor domain being prioritized is that the athletes' physical skills and level of fitness will be enhanced. However, as we have argued in previous chapters, athletes are more than machines to be programmed and sent out to perform. By not prioritizing the development of the cognitive and affective domains the coach goes against the body of evidence that suggests learning occurs in a social context thereby potentially disempowering the athlete and reducing his or her chances to learn.

Buck (2003: 48) notes that when practice is informed by a constructivist orientation to learning 'different ideas will arise', learner's responses will vary, 'teaching moments will appear and disappear quickly, [and] strategies will need to vary and flex. Uncertainty will create moments of "well, what now?" and "how will I proceed?" which in turn require constant situational decision-making (Chen and Rovegno, 2000)'. He goes on to point out that it is in these moments of uncertainty that 'meanings are reviewed and new learning occurs' (Buck 2003: 48). Moreover, the practitioner and the learner become 'co-learners creating a shared understanding from their shared experience' (2003: 48). One of the consequences of coaches adopting a constructivist orientation to learning is that the athletes and administrators may view them as not knowing their 'stuff' which may result in them having to deal with issues of credibility. This was illustrated when George and Merv voiced their annoyance at Denis's reluctance to tell the athletes what was the right move and when was the right time to adopt it. They viewed his reluctance as uncertainty, rather than a specific coaching strategy, and as a consequence did not respect him as a coach. A positive consequence of adopting a constructivist orientation to learning is that athletes will develop the confidence to produce new understanding of an issue rather than just reproduce existing understandings. This was illustrated when Tama and Victor expressed their enjoyment in designing new back line moves and how the camaraderie experienced by the back line resulted in them feeling confident to improvise in a game situation because they knew someone would be there in support.

An assumption informing constructivist learning theories is that knowledge is not 'out there' waiting to be found, rather individuals construct it. Yet, McMillan (1991: 39) argues that this does not result in the meaning of events being 'constructed as an inevitable response to external variables impacting on individuals'. Rather he contends that 'the meaning an individual gives to experience is constructed in conjunction with the meanings shared among peers and other persons', acknowledging that this 'does not mean that people who have shared the same experiences will share the same meanings for that experience' (McMillan 1991: 39). This is highlighted in the second vignette where different groups of athletes within the forward pack and back line construct quite different meanings of their respective coaches and coaching sessions even though they are all in the same team and attend the same sessions.

According to Bandura's notion of observational learning 'demonstration [or modelling] is a widely used technique in teaching a new skill' (Roberts *et al.* 1999: 79). It appears, from the second vignette, that many athletes, in the forward pack and the back line, valued Alex and Denis using models in the process of introducing a new skill or drill. Alex and Denis utilized models slightly differently, in that the former used high-status and skilful athletes as models on a regular basis, whereas the latter only sometimes used the experienced athletes, while at other times not differentiating between the experienced and the not so experienced athlete. Upon reviewing the literature associated with observational learning Roberts *et al.* (1999) made some generalizations about the consequences of observational learning in sport contexts that may be useful for coaches to heed. They include:

- modelling correct behaviour is more beneficial for learning than modelling incorrect behaviour;
- a high-status model will be more beneficial for learning than a low-status model;
- observing a model that is similar to the observer is more beneficial for learning than observing a model that is dissimilar;
- live and videoed models are equally beneficial for learning.

At first glance some of the generalizations may appear contradictory, for example a high-status model is better than a low-status one, and observing a model similar to oneself is better than observing a model that bears no resemblance. What happens if you are working with junior athletes with limited skills? On the one hand we are told that they learn better if the model has high status (e.g. an elite athlete), but on the other hand the research suggests they learn better if the model is similar to themselves. So how does a coach reconcile this? One way forward is not to rely on one form of modelling, as not all athletes in the team will learn the same way.

CONCLUDING THOUGHTS

As we stated in the introduction of this chapter, it was not our intention to position one group of learning theories as being better than another group, nor was the chapter designed to provide a detailed overview of learning theories. Rather we proposed to make explicit connections between some learning theories and coaching practices, and to discuss the possible consequence the practices have on athletes. We hope that by making connections via the vignettes and the subsequent discussion that we highlighted that coaches are knowledgeable about learning theories, that the learning process is complicated and that there is no causal relationship between a coach instructing and an athlete learning.

Lefrançois (2000) suggests that when thinking about learning it is useful to recognize there can not be a 'one size fits all' view of learning. Instead, there needs to be an acknowledgement that learning occurs in a range of circumstances, and the strength of a learner is in having an 'enormous range of competencies' (2000: 337). He reminds us that 'ideally, the human learner is flexible rather than rigid, open rather than closed, inventive rather than receptive, changing rather than fixed, and poetic rather than prosaic' (2000: 337). While Lefrançois's learner is an ideal, we believe it is still worth coaches considering this ideal when thinking about the athlete as a learner. If coaches systematically and rigorously examined a) what assumptions they hold of the athletes; and b) what view(s) of learning informed their practice, it would be possible to see how consistent these views and assumptions were with the learning outcomes that had been set for the athletes to achieve. Until there is some degree of consistency, the athletes will continue to learn *despite of*, rather than *as a result of*, the coach.

CHAPTER 7

▼ **'DEVELOPING' ATHLETES**

BY LISETTE BURROWS

■ Introduction   82
■ Developmentalism – what is it?   82
■ What does development do?   84
■ Doing development differently   88
■ Concluding thoughts   89

INTRODUCTION

Last night on television I saw a young man graduate with an honours degree in Science. The only thing that made that story 'newsworthy' was the fact that he was just 13 years of age. We don't expect achievements like this from young boys. We expect teenagers to be experimenting, searching for their identity, rebelling against their parents/caregivers. Graduating from university just does not fit our picture of what young people should be doing at age 13. Similarly when we coach a team of 5-year-olds in football we do not expect them to be executing finely honed passing, dribbling and kicking skills, positioning themselves strategically on the field or engaging in complex tactical play. We expect them to cluster around the ball like bees to a honey pot because 'that's the stage they're at'. Both of these expectations arise from developmental assumptions. In this chapter I outline what I mean by 'developmentalism'. Next, I explain why thinking about children 'developmentally' in coaching situations can be problematic. Finally, I sketch some alternatives that may help coaches to practise in less 'developmental' ways.

DEVELOPMENTALISM – WHAT IS IT?

Developmentalist notions are readily found within orthodox developmental psychology accounts of how people change. But, they are also readily found within the everyday common-sense assumptions that parents, coaches, teachers and children share about human change throughout a lifespan. Developmental statements 'make a claim about a person or group of people on the basis of age or "stage'"(Morss 2001: 2). 'He's too old for that', 'she's acting like a baby', 'she's a terrible two' and 'grow up, Johnny' are examples of developmental statements we hear every day in homes, schools and on sports fields. 'Developmentally appropriate practice' and 'sequential learning' are developmental concepts that we might hear teachers, psychologists and programme developers using. Developmentalism is an umbrella term used by some critical psychologists (for example, Baker 2001; Morss 1996) to refer to these kinds of statements and the assumptions that underpin them.

When we use developmental language we assume that people think and act in particular ways depending on their age and/or stage. We also assume that those ages and stages are universally recognizable; that is, if I say, 'Tom's a terrible teen', others will know what I mean. Chances are, in Western society at least, that people *will* know what a 'teen' means. Indeed, decades of experimental research in developmental psychology has 'proved' that teenagers exist, that they behave in particular ways (for example, they take risks, they are egocentric), and that all of this is very different from the world of 'grown-ups'. But are teenagers 'really' like that? Do all teenagers, feel, act, and think in similar ways? Is it necessarily the case that a 13-year-old thinks more about himself than others? Are all teenagers clumsy? Do they all eat lots of junk food? Are they all concerned with image? What happens to our theories of how people develop when something or someone interferes with them, like the boy I mentioned in the introductory anecdote? I'll come back to this question later in the chapter.

Another thing about developmental language is that it often suggests that what happens to us when we are young will influence how we 'turn out' when we are older. Contemporary concerns about childhood obesity, youth violence and drugs and alcohol are all linked to the notion that unless we 'catch them' early, a bleak future for young children awaits – whether this be as an obese adult, a violent parent, or a drug addict. Sport is no stranger to the 'catch them quick' notion either. 'Mastering the basics' is a catch phrase used by many coaches. The notion that children learn to walk before they run, creep before they crawl, and float before they swim, is an everyday understanding shared by many coaches and instantiated as 'fact' in motor-development literature. We do not teach things to children until they are 'ready' because we believe they need the fundamental motor skills *before* they can incorporate these into more complex motor scripts (like a game). Because we believe that early experiences determine what happens later in life, it is not uncommon to find children as young as 2 years old learning to throw, kick or bat a ball 'in preparation' for their participation in community and/or elite sport. Increasingly, young children are being encouraged to participate in sport not only for the recreational benefits it affords but also as a way of decreasing the likelihood that those children will grow up to be obese and unhealthy adults (Burrows and Wright 2003).

Because young children are presumed to have 'not yet developed' the cognitive capacity to think sensibly for themselves or to know what they need, parents are

'DEVELOPING' ATHLETES

often implicated as key facilitators of early experiences in sport and/or physical activity. Indeed, a 'good' parent/caregiver, in middle-class Western terms at least, is often portrayed as one who provides his/her children with early opportunities to participate in sport. When children are enrolled in sports clubs, coaches are charged with taking responsibility for the development of other people's children. In both parenting and coaching roles, the influence of developmental understandings of human change is palpable.

One of the other interesting features of developmental statements is their tendency to imply causal links between development in one sphere and development in another. In a New Zealand parenting magazine, for example, we read 'running, jumping and climbing in the early years set a child up for life. Movement is the key to developing self-esteem, confidence and learning' (*First Steps* 1996). In this statement, physical development through movement is explicitly connected to the development of emotional and intellectual capacities. Movement is accorded a primary role in 'setting a child up for life'. Similarly with sport, links are often forged in public and professional discourse between playing a game and becoming a better person – a person with capacities to work in teams, cooperate with others, set and achieve goals, and so on.

None of the above features of developmentalism are necessarily problematic unless we look at who misses out when we think of development like this. As Walkerdine (1984, 1993), Burrows (2002), and Stainton Rogers and Stainton Rogers (1992) suggest, the developmental 'story' of human change is just that – *one* amongst many possible tales of how people change. The fact that it has so much currency means that other ways of thinking about and practising human development are inevitably marginalized. Furthermore, as Walkerdine (1993) has suggested, developmentalism can actually work to construct the ways in which people recognize themselves and others. In other words, developmentalism *produces* the 'development' we think we observe in ourselves and others. In the next section I use some examples from coaching contexts to illustrate the more pernicious effects of developmentalism.

WHAT DOES DEVELOPMENT DO?

Developmental assumptions shape our view of what people can and cannot do at particular ages. In coaching, they provide a set of lenses through which we observe, monitor and classify children's progress. As I suggested at the beginning of this chapter, we do not consider teaching complex strategic moves to 5-year-olds because we know they will not understand them – it would be developmentally inappropriate. On the other hand, we *do* expect that 16-year-olds have mastered the basics of throwing and catching and that they can therefore participate in a game of basketball or cricket.

In a general sense, developmental psychologists tell us that children grow larger, taller, and more coordinated over time, exhibiting progressively more complex motor skills as they age. Developmental psychologists would also say that because children's mental structures change as they age, older children are more capable of abstract thought than young ones. The fact that most children *do* seem to be able to run faster, jump further, wield bigger cricket bats and understand game plans better at 12 years than 6 years confers a truth status to these developmental claims. We regard the processes of change that children go through en route to maturity as both natural and to some extent, predictable. We 'look' for these kinds of changes in children and worry if we cannot see them. But *whose* development defines 'the norm' against which these children are measured?

Since the 1960s, critical psychologists have been questioning the implied naturalness and universality of developmental 'norms' (Baker 2001; Broughton 1987; Burman 1994; Morss 1996; Walkerdine 1993). Space prohibits a thorough canvassing of this critique, yet what most of this work shares is an understanding that developmental milestones are cultural constructions rather than scientific truths. In other words, 'normal' is what a particular group of people with the power to define what 'counts' says is 'normal'. Commenting on the developmental accounts prevailing in American text books, Parker and Shotter (1990: 50) attest that 'what we have here are features of white middle class US society mapped onto models of development which are then treated as universal'.

The trouble with developmental 'norms' is that they tend to universalize tendencies and traits that relate to a particular sort of child – a masculine, European one – and stigmatize any child who fails to measure up to that idealized vision (Burman 1991, 1994; Walkerdine 1993). Once standards of 'normal' motor development, for example, are established, those deviating from the 'norm' are inevitably construed as in need of remedial assistance. The following excerpt drawn from a text widely used by physical educators clearly illustrates the evaluative consequences of employing developmental norms.

> Understanding the way people normally develop movement skills throughout the lifespan enables us to diagnose problems in those individuals who may be developing abnormally. . . . Also, because there is a link between all domains of behaviour, improvement in the motor domain may indirectly lead to improvements in intellectual or social development. Activities can therefore be devised to assist in the development of movement potential. To accurately create such a movement curricula, we must have a knowledge of normal motor development.
>
> (Payne and Isaacs 1987: 7)

Australian researcher Jan Wright's (1997b) critique of the hierarchy of skills development, supported by fundamental motor-skills programmes, provides another illustration of the consequences of normalizing particular kinds of development over others. She draws attention to the specificity of the skills included in Fundamental Motor Skills (FMS) assessment batteries widely used in Australia and New Zealand. She shows how skills like the overhand throw, catch and kick are intimately related to performance in competitive sports played predominantly by men. According to Wright, the lack of emphasis in FMS tests on motor skills which link to activities such as dance or gymnastics contributes 'to the (re) production of gender differences which construct girls and women as deficient, as lacking in comparison to a male standard' (Wright 1997b: 20). I would argue that the standards and norms informing motor-skill measurement marginalize not only girls, but all children whose interests and proclivities lie with skills requiring balance, flexibility or fine motor coordination.

Another problem with developmental claims is their evaluative tone. Because human development is represented as a linear process, people are assumed to be *progressing*, getting *better* at something, improving in an upwards and onwards sort of fashion. But what happens when development does not work like this? What happens when little Johnny stays short instead of developing the towering 6 ft 5 inch frame that was expected at 17 years? What happens if Mary never learns to 'run'? What happens when 'grown-ups' behave 'like children'? What generally happens is they get labelled as 'developmentally delayed' or 'immature'. These labels only acquire their pejorative tone *because* a norm or 'ideal' exists, yet as I have suggested those norms themselves may rest on shaky foundations.

It is not only those who do not fit the 'norm' who are positioned as under-developed when age- and stage-related claims and practices are enacted. Caregivers, coaches, teachers – any people who guide young people – also potentially feel the impact of developmental claims. A coach who fields a team of 'senior' athletes, some of whom have difficulty 'playing by the rules' or 'respecting the referee' will 'feel' the disapproval of her peers. A parent whose 5-year-old child can not throw the ball as far as the others in his team will worry. A coach whose teenage athlete fails to develop his 'full potential' under her tutelage will feel like she could have done more. When competency is linked with age, as it is in developmental claims, judgements are inevitable.

Developmentalism also actualizes particular power relations between adult coaches and young athletes. By virtue of being considered 'not yet an adult' (Mayall 1994), children are constituted as 'unknowing' alongside adults who 'know'. It is coaches who decide when their squad will do fitness activities, when they are 'ready' for the game and for how long, and under what conditions, they will practise specific skills. In certain circumstances coaches also involve themselves in planning athletes' nutritional intake, guiding their choice of clothing and controlling their social activities. As Mayall (1994) puts it, when children are construed as not yet able to make sensible, informed decisions about their well-being for themselves they become persons 'to whom actions are done' (Mayall 1994: 123). The benchmarks of 'normal development' mapped out in many coaching handbooks provide a set of lenses through which coaches can legitimately 'observe', exercise surveillance on, assess and remediate young athletes 'for their own good'.

Cross-cultural and historical research has repeatedly pointed to the multiple ways that childhood has been conceived of in different cultural and historical settings.

As Aries (1962) points out, prior to the nineteenth century, the notion of 'child-hood' itself did not exist. Rather children were regarded as 'mini adults' and afforded similar responsibilities to grown-ups. In contemporary times, the ideal end-point of child development in some Western communities is an individual, autonomous, rational self. For other cultural groups it is an interdependent adult capable of functioning in, and contributing to, a collective. Some societies expect their young children to be free to play, to 'make believe' and live unencumbered by fiscal responsibilities, while others require their children to participate in the world of work to keep their families afloat. Ideas about who children are, what they can be and how they should behave are inevitably connected to political, economic and cultural investments.

Even if you have difficulty thinking of development as social rather than 'natural', there are bound to be incidents in your experience as a coach that make you question the inevitability of normative ages and stages. At the beginning of this chapter I mentioned the 13-year-old who got an honours degree. There are golfers, runners and swimmers who also do surprising things that are out of step with our developmental expectations (for example, the 80-year-old who runs the marathon; or the teen golf champion). It is not only the 'exceptional' that alerts us to the problems of assuming age-related competency, though. Athletes of *similar* chronological age can differ markedly in their skills, aptitudes and behaviours, and the same child can act in different ways in different circumstances (e.g. on Monday he was great at goal kicking but on Thursday he couldn't get one ball between the posts). Precise claims about what children of particular ages can and cannot do simply cannot hold true for all children all of the time.

Despite abundant evidence contradicting the tenets of developmentalism, coaches, parents, officials and children themselves persist in holding expectations of what athletes are like based on their age. Many sports competitions use age as an organizing framework, and children's performances are regularly compared with those of others of the same age. Standards for judging performance and guiding coaching practices are inevitably informed by developmental notions that position some behaviours/skills as immature and others as mature. Children with disabilities, children whose proclivities lie outside the realm of what counts in 'developmental' terms and children for whom accomplishing 'fundamental motor skills' will take a lifetime, are just some of those rendered 'under-developed' or 'abnormal' when 'development' guides practice. Yet, what alternatives are there and do we not need something to help us decide what to do as coaches? It is not my intention to replace one orthodoxy – developmentalism – with another, nor to suggest that coaches should have no understanding of what their athletes may need at various points in their life trajectory. Rather, my intent is simply to encourage those working with athletes to think about the consequences of employing developmental assumptions and consider other ways of understanding children's change.

DOING DEVELOPMENT DIFFERENTLY

At one level, doing development differently might simply mean asking ourselves why we categorize athletes the way we do. For example, a starting question might be, is it 'fair' or 'pedagogically correct' to have 9-year-olds of widely variable strength and size playing together in competitive sports? In New Zealand, junior rugby grades use weight as an organizing framework for allocating athletes to teams. Wrestling and weightlifting clubs adopt a similar practice. In most other sports however, chronological age continues to function as the means for characterizing children as members of a team or coaching group. Re-thinking this mode of classification would be one step towards disrupting the restrictive (short 9-year-olds still have to get the ball in the standard hoop) and often discriminatory connotations (featherweight Johnny being squashed by heavy Karl) of age-related groupings.

A second strategy to disrupt developmental effects is to perpetually adopt a reflective stance towards our own pedagogical choices in terms of both content and delivery. Why do we always do the drills first and then play the game? Why do we presume athletes need to master the basics before moving on to the more complex task of using those fundamentals in a 'real' context? Why do we think we are the only ones with insights about what might make the team work more collaboratively? The authors in this book suggest that practices used in *Game Sense* (Thorpe 1997) are viable pedagogical alternatives to orthodox coaching practice. I suggest these ideas may also form viable anti-developmental alternatives for coaches. Lave and Wenger (1991) for example, have developed a concept called 'situated learning theory' that offers coaches a different way of regarding their athletes. Rather than assuming athletes are all at some pre-defined developmental stage, Lave and Wenger suggest that it is the *differences* of perspective and behaviour among co-participants that yield productive learning. They talk of 'communities of practice' where old-timers with knowledge and skills about something (for example, attacking the goal) work with newcomers (those who have not played before), each changing the other's way of doing something through the exchanges. This seems like a useful way to think about the coaching context. If age is a non-negotiable classification device, then a promising anti-developmental alternative would seem to be to regard the team as a community comprised of co-participants whose capacity to change (e.g. get better at attacking the goal) is not located in the minds and bodies of its individual children, but rather in the culture of the group and the relational possibilities it affords.

Rovegno's (1995) research on skill development in the physical education context may offer another alternative. She suggests that often coaches and teachers ascribe labels like 'immature' and 'mature' to children in relation to their skill level. Rather than continue to position young people as either advanced or retarded on some normative motor development scale, she emphasizes a holistic approach focusing on the relations between children and their environment. An approach like this means that children do not necessarily find themselves linking their competency to age and finding themselves wanting.

CONCLUDING THOUGHTS

Given what we know about the historical and cultural variability of childhood, why do we continue to use chronological age as a marker to shape our expectations of what children can achieve, think about and do? As Baker (2001) suggests, a grand narrative of child development as progressive, linear and gradual has been entrenched in the thinking and practice of Western peoples for centuries. The idea that children develop through a sequentially organized series of steps towards an ideal is so firmly embedded in both professional and everyday understandings, it seems impossible, at times, to imagine child development any differently, let alone do it differently. Just because we have always thought about development this way does not mean it is the best or only framework available for organizing human endeavour.

Age-related norms set up a notion of change over time that regulates, evaluates and excludes many children from positive experiences in sport. Some may argue that this is the nature of the beast – that is, sport is inherently selective, elitist and reliant on the exclusion of many to support the performance outcomes of a few. I would counter that whether you are a participation- or performance-orientated coach (or both) continuing to employ developmentalism as a bedrock for coaching children will always yield consequences, not many of them pleasant, for those at the centre of coaching practice – the athletes.

CHAPTER 8

▼ **UNDERSTANDING ATHLETES' MOTIVATION**

- Introduction   90
- What is motivation?   92
- Theories of motivation   93
- Exploring the social nature of athlete motivation   98
- Concluding thoughts   104

INTRODUCTION

Why do some athletes constantly strive for success while others opt to avoid competition and evaluation? Why do some athletes rise to challenging tasks while others prefer less engaging activities? Why do some athletes choose to drop out of sport while others decide to continue their participation? In order to best answer questions such as these and to also ensure that athletes enjoy optimal sporting experiences, we, among others (e.g. Duda and Treasure 2001; Weiss and Ferrer-Caja 2002), believe that coaches need an in-depth appreciation of the concept of motivation. In highlighting the need for coaches to possess a detailed understanding of athlete motivation, Weinberg and Gould (2003) point out that it is the ability to motivate athletes, rather than technical and tactical knowledge of a particular sport, that more often than not separates the excellent practitioners from the others. In further commenting on the importance of such knowledge to coaching practice, Smith and Smoll (1996) have contended that an athlete's success in sport, whether it is competitive triumph or an improvement in individual performance, is largely, though not solely, influenced by motivation. In particular, they have suggested that 'athletes who are not motivated to develop their skills will not achieve their potential' (Smith and Smoll 1996: 51).

In terms of the knowledge-base required in this respect, Finch (2002) has argued that it is not only necessary for coaches to have an in-depth comprehension of the many and various reasons why athletes choose to participate in sport, but they must also be aware of the diverse goals that individual athletes wish to achieve from their sporting experiences. Furthermore, she also suggests that coaches need to recognize how they may contribute to sustaining the long-term engagement of their athletes in sporting activity. However, despite an increased recognition that such an understanding of motivation is critical to the delivery of high quality coaching practice, Weinberg and Gould (2003: 52) contend that 'many [coaches] do not understand the process well'. Indeed, according to Finch (2002), coaches have traditionally failed to grasp the full complexity and subtleties of motivation in sport. In this regard, she describes how many coaches have viewed motivation as an internal personality characteristic that some athletes have more of than others, as an external stimulus or reward, or, alternatively, as explanations for behaviour. Such beliefs regarding motivation are problematic and, if adhered to, may have serious implications for coaching practice. For example, Finch (2002) suggests that coaches who view motivation as simply an innate ability may give up prematurely on athletes rather than helping them to understand and optimize their full motivation. Furthermore, she adds that those coaches who perceive motivation to be determined by external rewards (such as praise, medals and trophies) often fail to take into consideration the fact that athletes will not respond in a uniform manner to the same reward. Finally, Finch (2002) suggests that coaches who relate motivation to competitive success (i.e. 'we wanted it more than the other team') are guilty of confusing motivation with competitiveness.

In addition to the above shortcomings highlighted by Finch (2002), scholars have also argued that coaches and coach educators alike have, to date, not fully recognized that athlete motivation is influenced by wider social processes and values (Clews and Gross 1995; Duda and Treasure 2001). Here, Clews and Gross (1995: 91) note that 'the individual does not exist in a social vacuum; we are social beings and, as such, the environment in which we live exerts both a passive and dynamic influence on our behaviour'. Indeed, Finch (2002), in support of this viewpoint, argues that practitioners need to recognize that social and cultural factors, such as coaching philosophies and the nature of an athlete's relationships and interactions with significant others (such as coaches, peers and parents), will impact upon an athlete's ability to maintain optimal motivation in the long term.

Accordingly, in an attempt to somewhat unravel the complex and dynamic nature of athlete motivation within the coaching process, the broad purpose of this chapter is to explore both the personal and social nature of athlete motivation. In keeping with the book's general philosophy, the aim is not to provide prescriptions as to what coaches ought to do but, alternatively, it is to highlight the multifaceted nature of athlete motivation. Hence, following an introductory discussion, we explore the main theories relating to athlete motivation from a personal perspective, highlighting how these theories may inform coaching practice. Following this, the focus shifts to address the 'social infrastructure' (Clews and Gross 1995: 90) that influences athlete motivation. In particular, the purpose here is to examine how the interpersonal relationships that athletes have with coaches, peers and parents may impact upon their motivational orientation. In this way, it is hoped that this chapter will illustrate that athlete motivation is not determined by an inspirational speech from the coach, catchy slogans, or spectacular pre-match events but is, instead, a complex interaction of personal characteristics, environments, and cultures (Finch 2002).

WHAT IS MOTIVATION?

As highlighted above, athlete motivation is regarded as one of the most misunderstood aspects of the coaching process (Weinberg and Gould 2003), with coaches' definitions of this concept ranging from consequences and explanations of behaviour to internal characteristics and external influences (Finch 2002). This range of explanations is considered by many scholars to be the primary reason for the general lack of understanding of motivation among coaching practitioners (Duda and Treasure 2001; Finch 2002; Weinberg and Gould 2003).

In order to remedy this situation, Weinberg and Gould (2003) have suggested that coaches need to recognize that motivation is not adequately conceptualized by any one of these aforementioned outlooks. Instead, they contend that a more beneficial definition for coaches to adopt is that which considers motivation to consist of both the intensity and the direction of an athlete's efforts. In this respect, they consider the *direction of effort* to be concerned with identifying which situations an athlete may approach or be attracted to or, conversely, looks to avoid (e.g. a high school netball team, an injured athlete seeking medical advice, or a club tennis player actively selecting opponents who will challenge his or her game), while the *intensity of effort* refers to the amount of effort an athlete puts into a particular task or situation (e.g. an athlete not putting much effort into a netball practice session, or a club tennis player trying his or her hardest with every shot despite being well behind in a particular game or set) (Weinberg and Gould 2003; Duda and Treasure 2001).

It is important to note that while the direction-of-effort and intensity-of-effort components of motivation have been defined separately, these dimensions are, in practice, interrelated (Weinberg and Gould 2003). For example, if an athlete is highly attracted toward a particular sport, then he or she is likely to invest a great deal of effort in that particular situation. However, as Finch (2002) highlights, this may not always be the case. Here, she suggests that while an athlete may be attracted to a specific situation, they may fail to demonstrate any intensity of effort. Such a scenario could arise if an athlete does not enjoy a positive working relationship with the coach, if the grade of competition is too challenging or too easy, if the athlete receives no recognition for his or her efforts or performances, or if the athlete lacks any clear goals upon which to focus their efforts.

Finch (2002) suggests that coaches need to be aware of how motivation can be influenced by environmental sources (*extrinsic* motivation) as well as sources inside the athlete (*intrinsic* motivation). In this respect, *intrinsic* motivation refers to internal motives for participation, such as fun, skill improvement, enjoying challenges, and personal mastery of tasks (Finch 2002). In contrast, *extrinsic* motivation is concerned with external motives for involvement in sport, such as social status and approval from coaches, parents, peers and others, and material rewards (e.g. trophies, certificates, medals) (Finch 2002). To date, the available literature suggests that developing high levels of intrinsic motivation is the key to an athlete's sustained involvement in sport and physical activity (see Weiss and Ferrer-Caja 2002). Moreover, in addition to understanding how athlete motivation may be influenced by internal and external sources, coaches also need to be fully aware of the reality that an athlete's motivation is not a fixed property but is, instead, capable of altering across time and situations based on the athlete's interpretation of their sporting experiences (Duda and Treasure 2001). This issue will be further explored in the next sections of this chapter.

THEORIES OF MOTIVATION

In recent years, the concept of athlete motivation has been the subject of wide scale investigation by sport psychologists in particular (see Weiss and Ferrer-Caja 2002 for a detailed review). Perhaps the three most utilized theories in contemporary research are attribution theory, achievement-goal theory, and cognitive-evaluation theory (Finch 2002).

Attribution theory is based upon the work of Heider (1958) and Weiner (1972, 1979, 1985, 1986) and seeks to explain how athlete motivation is determined by the explanations (or attributions) athletes give for their successful and unsuccessful sporting performances (Finch 2002; Weinberg and Gould 2003). This theory contends that the potentially thousands of possible explanations for successful and unsuccessful performances can be classified into the attribution categories of *stability*, *locus of causality*, and *locus of control* (Weinberg and Gould 2003). In this respect, stability refers to the degree to which an athlete attributes success or failure to be either fairly permanent (e.g. an athlete's talent or ability) or unstable (e.g. good luck or poor coaching). The locus of causality aspect is concerned with identifying whether a factor is internal (e.g. effort) or external (e.g. the opponent's level of sporting prowess) to the individual athlete, while the locus of control refers to whether a factor is under the control of the athlete (e.g. implementing a race plan compared to an opponent's physical conditioning) (Weinberg and Gould 2003).

Researchers adopting this theoretical perspective on athlete motivation believe that attributions affect expectations of future success or failure and the emotional reactions of performers (Finch 2002; Duda and Treasure 2001). For example, if an athlete attributes success to internal reasons, he or she is more likely to feel pride and personal satisfaction and to continue with a particular sport or activity. Conversely, if an athlete believes sporting success is caused by external elements then he or she will not experience the affective responses that enhance self-esteem, which may have a detrimental impact upon an athlete's continued sport participation (Duda and Treasure 2001). Indeed, when athletes attribute success to unstable or external attributions they are less likely to have optimal achievement motivation than those who attribute their successes to stable and internal factors (Finch 2002). Moreover, if an athlete attributes failure to be the result of internal factors, then he or she is likely to experience negative emotions such as shame, guilt, and disappointment (Duda and Treasure 2001). Finally, when an athlete attributes sporting failure to external factors, quite different affective emotions may result, which could include feelings of frustration and anger (Duda and Treasure 2001). Obviously, such emotions may have a negative impact upon future performance and long-term sports participation.

In terms of its implications for coaching practice, this theoretical perspective suggests that coaches need to ensure that they carefully consider the feedback they provide to athletes regarding sporting successes and failures. In this respect, coaching practitioners should strive to ensure that their interactions with athletes about sporting performance are more likely to enhance motivation rather than undermine it (Duda and Treasure 2001). In order to achieve this, Duda and Treasure (2001) suggest that coaches could encourage athletes to feel accountable for their performances regardless of the outcome. In particular, they suggest that coaches may wish to persuade athletes that successes are the result of personal attributes and actions. Additionally, and perhaps more importantly, coaches may also seek to ensure that athletes believe there is always hope when failures are encountered. In this way, coaches could discourage athletes from thinking that 'I am not good at this . . . I never will be . . . and there's nothing I can do about it' (Duda and Treasure 2001: 49). In summary, attribution theory encourages coaches to strive to create a working climate that enhances each athlete's perceived control and competence (Duda and Treasure 2001).

Unlike attribution theory, which examines motivation in relation to athletes' explanations for performance, achievement-goal theory is concerned with explaining athlete motivation in relation to the goals an athlete sets for performance (Finch 2002). This theory, which is largely based upon the work of Nicholls (1984, 1989, 1992) in education, proposes that athletes define success according to two types of goals: *task involvement* and *ego involvement*. Athletes who adopt task-involvement goals are concerned with self-mastery and skill improvement. For these athletes, success is defined relative to the self, as the athlete places significant emphasis on the learning and/or improvement of skills or tasks (Duda and Treasure 2001). In contrast, athletes who adopt ego-orientated goals define success in terms of exceeding the performance of others (Duda and Treasure 2001). For example, if a tennis player defines success as winning the match, regardless of performance, then an ego-orientated goal is being employed. Unlike those athletes who adopt task-orientated goals, athletes who select ego-orientated goals judge their ability through subjective comparison with others (Finch 2002).

According to Finch (2002), an important point for coaching practitioners to note in this regard is that task and ego orientations are not dichotomous (i.e. you are not either one or the other but some of both). Specifically, she, among others (e.g. Duda 1993; Duda and Treasure 2001), highlights that athletes may be high on ego and task orientations, low on both, or, alternatively, high on task and low on ego. Furthermore, in drawing upon the work of Duda (1993), Finch (2002) also suggests that there are two commonly held misconceptions relating to achievement-goal theory of which coaches should be aware. First, she contends that practitioners should not perceive task-orientated athletes to be uninterested in winning. Second, she points out that it would be incorrect for coaches to view ego-orientated athletes as not caring about playing well. The key point for coaches to consider is how they define success and interpret losing, as, according to Finch (2002), it is these perceptual differences that have an impact upon motivation.

To date, research adopting this theoretical framework suggests that athletes who adopt task-orientated goals are more likely to persist with tasks, demonstrate a strong work ethic, and enjoy optimal performance in comparison to ego-orientated athletes (Weinberg and Gould 2003). Weinberg and Gould (2003) attribute this to the fact that task-orientated athletes are more likely to select realistic and moderately challenging goals, do not often fear failure, and base their perceptions of competence on their own standards of reference rather than against others. As a result, these athletes are less likely to experience feelings of disappointment, anger, and frustration, as they perceive themselves to have a sense of control over their sporting performances (Duda and Treasure 2001; Weinberg and Gould 2003). This contrasts with ego-orientated athletes who assess their perceived competence in relation to the performances of others, which is something that they cannot necessarily control. Accordingly, these athletes may experience difficulties in maintaining high levels of perceived competence, as, by default, at least half the competitors in any sporting competition must lose (Weinberg and Gould 2003). The negative consequences of taking an ego-orientated outlook to sporting performance include athletes showing less persistence in the face of adversity, choosing extreme goals (either too easy or very difficult), having weaker work ethics than their task-orientated counterparts, and making excuses for poor per-formances (Finch 2002). Furthermore, in addition to not developing their sporting skills to the maximum, ego-orientated athletes may also experience high levels of anxiety, which could ultimately result in them losing interest in a particular sporting activity (Duda and Treasure 2001).

In terms of its application to coaching practice, perhaps the most fundamental feature that this theory highlights for coaches is the need to consider how they can maximize an athlete's task orientation (Duda and Treasure 2001). Indeed, Duda and Treasure (2001) recommend that coaches should concentrate on this rather than attempting to reduce an athlete's ego-orientation levels, as this is perhaps a more realistic approach for the majority of coaches who do not work with full-time athletes or have access to sport psychologists. Duda and Treasure (2001) also believe that coaches should critically evaluate their practice in relation to task and ego goals, as by emphasizing certain cues, rewards, and performance expec-tations they can promote a particular goal state, which will affect the way athletes perceive the particular sport. In this respect, they suggest that the following questions may provide a valuable framework for such introspective analysis:

- How do you define success to athletes or children? Is it in terms of winning and losing or effort and improvement?
- Do you design practice sessions that optimally challenge athletes, or do you repeat well-learned skills that may stifle development even though they increase the likelihood of winning?
- How do you evaluate performance?
- Do you congratulate your athletes when they try hard and improve or when they win and out-perform others?
- How do you react when your team or athlete loses?

Finally, Duda and Treasure (2001) suggest that practitioners who work with young athletes also need to consider the potential impact that parents and guardians may have on the development of a child's achievement motivation. In particular, they highlight how, 'by making certain types of goals and feedback salient, a parent can influence young athletes' views about themselves, perceptions of the sport activity per se, and the criteria they use to evaluate success and failure' (Duda and Treasure 2001: 56). In this way, the efforts a coach makes to enhance an athlete's task-orientation levels may be compromised by parents who emphasize the outcome rather than the performance of a child. Accordingly, Duda and Treasure (2001) recommend that coaches may need to educate parents as well as the athletes themselves if they are to successfully promote high levels of task orientation among the latter. The impact of parents and significant others upon athlete motivation will be discussed in greater detail in the final section of this chapter.

The final theory of motivation presented in this section is cognitive-evaluation theory, which is based upon the work of Deci and Ryan (1985) and Vallerand *et al.* (1987). Unlike the two previous theories, which focus on the individual char-acteristics that may influence motivation, cognitive-evaluation theory is concerned with examining the relationship between intrinsic and extrinsic motivation and, in particular, the impact of rewards upon behaviour and performance (Finch 2002). Specifically, cognitive-evaluation theory suggests that athletes have two innate needs. These are to feel competent and to feel self-determining in their activities (Finch 2002). In this respect, Finch (2002) points out that any event, (such as the allocation of rewards or the feedback an athlete receives) that influences these two needs will have an impact upon an athlete's intrinsic motivation.

In particular, this theory contends that an athlete's intrinsic motivation is influ-enced by their *locus of causality*, which refers to the degree of control an athlete has over a particular situation (Finch 2002). In this respect, if athletes feel that they are forced into certain situations or, similarly, that their activities are initiated by someone else (e.g. coaches or parents), they have an *external locus of causality*. For example, Finch (2002) suggests that if an athlete feels controlled by a reward (e.g. being paid to play or compete), the motivation for his or her behaviour is extrinsic. As such, the controlling nature of the reward may conflict with his or her innate desire for self-determination, which, consequently, may have a negative impact on intrinsic motivation (Finch 2002). In contrast, athletes who feel that they decide upon and initiate their actions have an *internal locus of causality*. In this case, if the reward is not seen to control behaviour, an athlete's intrinsic motivation is likely to increase (Finch 2002).

In addition to the need for athletes to have some control over their activities, cognitive-evaluation theory also suggests that an athlete's intrinsic motivation will also be influenced by their perceived degree of sporting competency. Specifically, Finch (2002) highlights how events that provide the athlete with positive information are likely to increase his or her perceived competence, which, in turn, will have a positive impact upon intrinsic motivation. However, events that provide athletes with negative information about their capabilities typically lower their levels of perceived competence and, accordingly, reduce intrinsic motivation (Finch 2002).

Accordingly, in keeping with the preceding discussion on goal-achievement theory, cognitive evaluation theory suggests that in addition to carefully considering the feedback and working climate they provide, coaches need to recognize and, where possible, manage the messages that parents and significant others provide athletes with in relation to sporting competence and the control athletes have over their sporting involvement. With regard to the former, this theory posits that intrinsic motivation can be enhanced through the creation of stimulating coaching environments that emphasize 'self-evaluation, improvement and learning' (Weiss and Ferrer-Caja 2002: 130). In terms of the latter, Weiss and Ferrer-Caja (2002: 130) highlight how 'significant others (i.e. coaches, teachers, parents, peers), who are an important part of the social context, can affect self-determination through controlling versus informational salience'. Finally, this theory also explains why the commonly held belief that more rewards result in greater performance does not always work (Finch 2002).

In summary, this section has highlighted three leading psychological theories that are currently used to help us understand and explain athlete motivation. In terms of coaching practice, these theoretical frameworks have generally emphasized the need for coaches to build and maintain high levels of intrinsic motivation through the development of working climates that emphasize task mastery and provide athletes with a sense of control over their sporting involvement and performances. However, while such knowledge provides coaching practitioners with valuable frameworks which could, and should, be utilized to guide professional practice, it would be inaccurate for coaches to view motivation as a solely psychological process or attribute that exists inside individuals. Indeed, this section has alluded to the possible impact that significant others, in particular the parents of young athletes, may have on athlete motivation (Duda and Treasure 2001; Finch 2002). Accordingly, we believe that coaches also need to be aware of how the social and cultural contexts in which athletes operate may influence their motivation (Coakley 1998). Indeed, as outlined in the introductory chapter of this book, we contend that coaching exists in the complexities of modern day sport, which involves interaction between people of different race, class, gender, values, experiences and philosophies (Potrac *et al.* 2000). As such, coaching practitioners need to consider how the nature of athletes' social relationships and interactions with significant others (such as coaches, peers, and parents), both inside and outside of the immediate coaching environment, may impact upon their levels of motivation. It is this issue that will be considered in more detail in the next section.

EXPLORING THE SOCIAL NATURE OF ATHLETE MOTIVATION

The notion that social influences are important to understanding student motivation has long been recognized by educational researchers (Wentzel 1999). However, Wentzel (1999) contends that despite useful inroads being made, this area of inquiry remains inadequately theorized. Despite this current state of affairs, the available educational research on this topic has served to highlight how positive and supportive social relationships with teachers, parents, and peers have the potential to impact upon student motivation orientations towards school (Wentzel 1999). In transferring the findings of the educational literature to the sports coaching context, it would appear that, in addition to an understanding of the ways that various sets of psychological processes interact to motivate sporting performance, coaches would also benefit from an insight into how social encounters and experiences may impinge upon athlete motivation (Wentzel 1999). Given the relative paucity of literature addressing this topic, particularly in the sports science and coaching literature where this line of inquiry is still in its infancy (Smith 2003), this section does not provide the reader with an overview of 'specific mechanisms and processes that can explain social influences' (Wentzel 1999: 76). Instead, it aims to sensitize coaching practitioners to the various ways in which social interaction and socialization processes may come to bear on athlete motivation.

Coach–athlete interaction

According to Weiss and Ferrer-Caja (2002), the coach is a powerful socializing agent in the sporting domain. In this respect, they suggest that the ways in which coaches structure practice sessions and respond to athletes 'can significantly affect children's and adolescents' competence perceptions, global self worth, affect, motivational orientation, and actual participation' (Weiss and Ferrer-Caja 2002: 119). Indeed, surveys of athlete-participation motivation have identified the coach and coaching behaviour as major factors in determining whether athletes choose to continue with or drop out of a particular sport (Lee 1999; Weiss and Ferrer-Caja 2002). Consequently, given the enormous potential coaches have to influence the athletes in their care, we firmly believe that they should carefully consider the nature of their interaction with athletes if they are to help optimize athlete motivation. In this respect, we suggest that coaches need to not only focus on 'what' they say or do, but also to consider 'how' they say or do things, as well as reflecting upon the possible 'consequences' that may result from their interactions. In short, we contend that the nature of the working relationship that exists between coach and athlete will have a crucial impact upon athlete motivation (Jones *et al*. 2004). The quality of this relationship is not just determined by the technical and tactical knowledge that a coach imparts to his or her athletes, but also by the degree to which the coach connects with his or her athletes as social beings (Jones *et al*. 2004; Potrac *et al*. 2002).

In terms of developing positive working relationships with their athletes, Graham (2001) invites coaches to consider how their interactions with skilled or attractive students differ from those with unskilled and unattractive athletes. In this respect, he suggests that coaches may, albeit unknowingly, tend to privilege certain athletes over others. Given that athletes may make judgements about themselves through comparisons with others, such practice could serve to reinforce their feelings of incompetence and limited self-esteem and, as such, have a detrimental impact upon their levels of motivation (Graham 2001). In addition, Graham (2001) urges coaching practitioners to avoid placing athletes in situations that may cause them considerable embarrassment. In particular, he believes that, with young athletes in particular, coaches should refrain from incorporating activities such as allowing captains to pick teams, elimination games, and relay races into their practice, as they are potentially damaging to an athlete's self-concept (see Graham 2001; Byrne 1999).

Jones *et al*.'s (2004) examination of the coaching practices and philosophies of top-level coaches provides some interesting findings that coaches may consider in their quest to optimize athlete motivation. Specifically, their findings reinforce the contention that more can be achieved by a coach using positive interactions than negative ones. Indeed, the coaches in this study considered the use of praise to be a valuable tool for creating a supportive environment on the practice field, and maintaining high levels of morale and self-worth among the athletes. A similar finding was also reported by Potrac *et al*.'s (2002) examination of the interactions of a top-level English soccer coach. However, it would be unwise for coaches to adopt the belief that high levels of praise will automatically serve to enhance all athletes' levels of motivation in all coaching contexts. In this respect, Cushion and Jones (2001) have raised a question, not regarding the motives of the coach in providing a positive and supportive learning environment, but the success of such a strategy if the feedback was habitual, non-specific and consequently meaning-less for the athletes. Here, they suggest that a key point for coaches to consider is the meaning that athletes attach to such behaviour. As such, coaches need to take into account the specific needs and experiences of their athletes and determine how much praise to give and how often to give it is best for each athlete (Potrac 2001). In short, the coach needs to recognize the needs of the specific coaching situation and act accordingly (Jones 2000).

In comparison to the positive value ascribed to praise, negative interactions between coach and athletes are generally regarded as far from desirable (Jones *et al*. 2004; Potrac *et al*. 2002). Indeed, Potrac *et al*.'s (2002) findings suggest that while it was seen as occasionally necessary for a coach to 'lay down the law' or give a player 'a kick up the arse' during a practice session, the public berating of poor performances was considered totally unproductive. Indeed, as highlighted in Potrac's (2001) analysis of the working behaviours of top-level English and Norwegian soccer coaches, negative interactions are perceived to contribute towards lowering the confidence levels of athletes:

> If you keep hitting him with mistakes, you're not doing this, you're not doing that right, then he thinks f**k me I'm not doing anything right and so he loses confidence. So that is very important that, getting the player in the right frame of mind to work.
>
> (Potrac 2001: 83)

A further feature for coaches to consider in terms of their interaction with athletes is the possible contribution a coach's use of humour could have on the creation of a positive working relationship and, accordingly, athlete motivation. In the context of elite sport, Jones et al.'s (2004) findings revealed that humour could play a crucial role in defusing some of the tension that surrounds athletes in high-performance sport, as well as presenting the coach in a human light. In drawing upon the work of Graham (2001) in physical education, coach humour could also be important to developing an environment that fosters motivation in junior and participation-level athletes. However, he outlines that coaches should refrain from making sarcastic comments to and about athletes, as such behaviour may have a damaging impact upon an athlete's self-concept, as well as implying to athletes that sarcasm is acceptable in the coaching environment. Given the current paucity of research addressing the use of humour in the coaching process, we suggest that this represents a valuable line for future inquiry.

In developing upon the points made above, the coaches interviewed by Jones et al. (2004) suggested that the ultimate goal for coaches is to develop a climate whereby their interactions result in athletes striving to fulfil their individual potential, secure in the knowledge that, should they make a mistake, they will not be humiliated for so doing. Indeed, they considered such an atmosphere to have a valuable impact upon athlete motivation. This is perhaps well illustrated in the following extract:

> When you work with players on things that you feel they need to improve on you've got to make them comfortable to work . . . you give them a positive environment in which they think 'yes, things can be put right no problem'. So yes, it's very important that the player is relaxed enough to make mistakes in front of you. Like, for instance, David over there [a player] wasn't relaxed enough to make mistakes in front of me. He used to get bloody wounded. But if a player can say 'look Steve, I keep getting this wrong what am I doing?', then I can say 'look it's probably this or that and this is why'. If a player cannot say this, then there is no point doing the work because there is a barrier. It's very important that the

player is willing to do it wrong in front of you in order for both of you to put it right.

(Jones et al. 2004: 13)

Finally, if coaches are to optimize athlete motivation through their social interaction with them, we believe that coaching practitioners would benefit from developing a holistic understanding of their athletes (see Chapter 15 for a more detailed discussion). Specifically, we propose that an appreciation of, and sensitivity toward, athletes' identities (see Chapter 9 for more detail) and the lives that athletes lead outside of the immediate sporting environment could influence the nature of coach–athlete interaction and, ultimately, athlete motivation.

Parent–athlete interaction[1]

Byrne (1999) contends that alongside coaches, parents and guardians are capable of exerting considerable social influence upon young athletes' sporting participation and motivation. As such, he suggests 'coaches who choose to ignore parents do so at their peril' (Byrne 1999: 42). Indeed, the limited available literature on this topic highlights how parents 'are important transmitters of information about a child's competence through the mechanisms of modelling and reinforcement' (Weiss and Ferrer-Caja 2002: 118). Simply put, parents have the potential to reinforce or compromise coaches' efforts to develop a task-mastery-focused environment for young athletes. For example, by asking 'Did you win?', parents provide athletes with a clear message as to what they consider to be important (Duda and Treasure 2001).

In drawing upon Helstad's (1987) continuum of parental involvement in sport, Byrne (1999) highlights how 'underinvolved' and 'overinvolved' parents may have a potentially damaging effect on athlete motivation. With regard to underinvolved parents, he argues that children will not experience the full benefits of participation in sport if their parents do not take any interest in their activities. In particular, he suggests that a child's desire to please their parents and show them what they can do is an important facet of motivation. As such, he proposes that sport provides an ideal environment for young athletes to demonstrate effort, commitment, and the new skills that they have learnt to their parents. In this respect, he states that 'the smiling face of a parent to share in the successes and a hug to console in defeat go a long way to making sport an enjoyable experience' (Byrne 1999: 44). By comparison, a child's motivation for sporting involvement may decline if the athlete perceives his or her parents to have little or no interest in their sporting activity. Indeed, this state of affairs may result in a child not only making a judgement about the value of sport and physical activity in general, but also his or her self-worth. Accordingly, these athletes may interpret their sporting experiences to

---

[1] This section also refers to guardians and significant others

be stressful and unenjoyable (Byrne 1999). Obviously, such experiences may have an impact upon a child's long-term participation in sport.

Overinvolved parents can also have a detrimental impact upon a child's motivation. Such parents may be very critical of a child's performance, often subjecting the athlete to a minute analysis of a match or competition and suggesting improvements required for future performances (Byrne 1999). As a consequence of the pressure placed on them by parents, Byrne (1999) notes that these children may argue with officials because their parents expect it, work hard in training sessions but not enjoy them, and have trouble sleeping and eating prior to competition. Ultimately, the stress of having to conform to adult expectations is likely to result in athletes experiencing feelings of fear and dissatisfaction. Indeed, Byrne (1999: 45) suggests that 'external pressure from adults for children to take part in sport to win at all costs, to be number one, will undermine their motivation and turn play into work'. Accordingly, in order to optimize motivation in young athletes, it is crucial that coaches foster positive relationships with parents, as the failure to do so may result in the athlete receiving conflicting messages from the coach and his or her parents (Byrne 1999; Smoll 2001). According to Byrne (1999), such a scenario could not only impact upon athlete motivation but may also result in the sporting experience being an unenjoyable one for all concerned. In order to avoid this situation, Smoll (2001) suggests that the role of the coach is to both tactfully and diplomatically point out to parents the negative consequences of their actions and to highlight strategies that they may use to become more helpful and constructive in the sporting environment. For example, coaches could provide parents with codes of conduct that clearly outline the roles and responsibilities of the parent, reinforce desired side-line behaviours during competition and training, and stage coach–parent meetings at the beginning, middle and end of the playing season (Smoll 2001). Indeed, if coaches are to develop high levels of intrinsic motivation in young athletes it is essential that they are prepared to communicate with, and educate, parents.

Athlete–peer interaction

In addition to considering how their actions and those of parents may influence athlete motivation, a further factor for coaches to take into account is the possible impact that an athlete's interaction with his or her peers may have upon motivation (Smith 1999, 2003; Weiss and Ferrer-Caja 2002; Weiss et al. 1996). In the context of education, Harter (1997: 11) notes that peers not only meet important social needs by providing friendship and companionship to individuals, but that they also represent 'a very salient social reference group that invites intense social comparison'. In this respect, she highlights how peer approval or disapproval may have a major impact on an individual's self-concept (Harter, 1997). In a similar vein, Wentzel (1999: 89) notes that 'emotional distress has been linked consistently to peer rejection and lack of peer support'. In transferring these findings to the sporting domain, Smith (2003) suggests that given the importance of self-perceptions to quality physical-activity experiences, and in particular motivational processes, it is clear that an understanding of how peers shape self-perceptions is necessary for practitioners engaged in the fields of sport and physical education. Currently, the literature addressing this topic is very much in its infancy, particularly within the sports science and sports coaching domains. However, the limited available research highlights a number of issues that coaches would benefit from considering in terms of their professional practice.

In the context of sport, research suggests that peer acceptance and support may, in part, be determined by an athlete's sporting ability (Weiss and Ferrer-Caja 2002). Indeed, the research findings have illustrated that athletes who are perceived as being the most athletically talented are more likely to gain acceptance and status from their peer group. Conversely, athletes with lower ability have been found to have fewer opportunities to develop, maintain, and strengthen friend-ships with their peers (Weiss and Ferrer-Caja 2002). Indeed, the work of Evans and Roberts (1987) illustrates how athletes of lower ability may be 'locked out' of games, as the leadership roles and key positions are dominated by higher skilled athletes. Moreover, the lower ability athletes may also become the target of ridicule or be blamed for the loss of a particular event, match, or competition by their peers (Graham 2001). Such potentially painful and unpleasant experiences may negatively impact upon an athlete's self-concept, which has obvious implications for their continued participation in sport and physical activity (Graham 2001).

While the current research has tended to focus on sporting ability as a factor that contributes towards peer esteem and acceptance, it would be inaccurate to con-clude that this is the only factor that is important here. Indeed, coaches also need to consider how aspects of ethnicity, class, gender, and sexuality, among others, may impinge upon and influence athlete interaction and, as a result, the nature of the sporting experience. For example, Jones's (2002) investigation of black athletes' experiences in English semi-professional football highlights how the intentionally and unintentionally racist comments of the predominantly white peers and coaches had a detrimental impact upon the sporting experiences of the athletes. Similarly, research investigating female experiences of co-educational physical education lessons has revealed that, when participating in traditionally male-dominated sports such as soccer, female students may be subjected to ridicule by their male counterparts (Tinning *et al.* 2001). The consequence of such ridicule is that the female athletes may view their participation in this setting to be 'a waste of time' or nothing more than an 'opportunity for further humiliation' (Tinning *et al.* 2001: 128). In order to prevent athletes from having to endure such experi-ences at the hands of their peers, Weinberg and Gould (2003) suggest that coaches have a responsibility to encourage positive peer interaction and respect for others. Specifically, they believe that 'positive statements to team mates should be rein-forced, whereas derogatory remarks, teasing, and negative comments should not be tolerated' (Weinberg and Gould 2003: 498).

A final point for coaches to consider in relation to peer interaction is that many athletes, both young and old, 'enjoy sport because of the opportunities it provides to be with friends and make new friends' (Weinberg and Gould 2003: 497). This notion is well illustrated in the following vignette:

> More recently, I was conducting trials for a girls' 'Under 16' basketball team that I would be coaching at an inter-provincial tournament. After the second trial I 'cut' Mihi from the team. She was a good ball handler, was quick and played sound defence, however, I reasoned that I had other guards to choose from who could fit more easily into my proposed team patterns, to form the squad into an effective unit in the time we had available before the tournament. Also, while she was a good passer of the ball, Mihi did have a disturbing habit of predominantly passing to her two friends, and she tended to fire the ball at the hoop pretty much every time she caught sight of it. So, Mihi didn't come to subsequent practices – but neither did her two friends, who had made the cut and were the most useful players in the squad. It took me a while to pin all three players down to a face-to-face discussion, during which I came to the understanding that, for them, being in the squad primarily represented an opportunity to 'hang out' together doing something they enjoyed. Playing together – and travelling away to tournament – was their focus, rather than striving to become more skilful or seeking status through representing their province.
>
> (Salter 2000: 70)

Accordingly, where possible, coaching practitioners should attempt to provide athletes with opportunities to achieve these social goals. For example, coaches could schedule social events outside of practices and may also incorporate aspects of free time before and during practice sessions (Weinberg and Gould 2003). In drawing upon the work of Urdan and Maehr (1995), Weiss and Ferrer-Caja (2002: 160–161) state that a greater understanding of how 'social welfare goals (e.g. to become a productive member of society), social solidarity goals (e.g. to bring honour to one's family or raise esteem within one's group), social approval goals (e.g. to please parents, develop friendships, enhance peer acceptance), and social compliance goals (e.g. to become a good person)' influence motivation is required before we can adequately theorize athlete motivation.

CONCLUDING THOUGHTS

The purpose of this chapter was to highlight the complex nature of athlete motivation. Indeed, it is hoped that the reader has an initial insight into how athlete motivation is not solely influenced by the emphasis that coaches place on competition and task mastery, or the extent to which athletes perceive themselves to be in control of their sporting experiences. While these are undoubtedly important factors for a coach to consider in terms of their professional practice, it is also necessary for practitioners to be sensitive to how the social interactions that an athlete engages in with coaches, parents and guardians, and peers may impinge upon his or her motivation. In this respect, coaches should recognize that they are crucial to the motivational environment and can influence athlete motivation in direct and indirect ways (Weinberg and Gould 2003).

CHAPTER 9

▼ UNDERSTANDING ATHLETES' IDENTITIES

- Introduction   106
- What is identity?   107
- Gendered identity   108
- Sexualized identity   111
- Ethnic identity   115
- Concluding thoughts   117

INTRODUCTION

> Coaching is recognising situations, recognising the people and responding
> to the people you are working with.
> (Steve Harrison, Middlesborough Football Club, in Jones *et al.* 2004: 18)

The above quote is taken from a book that examines the philosophies and practices
of eight top-level coaches, who had enjoyed notable successes at both the international and national levels of sport. In reflecting upon what had made them
'successful', the respondent coaches highlighted the importance of understanding,
and relating to, their athletes as social beings and not just performing bodies. In
this respect, considerable emphasis was placed 'on getting to know them [the
athletes] and what makes them tick' (Jones *et al.* 2004: 18) in the quest to optimize
sporting performance.

While such inquiry has served to highlight the importance of recognizing and appreciating athletes as unique and individual beings, existing coach-education schemes
have tended to present sporting performers as a homogenous group (Jones 2000).
Indeed, far from recognizing how an individual athlete is shaped and influenced
by his or her gender, race, class, and sexuality, the bio-scientific approach, which
underpins contemporary coach education, has largely portrayed the athlete to be
little more than a mechanistic body that is 'serviced' by the coach (Jones 2000;

Potrac *et al.* 2000). In commenting upon the technocratic rationality that has underpinned much coach-education provision, Jones (2000) argues that coaches who are driven solely by mechanistic considerations may have difficulty comprehending and thus adapting to the complexities of coaching. Indeed, as Armour and Fernandez Balboa (2000) have suggested, coaching is not only about making connections to different scientific subjects and methods, but also, and perhaps more importantly, connections between other people and life in general.

Accordingly, the broad purpose of this chapter is to explore how athletes' identities may come to bear on the coaching process. In particular, following an introductory discussion of identity, we explore how notions of gender, ethnicity, sexuality and their interconnections may influence how an athlete views him- or herself and, as a result, how this sense of self could influence an athlete's participation in sport. In keeping with the general ethos of this book, the aim here is not to provide the reader with prescriptions as to what coaches should do but, instead, is to sensitize the reader to the critical concerns of culture as it relates to coaching practice.

WHAT IS IDENTITY?

It is useful to recognize that the term identity has been used in a number of contexts and is a highly complex concept that remains the subject of much debate in the fields of sociology and psychology (Brettschneider and Heim 1997). Despite this, Brettschneider and Heim (1997) suggest that identity can generally be understood to relate to how a person describes himself or herself to be distinctive or unique. The description could relate to *personal identity*, or *social identity*, the latter referring to how others share the former identity within the social environment. Indeed, while people may possess their own individuality, it is not wholly distinct from others in society (Haralambos and Holborn 2000). Through the process of socialization, an individual may come to internalize certain values and norms that are associated with a particular identity (Haralambos and Holborn 2000). An important point to consider when discussing identity is that an individual may possess several identities, which may sometimes be contradictory or unresolved, rather than have a single or unified concept of the self (Hall and DuGay 1996; Haralambos and Holborn 2000).

According to Jenkins (in Haralambos and Holborn 2000), individuals are never entirely free to choose the identities that they claim. In this respect, he argues that identity formation is not just related to social interaction but that it is also related to social groups and power relationships. Specifically, he contends that some groups have the power to assign particular identities to others in addition to claiming certain identities for themselves. Bradley (1997) suggests that such identities are a critical feature of social life, as they shape the way in which we view our social worlds.

For the purpose of this chapter, we consider identity to relate to our 'understanding of who we are and of who other people are, and reciprocally, other people's understanding of themselves and others' (Jenkins in Haralambos and Holborn 2000: 921). Additionally, rather than viewing identity to be a set of enduring personality traits that remain with us from childhood onwards, we consider identity to be both fluid and dynamic in nature (Bradley 1997; Tinning et al. 2001), as well as something that is 'constantly negotiated and performed in relation to changing contexts and circumstances' (Tinning et al. 2001: 97). In this respect, it is important to recognize that an individual's identities may not only be shaped by their social engagements with other people, but also through their interactions with what is written, filmed, televised, and photographed (Tinning et al. 2001).

GENDERED IDENTITY

Gender is the sociological concept that refers to 'all the differences between men and women which derive from social expectations about appropriate behaviour, interests, abilities and attitudes for masculine and feminine identity' (Kew 2000: 126). Traditionally, in most western countries, masculinity has been principally associated with notions of independence, decisiveness, aggression, toughness, strength, and power. Conversely, femininity has been largely characterized by qualities such as fragility, sensitivity, and a dependency on men (Coakley 2001; Horne et al. 1999; Tinning et al. 2001). Tinning et al. (2001) believe that these particular conceptions of masculinity and femininity may not be as powerful as they were in previous centuries. Nonetheless, they argue that the dominant discourses of femininity still reinforce heterosexuality, nurturing and being supportive, while the dominant discourses of masculinity put pressure on young men, in many social contexts, to earn enough money to support a family, be independent and physically strong.

In this respect, Tinning et al. (2001) note that the body is becoming an increasingly important source of an individual's identity or identities. In drawing upon the work of Schilling (1993), they suggest 'the more people attach value to how we look and what we do with our bodies, the greater the likelihood that our self-identities will be tied to them' (Tinning et al. 2001: 98). Consequently, we believe that coaching practitioners should be sensitive to how notions of masculinity and femininity may be intimately linked to an athlete's body and would benefit from an awareness of the discourses associated with the male and female body in contemporary society.

Before proceeding with an examination of masculinity and femininity as it relates to athlete identity and coaching practice, it is perhaps useful to first outline the concept of 'hegemony'. Hegemony is the sociological concept that refers to the ability of dominant social groups to 'use their power and influence to promote and shape attitudes, values, beliefs, and worldviews' (Sage 1998: 20) that serve to maintain their privileged position in society. In this respect, Sage (1998) states that

> the ways of life and versions of culture and civilisation of the dominant actors are fashioned in a direction that, while perhaps not yielding

unquestioned advantage for narrow dominant interests, persuades the masses to embrace a consensus that supports the existing social arrangements.

(Sage 1998: 22)

In the context of gender relations, hegemonic masculinity refers to the dominance of one form of masculinity over others (Connell 1995). According to Connell (1995), hegemonic masculinity is not fixed in nature across time and place but is, instead, the masculinity that occupies the hegemonic position in a particular social setting. As such, the dominance of a hegemonic masculinity is open to challenge from other masculinities and women (Connell 1995). In contemporary Western society, the dominant or hegemonic masculinity has tended to be that of white, middle-class males, as opposed to the masculinities of non-whites and homosexuals (Connell 1995; Sage 1998), which are considered to be 'marginalised' and 'subordinate' masculinities, respectively (see Connell 1995). However, this is not to say that non-white and homosexual masculinities are disadvantaged in all social settings. For example, in certain contexts, such as the Gay Games, gay men occupy the hegemonic masculine position. Despite this, the main hegemonic form of masculinity, as indicated above, has tended to emphasize heterosexuality as an important male trait. Failure to comply with these values is not without its consequences. For example, the fear of being labelled a 'poofter' or a 'fag' may cause some males to not participate in what have been traditionally labelled feminine sports and activities, despite their interest in and enthusiasm for them (Coakley 2001; Tinning et al. 2001). This is well illustrated in the movie Billy Elliot, where the main character's decision to pursue a career in ballet is, initially, met with a mixture of shame, anger and ridicule from his family and significant others.

In terms of coaching practice, it is perhaps useful for coaches to be sensitive to how sport has provided a particularly fruitful arena for legitimizing and maintaining the hegemonic masculinity while marginalizing or excluding others (Connell 1995; Hickey and Fitzclarence 1997; Kenway and Fitzclarence 1997; Miedzian 1991). In this respect, Tinning et al. (2001) suggest that coaches may benefit from a sensitivity toward the ideal male body promoted in magazines, television, films and sports, which is one that is muscular, strong, and powerful. As a consequence of these images, some male athletes may have concerns about subjecting their bodies to public evaluation in the sporting context for fear of ridicule, especially if they believe their bodies do not conform to social expectations. Additionally, Hickey and Fitzclarence (1997) suggest that coaches need to recognize how sport is a cultural practice, and acknowledge that what is taught in the name of sport is more than the drills prescribed in the coaching manuals. For example, in the context of Australian Rules Football, Hickey and Fitzclarence (1997) note that, through both formal and informal channels, boys learn to adopt a masculinity that is racist, homophobic and patriarchal, in addition to being violent and aggressive. They go on to suggest that the cultivation of values such as strength, dominance, and aggression in sport is problematic. Especially, they argue, when boys and men are taught to behave in ways that, outside of the sporting environment, would be deemed to be dysfunctional and deviant.

In drawing upon the work of Miedzan (1991), Hickey and Fitzclarence (1997) state that sport has become a space where violence is tolerated, women are marginalized and where abusive behaviour is explained away with the platitude 'boys will be boys'. In this respect, Coakley (2001) suggests that the record of men's destructive and violent behaviour may be, in part, explained by the hegemonic masculinity that is promoted in contemporary sports. Indeed, he notes that

> as boys and men apply this ideology to their lives, they learn to view manhood in terms of things that jeopardise the safety of and well-being of themselves and others. They may ride the tops of elevators, drive cars at breakneck speeds, play various forms of 'chicken', drink each other under the table, get into fights, use violence in sports as indicators of manhood, use dangerous substances to build muscles, avoid interacting with females as equals, keep sexual scores in heterosexual relationships, rough up girlfriends or wives, rape, or kill 'unfaithful' women. Some men learn that size and toughness allow them to get away with violating norms and that status depends on making others fear or depend on them. If men take this ideology far enough, they may get in the habit of 'forcing their way' on others through physical intimidation or coercion.
>
> (Coakley 2001: 235)

Hickey and Fitzclarence (1997) contend that coaches, through the familiarity, legitimacy and authority they possess are important agents in the quest to bring about social change in this regard. They suggest that coaches could benefit from an in-depth understanding of young males' interpretation and construction of masculinity within the culture of a particular sport. For example, while the hegemonic practices in rugby, surfing, dance and skateboarding contexts are not the same, they all have 'common-sense' assumptions of what it means to be a male in that specific setting. Despite the differences in what is viewed as 'common sense', the task for coaches is to challenge behaviour that threatens the rights and identities of others. This could include: recognizing the way in which power is invested in the hierarchical structures of sports coaching and how this recreates class and race inequalities; reducing the level of covert or overt violence in sports; and assisting boys and men to develop positive relationships between men, and between men and women (Connell 1995; Jones 2000; Schempp and Oliver 2000). In this respect, Hickey and Fitzclarence (1997) propose that the following strategies may be useful for coaches who wish to create a climate that enables multiple masculinities to be valued:

■ Examine the way individuals within a group learn to create a 'them' and 'us' mentality by isolating the 'other' in order to assert the authority of the dominant group.

- Do not accept the rationalization of violent behaviour (e.g. 'I just flipped out', 'I have a short fuse', 'boys will be boys'), as these rationalizations distance the aggressor from taking responsibility for their actions.
- Identify how many of the attitudes and behaviours believed to be 'normal' within the culture of the sport parallel forms of social disharmony and deviance outside of that specific setting.

However, while Hickey and Fitzclarence (1997) believe that new pedagogical strategies and practices, such as those outlined above, are needed to support coaches in their efforts to assist young males explore their masculinity, they warn that this is a far from straightforward process. This is due to many of the behaviours we may want to change being embedded in traditions, customs, routines and habits. One consequence of this is that the behaviours are difficult to recognize and challenge because they do not operate at a rational level.

Coaches may also have to contend with similar issues to those discussed above when working with female athletes. For example, Coakley (2001) highlights how the media promotes 'heterosexualised hard bodies' as the most desirable body type for women. Indeed, this image is highly prevalent in magazines, newspapers, and television commercials, which emphasize, among other attributes, 'thinness, bust size, lip shape, hairstyles, body hair removal, complexion, [and] allure . . . that "make" the woman' (Coakley 2001: 208). As a result of the prominence of such images, female athletes, particularly adolescents, may adopt these discourses as frameworks against which to evaluate their bodies. This is a particularly problematic state of affairs, as the body shape promoted in the media is often an image that most women can only obtain through depriving themselves of food and nourishment (Coakley 2001). As such, the public display of the body (e.g. getting changed in the locker rooms, wearing a team uniform in competition), which is an integral feature of sporting participation, may cause some females not to participate in sport until they are 'thin enough to look "right" and wear the "right" clothes' (Coakley 2001: 210). Furthermore, the pressure to conform to social expectations regarding body shape may manifest itself in the form of eating disorders. For example, Benson and Taub (1993: 360) suggest that 'swimmers may be especially vulnerable to disordered eating due to the display of their bodies in a tight and revealing uniform'. Indeed, the available research (e.g. Johns 1998; Ryan 1995) on female athletes in general indicates that 'an alarming number of women use laxatives, diet pills, diuretics, self-induced vomiting, binges, and starvation diets in conjunction with their training' (Coakley 2001: 211). Obviously, the consequences of such actions can be extremely painful for the athlete both psychologically and physiologically.

However, it would be naive to believe that such actions only result from the dominant images of the female body provided by the media. Indeed, the research of Reel and Gill (2001) and Johns (1998), among others, has highlighted that coaches and peers may also have a significant impact upon how a female athlete views her body and, ultimately, the self. In this respect, they note how the perceived relationship between body fat and performance espoused by many coaches may impact upon a female athlete's sense of identity. This is clearly illustrated in the work of Johns (1998), who found that the gymnastic coaches in his study considered 'systematic weight loss' to be crucial to the development of aesthetically pleasing gymnasts. In this study, the coaches were found to exert great pressure on the gymnasts by strictly monitoring their eating and frequently measuring their weight, especially in the lead up to competitions when the gymnasts were required to diet. In this respect, his findings suggested that they tacitly supported, and perhaps encouraged, the gymnasts to achieve rapid weight loss through a severely limited dietary intake. Such pressure from the coaches has its consequences. Specifically, Johns' (1998) findings revealed how, as a result of the coaches' actions, the gymnasts perceived themselves to be 'fat' regardless of how much weight they lost, as illustrated in the following reflections:

> For sure the coaches definitely had a strong influence over what you understood to be the right thing to do, because ultimately you were performing for them, for the sport, and for the country. When it came to the problem about weight they would say, 'Sarah looks a little heavy on the floor, she really should lose some weight, and she'll represent us well'. As a young athlete you automatically become concerned about your weight, and you begin to blow things out of proportion and see yourself as an elephant.
>
> (Johns 1998: 55)

> Another instance really sticks out in my mind, and it was with my team mate and very good friend, [name deleted], who was completely bulimic and was extremely thin. Even though I was healthy and was pretty thin myself, I was being compared to her, but I looked fat and they were saying things like, 'See, [name deleted], she is really looking good, and that is what you have to be like'. Unfortunately, they did not know, or they pretended not to know, that she was barfing her brains up behind closed doors, and then in front of the coaches was the picture of goodness not eating a thing.
>
> (Johns 1998: 57)

In addition to the coach having the potential to exert a strong influence upon how an athlete may perceive her body, Reel and Gill (2001) suggest that comments made by team members may also contribute toward an athlete's view of her body. In this respect, they note that through interactions and comparisons with their peers, an athlete may arrive at a particular judgement regarding her body shape and, ultimately, herself. In order to reduce the possibility of an athlete developing negative feelings toward her body, Reel and Gill (2001) suggest that coaches should adopt a number of strategies. For example, they should strive to ensure that they avoid group weigh-ins, educate athletes with regard to nutrition and the relationship between body fat and muscle, discourage team members from making weight-related comments to other athletes, and evaluate their own beliefs regarding the weight–performance relationship.

As an example of the interconnectedness of identities, in this case gender and sexuality, a further issue for coaches to consider is how the fear of being labelled a lesbian may impact upon female athletes. In this regard, it may not only influence the sports that female athletes may choose to participate in, but also the effort that they put into a particular sporting activity and their willingness to engage in training programmes. Especially, if the result of the training is the development of bodies that differ from the prevailing images of femininity and 'heterosexualised hard bodies' (Choi 2000; Coakley 2001; Kew 2000). While coaches are unable to eradicate the constraints placed on some women by existing homophobic discourses, they may be able to create a working environment that promotes the view that developing strength and muscle is a form of personal empowerment for female athletes (Schempp and Oliver 2000; Heywood 1998). Indeed, coaches, through their professional practice, may seek to challenge existing conceptions of femininity. This does not mean that coaches should advocate that females adopt traditionally masculine behaviours, rather they may encourage 'girls and women to explore and connect with the power of their bodies' (Coakley 2001: 237).

SEXUALIZED IDENTITY

Sexuality, in broad terms, refers to the sexual behaviour and sexual characteristics of human beings (Giddens 1997). Giddens (1997) notes that while heterosexuality is the basis for marriage and the family in almost every society, there are many other sexual tastes and inclinations, which include lesbian women, gay men, bisexual men, bisexual women, transvestite men, transvestite women, transsexual women and transsexual men. This section will principally focus on the identities and experiences of gay men and lesbian women in sport.

Before proceeding with the exploration of sexual identity as it relates to coaching practice, it is perhaps worthwhile providing some background information relating to homosexuality. While homosexuality exists in all cultures, the notion of a homosexual person is a relatively recent one (Giddens 1997). Here, in drawing upon the work of Weeks (1986), Giddens (1997: 104) indicates that the term homosexuality originates from the 1860s, and was used to describe 'a separate type of people with a particular sexual aberration'. Indeed, homosexuality was, until several decades ago, not only frowned upon in nearly all Western societies but was also considered to be a criminal activity. The history of homosexuality might explain why many people are still hostile towards homosexuals (Giddens 1997).

According to Coakley (2001), gay men and lesbians are often feared, marginalized, ignored, and, in extreme circumstances, subjected to vitriolic criticism, defensive reactions, and physical assault in contemporary Western society. As such, it is perhaps not surprising that many gay and lesbian athletes prefer not to reveal their sexual orientation to their team mates and coaches. Indeed, the consequences of 'coming-out' in the sporting context, according to the existing research (see Griffin 1998; Pronger 1999; Squires and Sparkes 1996), include, among other things, experiencing a sense of isolation, angry hostility, and, for elite athletes, the loss of sponsorship and endorsements. This is perhaps well illustrated in the following vignette:

> After joining (the campus lesbian and gay student group) I enjoyed the sense of community I had with other students. I was an anomaly, an out lesbian softball player who wanted to take on the world. I became one of the poster children who were invited to classes or dorms to talk about lifestyles and answer questions. While I was becoming more and more open about who I was, I found myself sitting on the bench more and more. I was there (on the team) as an athlete not a lesbian, but no one in the team could separate the two in their minds and accept me for who I was, so I had a pretty horrible season. On away trips, no one wanted to stay in the same room with me at hotels. Other players preferred sleeping on the floor in other rooms rather than staying in a room with a lesbian. Players shunned me and generally made my life miserable. My coach, who was also rumoured to be a lesbian, was no help. When I was in the health centre with a back injury, no one on the team checked on me.
>
> (Griffin 1998: 98)

With respect to the lesbian experience in sport, Griffin's (1998) work has revealed that there are many myths surrounding lesbian athletes. Among these myths are the misplaced beliefs that lesbian athletes are sexual predators who prey on their team mates in order to recruit them to their lifestyle, and that heterosexuals will become lesbians just by associating with lesbian team mates and opponents. Indeed, the latter view has tended to present lesbianism as a virus with which a heterosexual athlete can become 'infected' (Fasting 1997). The limited available research exploring the sporting experience for gay athletes has reported similar findings (e.g. Pronger 1999; Woog 1998). Indeed, in a similar fashion to lesbian athletes, gay male athletes tend to be feared, mistrusted and stigmatized. In this respect, Coakley (2001) notes that some heterosexual men adopt threatening anti-gay behaviour in the locker room that keeps gay men silent about their sexuality as well as fearful of behaving in a way that could be identified as 'gay'. According to Messner (1996), such practices have served to generate feelings of shame among men who have strong feelings toward other men. This is well illustrated in the following quotation:

> I could have been a very good major-league player if I was not so emotionally screwed up when I was playing. I was very hard on myself, and I think it all translates back to that feeling of, 'I'm not worthy'. I'm bad because I'm a gay man on the Dodger Stadium field. I don't belong out here. This is wrong. I hate myself. . . . I remember walking in the clubhouse every day and feeling that people could see the kiss I gave my lover when I

walked out the door. . . . Then you sit down and start talking about strip clubs.

(Wine 2003)

Given such findings, we argue that coaches should attempt to provide an environment that challenges the existing stereotypes regarding gay and lesbian athletes. In this respect, coaches could begin this process by critically reflecting upon their own beliefs regarding gay and lesbian athletes. In addition, they may also wish to examine how their current practice may serve to reinforce the dominant homophobic discourses in sport (Schempp and Oliver 2000). For example, by using, or not challenging, the use of language such as 'fag', 'poofter', and 'dyke', coaches may be guilty of reinforcing institutionalized homophobia (Coakley 2001). In addition to examining their own beliefs and practices, coaches may also consider how they provide a coaching environment that supports gay and lesbian athletes. This could include dealing with athlete sexuality in a positive, supportive and sensitive manner by challenging derisory comments, jokes, and other practices that are homophobic in nature (Schempp and Oliver 2000). For example, in terms of athletes engaging in public displays of affection, coaches could strive to create an environment that is conducive to gay or lesbian athletes as well as heterosexual performers. Such actions would require some courage on behalf of the coach, and may prove to be a far from unproblematic process. However, as Coakley (2001:238) notes, 'the listener who stands by and says nothing in response to this language perpetuates inequities'.

ETHNIC IDENTITY

Unlike the concept of race, which has been used to classify people according to physical characteristics, ethnicity refers to 'categories of people who share a common cultural identity and heritage' (Nixon and Frey 1998: 227). In particular, ethnicity is determined by cultural characteristics, such as traditions, values, norms and ideas, which constitute a particular way of life (Coakley 2001). In most Western societies, ethnic groups that do not identify with the majority ethnic group, which is often white, are often subject to inequality, discrimination, and oppression (Thompson 1998; Tinning et al. 2001).

In the realm of physical education, Tinning et al. (2001) suggest that, in tandem with events in the wider society, the interests, needs, and experiences of minority groups are often disregarded. This particular state of affairs is mirrored in the sports coaching context. Indeed, while coach education has begun to address the need to cater for athletes with different skill and performance levels, it has largely ignored issues relating to the needs and requirements of different cultural groups (Jones 2000). As a consequence of those issues being ignored, there has been a proliferation of stereotypes and assumptions among coaches relating to athletes from different cultural backgrounds. For example, Afro-Caribbean athletes are often believed to be physically powerful but lacking in leadership and decision-making skills, while young Muslim males are widely perceived to prefer academic pursuits to any involvement in sport and physical activity (Fleming 1991; Kew 2000; McCarthy *et al.* 2003). Similarly, Tinning *et al.* (2001) note that Muslim girls are often considered to be problematic by educators and coaches due to their apparent resistance to sport and physical activity.

Accordingly, in drawing upon the work of Schempp and Oliver (2000), we believe that it is crucial for coaches to develop an understanding of, and sensitivity toward, the ethnic heritage of their athletes if they are to provide individuals with positive sporting experiences. For example, in the context of Muslim males' involvement in sport, an appreciation of how religious requirements may constrain sporting involvement could help to dismiss stereotypical beliefs regarding lack of interest. This is illustrated in the following quote taken from Fleming's (1991) work with Asian schoolboys:

> It's quite difficult for me. I have to pray five times a day. If I have to pray at 12 o'clock and there's a match, I can't play. . . . If it's a matter of 'life and death', you can pray afterwards. But sport doesn't count as a matter of 'life and death'.
>
> (Fleming 1991: 37)

Furthermore, Tinning *et al.* (2001) suggest that an understanding of Islamic religious practices and beliefs regarding modesty may help us understand the issues that Muslim females have to contend with in relation to sport. In this respect, they highlight how Muslim females may, if they expose their bodies and legs to non-Muslims and males, have feelings of guilt and shame. As such, they suggest that, rather than Muslim females being 'problematic', it is the traditional sporting uniform of skirts or shorts that is a major barrier to their participation in sport. From such a discussion, it is clear that coaches would benefit from a detailed insight into how Muslim identities may come to bear on an athlete's sporting experience. In much the same way, coaches in Aotearoa/New Zealand could benefit from an appreciation of how being Māori or Pacific Islander may provide particular cultural resources that impact upon, and determine, the sense athletes make of their sporting experiences (Salter 2000). For example, an understanding of Māori beliefs regarding the process of interaction may enable a coach to recognize why a Māori athlete communicates and responds to teammates and coaches in the way that he or she does. In this respect, we contend that coaches would, among other things, benefit from an appreciation of the cultural significance that Māoridom attaches to 'manaakitanga (the showing of kindness, hospitality and respect), aroha-ki-te-tangata (love of your fellow man/woman), whanaungatanga (familiness), wairua (spirituality) and awhinatanga (helping, assisting)' (Bevan-Brown in Salter 2000).

THE ATHLETES

CONCLUDING THOUGHTS

While the concepts of gender, ethnicity and sexuality and how they may influence athlete identity have been discussed separately, they are, in reality, inextricably linked. As such, it is in their intersections that the key areas of understanding for coaches lie. Indeed, by recognizing that athletes are social beings rather than mechanistic bodies, coaches stand to gain an important insight into how 'the socio-cultural dynamics which shape identities in the wider society also impinge upon teaching/coaching and learning in sport, and ultimately the ability to perform well' (Jones 2000: 8). In this respect, Jones (2000) believes that an awareness of social prejudices that may cause an athlete self-doubt or similar problems is essential if a coach is to understand the totality of the athlete's performances. Indeed, he concludes that it is only by understanding the social aspects of the coaching process in a thoroughly practical way that coaches can possibly mediate tensions and overcome difficulties.

▼ END OF SECTION TWO: TASK

It's 11a.m. on a Saturday morning and the children of Parkway United Under-11 football team are milling around outside the changing rooms eagerly awaiting the start of practice. While the coach, Ian McPherson, makes some last-minute arrangements to the equipment and practice areas, the children are busy keeping themselves occupied. Some of the boys and girls are 'showing off' their latest ball skills, while others tell jokes and discuss what the weekend holds in store for them. Amidst the noise and laughter of young voices, one child stands alone clutching his water bottle and soccer ball with a look of apprehension upon his face. David, whose parents have just moved to the area, is new to the team. This is his second week at practice and he is anxious to make friends and become accepted by the group. Whilst in the process of marking out one of the practice grids, Ian looks up and notices how David seems to be ignored by the other children but decides to take no action on this occasion.

With the practice areas neatly marked out, Ian signals the start of the training session with a short blast on his whistle. The children run over to Ian, as they like him and enjoy their coaching sessions with him – well most of them anyway. Ian begins the session with a warm-up game of soccer tag, which has proven to be popular with the children. The game involves one boy and one girl attempting to tag the other children by kicking the ball against them. Ian chooses Rachel and David to be the kickers. On a signal from Ian, the rest of the team move around the practice area and attempt to avoid the balls which are being kicked at them. After a minute or two, it becomes apparent that David lacks the physical skills to hit the other children. Indeed, many of the children begin to mock him while Rachel complains that it's not fair having to partner David, as 'he's rubbish'. Ian lets the game go on for a minute or two longer before replacing David as one of the kickers. The new kicker, Austin, is one of the more highly skilled players on the team. The change of partner seems to reinvigorate Rachel's enthusiasm for the game and she announces to the rest of the team that the kickers 'will now show everyone how to play this game properly'.

They begin by targeting the slower moving children who, upon being tagged, have to sit on the sidelines and watch while the kickers try and tag the other children. Simon and Clare who are tagged early on in the game share their frustration at 'always being out first' and having to 'wait ages for another go'. The numbers on the sideline steadily grow, until only David and Matt, who is the team's best player and captain, are the only two still to be tagged. John, Matt's best friend on the team, begins to cheer for Matt from the sideline and urges Rachel and Austin to tag David. Soon, the other children are cheering for Matt, while David appears to receive no such support from the audience of his peers. Meanwhile, Rachel and Austin have decided to target David and deliberately make no serious efforts to tag Matt. In her efforts to tag David, Rachel mistimes her kick and sends the ball into David's face. David is knocked to the ground. The rest of the team find the incident hilarious and burst into laughter. Ian rushes over to check that David is okay. Upon seeing that no real harm has been done, Ian announces Matt the winner and instructs the team to give Matt a big cheer for being the winner. He also invites the group to congratulate David for his efforts. This request is received with a mixture of half-hearted clapping and some enthusiastic booing.

Following the warm-up, Ian picks two captains who are to select teams for a series of soccer relay races. The captains choose one individual at a time until all the children have been selected for one team or the other. David hoped to be picked early but instead finds himself standing alone while all the other children, who have been picked ahead of him, are lined up behind their respective captains. By default, David has to join Matt's team so that both teams have even numbers. As David makes his way towards his relay team, Matt turns to the other team captain and says 'you can have him, we'd rather be a player short than have him in our team'. Hearing this, a visibly upset David starts to make his way from Matt's team to the other one when he hears Ian say 'Don't be silly, David. Matt was only joking. You're in his team for the relay races'.

The first relay involves dribbling around a series of cones and back again before passing the ball to the next team member. Matt's team develops an early lead, as the better skilled players position themselves early in the team order. However, the lead is gradually reduced with each team member that subsequently completes the course. This is, in part, due to the fact that the other relay team have made the less skilled players go first and saved their better players till last. By the time David, who is the last person to go in Matt's team, receives the ball he only has a short lead over the other team. The lead doesn't last long as David clumsily makes his way around the dribbling course, and Rachel, his opponent, demonstrates superior skill. Soon both players are neck and neck, which brings shouts of encouragement and calls for greater effort from their team-mates. David loses control of his ball, sending it off the marked course, which presents Rachel and her team with an easy win. Indeed, by the time David has regained control of his ball, Rachel's team are loudly celebrating their victory. David completes the course to a chorus of laughter from the other team and is then accused of letting the team down by Matt and some of his team-mates.

Ian informs the group that the relay competition will consist of three races and, as such, both teams 'still have plenty to play for'. As the teams prepare for the second race, Matt turns to David and says 'Don't let us down this time, you useless idiot'. Ian starts the race and observes his charges make their way around the dribbling course he has devised. Halfway through the race, a teary-eyed David asks Ian if he could sit out as he has a sore stomach. Ian allows David to rest and encourages him to join back in as soon as he feels ready to do so. As the session progresses, Ian repeatedly asks David if he is ready to join back in again. However, his promptings are met with a shake of the head on every occasion. Following a series of relay races, passing drills, and a small-sided game, Ian signalls the end of the session with one final blast of his whistle. As the children make their way back to the changing rooms where their parents are waiting to collect them, Ian is surprised to see a smiling David leading the dash for home.

1   How might David's motivation for continuing to participate in soccer be influenced by the actions of his peers?
2   What impact might their actions have on David's self-concept?
3   How might Ian better manage the social climate of the group? Why should he adopt the strategies you suggest?
4   What advice would you give Ian in relation to the tasks he selects and how he implements them with the team? What alternatives would you suggest and why?
5   Describe the learning theories that inform Ian's practice. Justify why you think this.
6   Explain some of the consequences for David of Ian being informed by these theories.
7   Describe some of the practices Ian could have adopted in his practice session that would have supported the view that learning occurs in a social context.
8   Using Nixon's (1984) framework outlined in Chapter 12, discuss what actions Ian could have taken if David had a) an intellectual or b) a physical disability.

SECTION THREE
COACHING
CONTENT

10 Examining coaches' content knowledge   123

11 Assessing athletes' understanding   130

12 Coaching athletes with a disability: exploring issues of
    content   139

CHAPTER 10

▼ **EXAMINING COACHES'
CONTENT KNOWLEDGE**

- Introduction   123
- What is content knowledge?   124
- Additional things to consider when thinking about content
  knowledge   125
- (Re)thinking coaches' knowledge   128
- Concluding thoughts   129

INTRODUCTION

> There is no curriculum that youth sport coaches must adhere to, and they
> have little or no supervision. Most youth team sport coaches work in isola-
> tion and therefore have tremendous freedom in the content they select to
> teach, and the way they structure the training programs.
>
> (Gilbert and Trudel 2001: 67–68)

The freedom coaches have to select the content they use in their practice sessions
may be part of the reason why discussions on content have not had a high profile
with sports scientists. Yet being aware of some of the educational discussions that
surround the notion of content knowledge may assist coaches to provide athletes
maximum opportunities to learn. The purpose of this chapter is to introduce, into
the sports coaching context, a discussion that highlights the complexity of a coach's
content knowledge by drawing on the work of Shulman (1986) and Metzler
(2000). The chapter begins with a discussion of the work of these two scholars.
Specifically, it discusses how Shulman breaks down the notion of content knowledge into three sub-sets: subject-matter content knowledge; pedagogical content
knowledge; and curriculum content knowledge, and how Metzler breaks the three
sub-sets of content knowledge into three more categories: declarative knowledge,
procedural knowledge, and conditional knowledge. In keeping with the book's general philosophy, we then proceed to highlight other aspects of content knowledge

not explicitly discussed by Shulman (1986) and Metzler (2000) but which we consider to be useful for coaches who strive to become quality coaches. We conclude the chapter by questioning the desire many have for 'certainty' and getting things 'right' (Cassidy and Tinning 2004) and what this means for coaches' content knowledge.

WHAT IS CONTENT KNOWLEDGE?

As mentioned above, content knowledge has been described as comprising of three sub-sets: subject-matter content knowledge (SMCK), pedagogical content knowledge (PCK), and curriculum content knowledge (CCK) (Shulman 1986). Subject-matter content knowledge is explained as the knowledge a coach has, or has access to, that represents the extent of the activity being coached. To be considered to have adequate subject-matter content knowledge a coach has to have knowledge of the range of activities that can be included in a session, the skills, tactics, strategies that can be adopted by athletes, and the rules of the activity being coached. Pedagogical content knowledge is considered to be the knowledge the coach needs to be able to teach (or communicate) the subject-matter content knowledge to the athletes. PCK enables the coach to make the subject matter 'comprehensible to others' (Shulman 1986: 9). For example, a coach needs to know when, why and how to adopt particular coaching method(s), and how to recognize athletes' learning preferences. Shulman's definition of curriculum is premised on a particular understanding of the term, namely that it is a set of materials such as a coaching manual. Consequently, curriculum content knowledge is viewed as the knowledge of available resources that the coach needs, and the knowledge of how to implement the activities into a coaching session so that the athletes learn what it is that the coach wants them to learn. For example, a basketball coach needs to be able to access the most recent sport-specific coaching manuals and be able to adapt the drills outlined in the manual to suit the situation in which she or he is working and achieve the desired learning outcomes for the athletes.

While Shulman's (1986) framework is a useful starting point for discussing content knowledge, Metzler (2000) argues that for teachers, and we would argue coaches, to become intimate with the content knowledge of their sport or activity it is useful to further break each of Shulman's (1986) sub-sets of content knowledge into three further categories. The categories identified and described by Metzler (2000) are:

- *declarative knowledge (DK)* – that which a coach can express verbally and/or in a written form;
- *procedural knowledge (PK)* – that which a coach can apply before, during and after the coaching session;
- *conditional knowledge (CK)* – that which informs a coach regarding when and why to make decisions so that they fit a particular moment or context.

According to Metzler (2000) there is a strong relationship between all three types of knowledge, with declarative knowledge being a 'prerequisite' for conditional and procedural knowledge. What this means in a coaching context is that a coach must have a basic knowledge of the sport or activity before she or he can attempt to run a practice session. Once the coach can operationalize the knowledge in one setting or with one group, conditional knowledge enables the coach to adapt the practice sessions to other settings and with other groups, and to '"know why" before acting to "make it happen"' (Metzler 2000: 22).

To some, this discussion of sub-sets, and categories of sub-sets may sound excessive. But when the categories and sub-sets are applied to a coaching situation it highlights the various forms of content knowledge that coaches need to be aware of if they are going to coach in a way that provides athletes with maximum opportunities to learn. The following framework utilizes the sub-sets of Shulman's (1986) content knowledge and Metzler's (2000) associated categories to highlight the wide range of content knowledge a coach needs to have if he or she is to become a quality coach. The framework is deliberately designed around a generic, rather than a sport-specific, coach so it can be applied to a diverse range of sports and activities.

SMCK:
DK – Knowledge of relevant information e.g. knowledge of rules, biomechanics and psychology;
PK – Being able to model and adjudicate the rules of the game in the coaching session;
CK – Knowing what tactics to employ against what opposition.

PCK:
DK – Knowledge of the different coaching methods a coach can adopt;
PK – Being able to apply various coaching methods in the coaching session;
CK – Changing the coaching methods to suit the learning preferences of the athletes.

CCK:
DK – Knowledge of what coaching resources are available;
PK – Being able to incorporate the ideas and activities into the coaching session;
CK – Using words to explain the drills that suit the context and the type of athletes.

ADDITIONAL THINGS TO CONSIDER WHEN THINKING ABOUT CONTENT KNOWLEDGE

Subject-matter content knowledge can be somewhat limiting if it only focuses on the knowledge of the activity being coached rather than on the principles informing the knowledge. Generally, the SMCK of a soccer coach has been considered to be the skills, tactics and strategies that can be found in a soccer coaching manual. However, if the SMCK of a soccer coach is also to be considered to be based on principles, such as creating space on attack, then the coach has licence to draw on many of the skills, tactics and strategies that can be found in other invasion games such as hockey and basketball. To assist teachers and coaches work with generic principles some scholars have classified games (read sports) into four forms: invasion (e.g. basketball, football and hockey); net/wall (e.g. tennis, volleyball, squash); striking/fielding (e.g. cricket, baseball); and target (e.g. golf, croquet, snooker) (Bunker and Thorpe 1982; Thorpe 1997). By knowing about, and utilizing the games classification system, a coach can make coaching sessions more varied and interesting by selecting activities from different sports within the same category to explore and develop common movement principles. Further, the coach can utilize activities (within the same category) that are not specific to the sport he or she is coaching to develop tactics rather than only focusing on sport-specific techniques (Werner *et al.* 1996). Examples already exist on how a focus on generic invasion game tactics, relating to scoring and preventing scoring, can improve soccer playing performance (see Mitchell 1996), and how a focus on generic net/wall game tactics, such as setting up to attack, can improve volleyball playing performance (see Griffin 1996). Further, it has been documented how Wayne Smith (assistant All Black rugby union coach) uses these principles at the elite level (Kidman 2001)

It is useful for coaches to remember that the subject-matter content of any activity or sport is not written in stone. As such, we believe that coaches can question 'why the subject matter is so, on whose authority it is so and under what conditions could this change . . . [and] why one topic is privileged over another' (Rossi and Cassidy 1999: 193). These questions become important ones to ask because knowledge about our world is increasing exponentially. New so-called experts are being created which makes it difficult to 'know *who* and *what* to believe' and what knowledge, if any, can be considered 'permanent' (Tinning 2002: 384). One consequence of this rapid increase in knowledge is that social practices, such as coaching, are constantly being assessed and revised in light of new information. Yet, it is worth noting that the very process of examining the practices in turn alters the practices (Giddens 1990).

Consistent with the above discussion, we do not consider Shulman's (1986) conceptualization of content knowledge to be immune to examination and reformation in light of the new information. For example, Cochran *et al.* (1993) refer to PCK as content *knowing* to emphasize the dynamism associated with coming to know. Additionally, Geddis and Wood (1997) contend that the transformation of subject-matter content knowledge into pedagogical content knowledge requires recognition of the learner, the context, the place and time. Similarly, Rossi and Cassidy (1999) consider that a weakness in Shulman's (1986) conceptualization of pedagogical content knowledge is that it supports a compartmentalized view of the pedagogical act by focusing on teaching at the expense of the learner. An alternative to compartmentalizing the pedagogical act is to draw on the work of Lusted (1986) who views pedagogy as a process rather than an act thereby recognizing that a dynamic relationship exists between the teacher (read coach), the learner (read athlete) and content. As mentioned in the introductory chapter, this book is organized around Lusted's notion of the pedagogical process.

COACHING CONTENT

Defining the curriculum is not as straightforward as Shulman's (1986) categories may suggest. The reality is that over the decades intense debate has surrounded the term (Marsh 1997). Curriculum has been defined as 'that which is taught in school', 'a set of subjects', 'content', 'set of materials', or 'a set of performance objectives' to name a few (Marsh 1997: 3). Despite there having been debate about the meaning of curriculum in the educational literature, in the coaching context there has been little evidence of such a debate. In the following section we refer to curriculum as a set of materials. In the coaching context, sets of materials are often published by national sporting organizations (see, for example, Fortanasce *et al.* 2001; Jobson 1998; Readhead 1997). These are distributed to, or purchased by, coaches in an attempt to increase their knowledge and indirectly improve the skills and knowledge of the athletes. This material can be thought of as the overt, formal or official curriculum. However, as a number of researchers have pointed out (see Dodds 1985; Kirk 1992; Marsh 1997) students, and we would also argue athletes, gain knowledge, values and skills not only from the formal, overt or official curriculum but also from the informal, covert or hidden curriculum.

One of the early physical education researchers to question the curriculum was Dodds (1985) who argued for the curriculum to be viewed on four levels; overt, covert, null, and hidden. In this section we do not focus on the overt curriculum which Dodds (1985: 93) described as 'those publicly stated and shared items that teachers want students to acquire'. Instead we focus on the other three forms of curriculum because in our opinion, Shulman's (1986) framework does not adequately consider these. The covert curriculum can be considered to be those learnings that a coach has not formally stated in any coaching plans but would be intentionally communicated to the athletes when implementing the formal plan. For example, a coach could consciously and intentionally communicate to the athletes the value of perseverance and obeying the referee. The null curriculum represents those ideas, concepts and values that are knowingly excluded from the formal coaching plan. For example, a junior level athletics coach may choose not to coach javelin because he or she considers it to be too dangerous for junior athletes (Tinning *et al.* 1993). The hidden curriculum can be thought of as the learnings of 'attitudes, norms, beliefs, values and assumptions often expressed as rules, rituals and regulations. They are rarely questioned and are just taken for granted' (Marsh 1997: 35). Whether or not the hidden learnings are judged to be negative or positive depends on the perspective of the individual concerned. This is illustrated in the practices of a basketball coach, who largely focuses on rebounds and shooting from close under the ring. The smaller athletes on the team may learn from the hidden curriculum that they are not very good shooters or rebounders. Yet, the taller athletes on the team may learn that they are good basketball players because not only can they successfully shoot and rebound the ball but they receive positive feedback from the coach and their peers which in turn increases their social status within the team.

Not only are hidden messages portrayed in what the coach chooses to do and say, but they are also communicated by the tone of the coach's voice or by non-verbal communications such as gestures (for further discussion see Chapter 3 on feed-back). Moreover, the routines, dress, body shape, the coaching methods adopted and the expectations coaches have of the athletes also carry hidden messages. While we recognize that there will always be some hidden messages, by reflecting on the possible covert, null, and hidden curricula coaches can gain some insight into the way a whole range of practices can cause athletes to have pleasant and unpleasant experiences of the coaching process. What is more, by reflecting on the various forms of curricula it may be possible for coaches to develop practices that increase athletes' opportunities to learn. Some coaches may consider the individual incidents that make up the hidden curriculum to be trite or insignificant, since having one or two negative experiences never damaged anyone for life. We agree that one or two negative experiences do not damage people for life. Yet, we agree with Tinning *et al.* (1993: 108) that there is a powerful cumulative effect of the learnings associated with the hidden curriculum and these can be compared to 'the silt in a river bed which eventually hardens to form mudstone'.

(RE)THINKING COACHES' KNOWLEDGE

Viewing content knowledge of coaches as stable is driven by the modernist desire for certainty and for getting things 'right' (Cassidy and Tinning 2004). In reviewing Daryl Siedentop's engagement with content knowledge in a physical education context, Tinning (2002) highlights the way contemporary knowledge has changed, and goes on to point out that some social analysts even claim that there is no permanent knowledge. What this means for the coaching community is that maybe it is time for coaches and deliverers of coach education to become more sceptical, and modest, in what they claim they can do, and recognize that coaching knowledge is not static. What may also be required is a willingness by coaches to experiment, continually adapt coaching practices and recognize that the coaching process can not be controlled completely.

While the above may be good in theory, it is not helpful to view the content knowledge of a coach as separate from his or her identities (for further discussion of identities see Chapter 9). Much of the knowledge that enables coaches to 'go on' in their coaching life is practical in character, and it is this knowledge that enables them to simply 'do' things while concentrating on other activities that require conscious effort. Associated with this practical knowledge is the way actions of coaches conform to social conventions, as well as being influenced by their own personality and characteristics (Rossi and Cassidy 1999). For example, when a coach begins to coach, he or she may choose to teach skills and drills with which they are very familiar, wear the 'right' gear and adopt an authoritarian approach. These practices are part of the routines and regimes associated with being a coach and are some of the ways anxieties associated with coaching can be reduced. But as mentioned above, there are hidden meanings associated with these practices which need to be acknowledged if the coach is going to progress to become a quality coach.

CONCLUDING THOUGHTS

As we have illustrated in this chapter, a coach's content knowledge is multifaceted. Recognition of this enables a coach to move towards developing a comprehensive knowledge of the practice of coaching. While Shulman's (1986) and Metzler's (2000) frameworks are useful to assist us to understand the complexity of content knowledge it is imperative that our exploration does not end here. Rather we urge coaches to take cognizance of the work that has been conducted in areas such as education and physical education. There is plenty of scope for sports coaches and coaching researchers alike to consider a range of issues associated with content knowledge. For example, over ten years ago, Kirk (1992) argued in the physical education teacher education context, that the term hidden curriculum had become *passé*. While this may be the case in physical education, this does not appear to be so in the sports coaching context. As such we believe it is a term that is still worthy of exploration because, as Kirk (1992) rightly points out, it is concept that is ignored at one's peril. One alternative way of considering the idea of the hidden curriculum is to utilize the notions of discourse and ideology since these concepts create an opportunity to link learning with wider socio-cultural practices in society (Kirk 1992). (For further discussion of the discourses in sports coaching see our Chapter 13.)

CHAPTER 11

▼ **ASSESSING ATHLETES' UNDERSTANDING**

- Introduction   130
- The purposes of assessment (*Why?*)   132
- Forms of assessment (*When?*)   132
- Meaningful and authentic forms of assessment (*How?*)   134
- Concluding thoughts   138

INTRODUCTION

Assessment has not been a 'hot topic' amongst coaches nor has it had mass appeal amongst the coaching science research community. According to the annotated bibliography compiled by Gilbert (2002), only 4 per cent of articles in the coaching science literature have focused on assessment. When a review of the assessment articles was undertaken it was clear that the focus of many of them was on the coach's behaviour, with researchers using quantitative assessment tools to assess the behaviour (see for example Côté *et al*. 1999; Cunningham *et al*. 2001). However, since the late 1990s some researchers have begun to use mixed methods, utilizing interviews as well as systematic observation systems or questionnaires to understand the assessment process in coaching (see DeMarco *et al*. 1997; Gilbert *et al*. 1999). On the odd occasion when athletes have been the focus of the research, they have been asked to complete an athlete satisfaction questionnaire (see Riemer and Chelladurai 1998). A consequence of this research agenda is that the focus is once again on the coaches' behaviour. Interestingly, Gilbert (2002) grouped the articles that focused on the evaluation of coach education programmes (see for example Gilbert and Trudel 1999; MacLean and Zakrajsek 1996) under the assessment coaching theme. But as we will discuss below, the terms assessment and evaluation are not synonymous, nor is evaluation a sub-set of assessment.

A possible limitation of Gilbert's (2002) annotated bibliography is the lack of recognition of evaluation as a separate or overarching coaching theme. When we conducted an independent review of the coaching science literature on *evaluation* and *sport coaching* forty-five articles were identified. This number is nearly twice the number of articles that Gilbert identified under the theme of assessment. However, in Gilbert's defence he did limit his search to academic review journals, and a noticeable feature about the evaluation articles was that many were published in professional magazines/journals, and were relatively short in length, and as such did not go into details regarding the research that informed the findings. Evaluation can be considered to be loosely comprised of four elements: programme evaluation; curriculum evaluation; evaluation of the opportunities created for learning; and student assessment (Kemmis and Stake 1988). In this chapter we specifically focus on assessment, particularly athlete assessment. In some educational literature, assessment has been described in terms of judging and measuring the quality of a learner's performance, in particular measuring learning as 'an outcome of performance' (Kemmis and Stake 1988: 21). Moreover, it has been argued that the 'goal of assessment' is to put 'a value on the achievement of students' (1988: 21). But as we will point out below, there are multiple purposes for assessing the learner. Due to the paucity of attention given to understanding assessment in the coaching science literature we hypothesize that coaches will only have a limited understanding of the issues surrounding assessment. Therefore the purpose of this chapter is to introduce, into the sports coaching context a discussion regarding some fundamental issues such as the purpose of assessment and forms of assessment, and to make some suggestions for making assessment meaningful and authentic.

As highlighted above, there appears to be limited coaching science literature that focuses explicitly on assessing what athletes learn. We find it surprising that there is such a gap, because arguably many athletes, parents of athletes and administrators would expect that one of the roles of the coach would be to maximize learning opportunities for the athletes. One consequence of there being limited discussion on the assessment of athletes' learning in the coaching science literature is that there are few resources available to coaches to assist them to understand how to assess what an athlete is learning. Utilizing various assessment practices is a way a coach can maximize athlete learning as well as demonstrate accountability. If coaches are going to maximize the learning opportunities of their athletes then they need to be aware of what they are trying to achieve as a coach. This needs to be more specific than 'I want the athletes to win'. A coach needs to be able to specifically identify intended learning outcomes for the athletes and work towards achieving them. According to the New Zealand Ministry of Education (1999: 55) a learning outcome is the 'expected learning that occurs as a result of a particular learning activity'. Once a coach has decided upon the learning outcomes for the season, and the specific sessions, a decision has to be made regarding *what* is going to be assessed, *how* it is going to be assessed and *when* it will be assessed. In this chapter we do not discuss *what* is to be assessed since that is sport-specific. Rather the discussion is structured around *why* something is to be assessed, *when* assessment is to occur, and finally *how* assessment practices can be authentic and meaningful to the athletes and coach.

THE PURPOSES OF ASSESSMENT (*WHY?*)

As mentioned above, assessment is often thought of in terms of assessing a learner's performance, or putting a value on an achievement (Kemmis and Stake 1988). Yet as Tinning *et al*. (2001) point out, there are other purposes of assessment which include: diagnosis; providing feedback; motivation; certification; selecting and screening; and accountability. Not only are there multiple purposes of assessment, we contend that assessment is not a neutral exercise. Broadly speaking assessment serves educational, as well as social and political purposes (Tinning *et al*. 2001). In a coaching context, 'educational ends' are advanced a number of ways. Assessment can be used to assist coaches and athletes ascertain the latter's progress to see if learning is occurring. It can further be used to diagnose the usefulness of the programme and make changes where necessary to maximize an athlete's learning. What is more, assessment provides the opportunity to provide feedback to the learner with the intention of improving performance. Finally, assessment can be used to hold learners accountable (Tinning *et al*. 2001). In a coaching context, the 'social ends' of assessment are achieved when it is used to reveal those athletes who need more attention in order to achieve the learning outcomes. Viewed this way, assessment can also be used to motivate and reward athletes (Tinning *et al*. 2001). When assessment is used for 'political ends' it is used to sift, rank or sort athletes in what is often a competitive environment. The results of assessment can be used in team selection, thereby affording opportunities to some athletes at the expense of others. Furthermore, in a coach education context, assessment can be used to certify some coaches and not others (Tinning *et al*. 2001).

FORMS OF ASSESSMENT (*WHEN?*)

The various forms of assessment can be viewed on a spectrum from formal, more structured forms at one end, to informal, less structured and more integrated forms at the other (Siedentop and Tannehill 2000). The following quote illustrates a formal form of assessment in a volleyball context:

> We frequently see the set in volleyball assessed by the number of times a student [read athlete] can set the ball against the wall above a 6-foot line. Although this may demonstrate how many times the student can set the ball in this fashion, it certainly does not indicate how well the student will perform receiving a pass from a teammate and setting it to the hitter in a game of volleyball.
>
> (Siedentop and Tannehill 2000: 180–181)

In contrast, an informal form of assessment in volleyball can occur when a non-player records statistics on the sets (successful and unsuccessful) the athletes attempt during a game (Siedentop and Tannehill 2000). These statistics provide coaches and athletes with information regarding what the athletes are able to do in a game situation (Siedentop and Tannehill 2000). In conjunction with formal and informal forms of assessment there are summative and formative forms of assessment. Formative assessment provides information to feed into the instructional process, while summative assessment supplies a final judgement on what has been learned (Seidentop and Tannehill,2000). The former provides evidence that learning is occurring while the latter determines whether or not learning has occurred.

Those who have had an orthodox Western-type school experience will have had plenty of experience of summative assessment practices (e.g. school exams) and may also recognize the flaws in this form of assessment. For example, how many times was it possible to recall information asked for in an examination but impossible to recall the same information the next day? Or how many times was it impossible to recall information when a question was asked out of context but once the context was given the information was able to be recalled? Summative assessment practices generally occur in controlled settings and when a sequence of instruction has been completed. Moreover, they are often standardized, contrived, and able to be measured although not generalizable. Finally, they are often used to make a judgement on what has been learned for comparative or grading purposes (Seidentop and Tannehill 2000; Tinning *et al*. 2001).

An example of a summative assessment practice in a coaching context is the testing of the fundamental motor skills of junior athletes. This can occur at the start of a playing season, which can also be thought of as the end of the previous season, since the pre-season selection process is making a judgement on previous learning for grading purposes. It is possible that in a pre-season selection process coaching staff assess the athletes by comparing their motor skills against a check list that compartmentalizes the skill in an attempt to judge what part of the skill can, or can not be performed (for an example of a check list see Seidentop and Tannehill 2000). Another example is when athletes are required to perform the Beep Test or Coopers 12-minute run in the process of having their cardio-vascular fitness assessed. At the end of the testing they are awarded a number or a level. A limitation of these testing regimes is that the athlete may be required to undergo these tests in front of an audience of significant others such as their peers, family members and coaching staff who can put undue pressure on the athlete to perform. What is more, data gathered in this type of situation does not reflect a holistic or applied understanding of knowledge, rather it is a one-off snap shot of a particular type of knowledge.

Despite summative assessment practices still dominating (in the psyche at least) there are other forms of assessment that can be adopted to assess whether learning is occurring. These are known as formative forms of assessments. Formative assessment practices generally provide learners with feedback on their progress rather than judging them correct or incorrect. They are also often viewed as one step in the learning process and used to motivate the learners to want to achieve (Siedentop and Tannehill 2000).

One way formative assessment practice can be used in a coaching context is by collecting game statistics on an athlete throughout the season. For example, at the start of the season a basketball coach and athletes may set the following learning outcome: *The athlete will be able to extend her physical competence by successfully completing twenty defensive rebounds in a competitive game situation.* Over the course of the season the coach co-opts a non-player to collect statistics on the number of defensive rebounds the athlete successfully completes each game. After each game the athlete can view the statistics and is able to monitor her progress against the learning outcome. If the learning outcome is realistic, the process of being able to track her progress can motivate the athlete to want to achieve. Equally, the coach is able to monitor the progress of the athlete and is able to modify, if necessary, his or her coaching practices to support the athlete achieve the learning outcome.

In adapting Siedentop and Tannehill's (2000) aims of formative assessment to the sports coaching context, we contend that the first aim is to provide feedback to coaches and athletes so that learning, and learning difficulties, can be monitored and identified respectively. The second aim is to inform the review of the coaching practice, while the third aim enables athletes to maintain a record of their performance, assess their own performance and to identify weaknesses in their play.

MEANINGFUL AND AUTHENTIC FORMS OF ASSESSMENT (*HOW?*)

In the educational context, there has been a move to emphasize meaningful and authentic learning outcomes and assessment incidents that reflect real-life situations. Authentic assessment tasks involve learners solving realistic problems by applying new information to prior knowledge and skills (Siedentop and Tannehill 2000). What is more, authentic assessment is ongoing, focused on a range of learning outcomes, can be viewed as a learning tool, and is conducted informally and formally. Some examples of authentic assessment include a golfer handing in a score card to illustrate her or his competence on the golf course. Or a 5000m runner using a heart-rate monitor to record the amount of time spent within the training heart-rate zone on a run (Siedentop and Tannehill 2000).

When considering how to design authentic and meaningful assessment it is important for a coach to incorporate what he or she, and the athletes, want to achieve and then design the practices around achieving the stated outcomes. This is different from what often happens, namely that the coach will think about what activities he or she knows and have the athletes perform these. However, getting coaches to decide upon what learning outcomes they will focus on for the season requires them to change the questions they initially ask themselves. The questions need to be shifted away from:

- How long is the season?
- How many training sessions are there?
- What will I put in the programme?

towards:

- What are the important outcomes? (Remembering that the learning outcomes have to be meaningful and authentic otherwise why will the athletes bother trying to attain them?)
- What must the athletes be able to demonstrate to show that they understand the content?
- What opportunities do the athletes have to demonstrate their skill and knowledge in a way that is unique to them?

(Siedentop and Tannehill 2000)

Designing assessment that is authentic and meaningful is consistent with a constructivist view of learning. This view 'assumes that for learning to occur learners need to actively engage with their environment' (Kirk and MacPhail 2000) (see our Chapter 6 for a discussion on a constructivist orientation on learning). As such, it is useful for coaches to incorporate a range of tasks that cover a variety of learning styles, brief the learners as to the tasks being assessed, and provide them with clear criteria and relevant feedback (Tinning *et al.* 2001). Also, both coach and athletes need to be clear about *what* is being assessed, *how* it will be assessed, *when* it will be assessed, *who* is being assessed and *why* the assessment is occurring (Tinning *et al.* 2001).

One assessment strategy that specifically provides an authentic picture of athletes' skill and tactical abilities in a team-game situation and satisfies many of the above suggestions is the Game Performance Assessment Instrument (GPAI) (Griffin *et al.* 1997; Oslin *et al.* 1998). The GPAI is a generic template that was designed to enable observable behaviour to be coded in a game situation. The designers of the GPAI claim that an athlete could demonstrate seven components of a game performance. These include:

- *Base*: ability to return to a recovery position between attempting skills;
- *Adjust*: ability to move offensively or defensively, as necessitated by the flow of the game;
- *Decision making*: ability to make legitimate decisions about what to do with the ball, or similar, during a game;
- *Skill execution*: proficient performance of specific skills;
- *Support*: off-the-ball movement to a space thereby making it possible to receive a pass from a team mate who has possession;
- *Cover*: ability to provide defensive help for a team mate attempting to use the ball, or similar, or moving towards the ball;
- *Guard or mark*: ability to defend an opponent who may, or may not, have the ball.

(Griffin *et al.* 1997)

In addition, each component has three aspects of performance: 'decisions made (appropriate or inappropriate), skill execution (efficient or inefficient), and support (appropriate or inappropriate)' (Metzler 2000: 363).

Once a coach has made the decision to use the GPAI she or he has to choose which of the above seven components to focus on, as well as deciding on specific criteria within each component. Using an example from field hockey we illustrate how a coach can assess athletes' tactical and skill ability by assessing skill execution, decision making and support in relation to maintaining possession.

Maintaining possession	Criteria
Decision making:	Athlete attempts to pass to an unmarked team mate;
Skill execution:	Reception: control of pass; Passing: ball reaches target;
Support:	The athlete attempts to support the ball carrier by being in, or moving into an area where he or she could successfully receive a pass.

Once the assessment components and criteria have been identified the coach can then design a template to support the collection of the data as it occurs in the game (for example see Table 11.1).

It is possible to analyse an individual athlete's overall game involvement as well as performance in relation to specific criteria using the following formulas:

Game involvement = number of appropriate decisions + number of inappropriate decisions + number of efficient skill executions + number of inefficient skill executions + number of appropriate supporting movements.

Decision-making index (DMI) = number of appropriate decisions divided by number of inappropriate decisions.

Skill-execution index (SEI) = number of efficient skill executions divided by number of inefficient skill executions.

Table 11.1 An example of a GPAI template

	Decision making		Skill execution		Support	
Name	A	IA	E	IE	A	IA
Tui	✓✓✓✓✓	✓	✓✓✓✓	✓	✓✓✓	✓✓
Bea	✓✓	✓✓✓✓	✓✓	✓✓	✓✓✓	✓
Max	✓✓	✓	✓✓✓	✓	✓✓	
Carl	✓✓✓✓	✓✓✓	✓✓	✓✓✓✓	✓✓✓✓✓	✓
Jon	✓✓		✓✓		✓✓✓✓	✓✓

Key: *A* = Appropriate, *IA* = Inappropriate, *E* = Efficient, *IE* = Inefficient.

Support index (SI) = number of appropriate supporting movements divided by number of inappropriate supporting movements.

Game Performance = [DMI + SEI + SI] divided by 3 (Number of indexes).

To demonstrate what these formulas look like in practice we have used Tui's GPAI data documented in Table 11.1:

Game involvement = 5 + 1 + 4 + 1 + 3 = 14
Decision making = 5 / 1 = 5
Skill execution = 4 / 1 = 4
Support = 3 / 2 = 1.5
Game performance = (5 + 4 + 1.5) / 3 = 3.5

The final game performance score represents a ratio between appropriate and inappropriate as well as efficient and inefficient instances. An athlete obtains a higher GPAI score when he or she demonstrates more positive than negative instances. According to Metzler (2000) the GPAI scoring system encourages athletes to make clever tactical decisions rather than simply encouraging a high number of plays.

Another way to assess tactical decision making and skill execution as well as an athlete's 'ownership' of their learning is for a coach to incorporate some form of self-assessment. This is where the athletes have the opportunity to critically analyse aspects of their own performance in relation to their own goals, their coach's goals or peer performance standards. Some examples of self-assessment tasks are keeping a portfolio or a journal. A portfolio is a collection of material that documents an athlete's effort, progress and achievement toward a goal or goals. Items suitable for inclusion in the portfolio include: video recordings of games, newspaper cuttings that mention the athlete or team, certificates of achievement; 'Most Valuable Player' awards; data sets that compare skill execution before and after a coaching session; and peer assessment by athletes who work alongside the player in the team, for example, half back (scrum half) and first five eight (fly half) in rugby union and goalie and fullback in hockey and soccer. A portfolio is in itself not an assessment strategy until the following requirements have been considered and negotiated:

- An assessment purpose is determined;
- How and what to select for inclusion are defined;
- Decisions on who may select portfolio materials and when they may be selected are articulated;
- Criteria for assessing portfolio are identified.

(Herman *et al.* in Siedentop and Tannehill 2000: 191)

Journals also allow athletes to reflect upon and share their thoughts, feelings and impressions about their performance and/or event. A journal serves as a means of an athlete describing a situation, how they reacted to that situation, having the opportunity to reflect upon their actions, and using those reflections to learn. While many coaches may think that journals would be no use in a coaching context, it is important to remember that the assessment strategies are linked to the learning outcomes. Journals may be appropriate if a goal is to increase the athletes' ability to think tactically. A coach may pose some key questions and then request that the athletes write in their journals what they did and why.

CONCLUDING THOUGHTS

While assessment may not be a 'hot topic' amongst coaches or the coaching science research community it is nonetheless an extremely important topic in the coaching process since assessment is a tool to measure whether or not learning has occurred. Given that many, if not all, coaches wish to improve the performance of their athletes, and that a common response from athletes when asked why they play sport is to 'learn more skills', it seems surprising that assessment is not a 'hot topic' of conversation and analysis. By neglecting to consider the complexities associated with assessment, coaches are unable to gain an accurate picture of what the athletes are learning. Not only that, but they also limit their ability to diagnose, motivate, select athletes and demonstrate their accountability to governing boards, sponsors, and athletes. When considering what form of assessment, and what assessment tasks to adopt, it would be useful for coaches to keep in mind the purpose of assessment.

CHAPTER 12

▼ COACHING ATHLETES WITH A DISABILITY: EXPLORING ISSUES OF CONTENT

■ Introduction   139
■ Viewing athletes with a disability   140
■ Integrating athletes with and without a disability   142
■ Concluding thoughts   145

INTRODUCTION

According to DePauw and Gavron (1995), athletes with physical, mental and emotional disabilities have historically been subject to disenfranchisement and exclusion in sport. This state of affairs is hardly surprising given that Western societies have traditionally portrayed individuals with disabilities in terms of their 'deficits' and as 'victims' in need of support, and protection from their able-bodied counterparts (Ballard 1993; DePauw 2000). In the context of sport, Nixon (1984: 184) argues that such discourses have resulted in many people, such as coaches, finding it particularly difficult to associate individuals with disabilities with 'vigorous activity or demanding roles'.

DePauw and Gavron (1995: 3) believe that athletes with disabilities are 'beginning to receive the recognition they deserve and, more importantly, acceptance as athletes'. They attribute this to increasing public awareness and the performances of elite athletes with disabilities. With regard to the former, DePauw (2000) highlights how the disability rights movement, and the emerging field of disability studies, has challenged the popular belief that disability is 'pitiful' and 'tragic'. In this respect, coaches and administrators in both performance and participation sports have been encouraged to focus on the abilities of athletes with disabilities rather than focusing on the frailty of the athletes. Furthermore, DePauw and Gavron (1995) contend that the performances of elite athletes with disabilities leave no question marks regarding their sporting ability. They note that there are only seconds, or tenths of seconds difference between athletes with and without disabilities in sports such as swimming and downhill skiing. In addition, they highlight how athletes with disability bench press up to 600 pounds (272 kilograms) in competition, while athletes with single leg amputations have jumped 6 feet, 8 inches (2.03 metres). However, it is important to note that the celebration of the sporting performances of athletes with a disability, which often includes the portrayal of their achievements as 'heroic', can also contribute to reinforcing the minority status of this diverse group of athletes (Nixon 1984; Thompson 1998).

The purpose of this chapter is twofold. Initially, the emphasis will be placed on providing an overview of the dominant societal discourses related to athletes with disabilities. In particular, this section will examine the medical and social models of disability and explore how they may influence coaches and coaching practice in the context of disability sport. The second section will focus on the issue of integration. Specifically, using Nixon's (1984) work as a framework for discussion, this section will explore some of the issues that coaches may want to consider when choosing to combine athletes with a disability with their able-bodied counterparts. As highlighted in the earlier chapters of this book, the purpose here is not to provide micro-level prescriptions of what coaches should do, but instead is to encourage reflection and critical analysis on behalf of the reader.

VIEWING ATHLETES WITH A DISABILITY

Western society has, according to Thompson (1998), traditionally focused on the medical aspects of disability and the limitations that arise for the individual as a result of his or her impairment. In drawing upon the work of Barnes (1990), Linton (1998) and Oliver (1990), DePauw (2000) argues that the medical model has portrayed disability to be a physiological or psychological condition and to be a problem of the individual. Indeed, in synthesizing the work of Fine and Asch (1988) and Wheeler (1998), DePauw (2000) further suggests that there are a number of prevalent assumptions surrounding the medical model of disability, which include:

■ Disability is located in biology, it is a given;
■ Disability is a medical issue, not a social issue;
■ Having a disability means needing help and support;
■ When a person with a disability has a problem, the assumed cause of the problem is the impairment;
■ The person with a disability is a victim.

(DePauw 2000: 365)

Thompson (1998) contends that the dominance of the medical view is so strong that it is often uncritically accepted as the best way of conceptualizing disability. Indeed, Oliver (1990: 7–8) notes that 'these ideologies are so deeply rooted in social consciousness that they become "facts"; they are naturalised. Thus everyone knows that disability is a personal tragedy for individuals so "afflicted"; hence ideology becomes common sense'. The consequence of this particular discourse on disability is that 'it casts human variation as deviance from the norm, as pathological condition, as deficit' (Linton 1998: 11). Thompson (1998) contends that there are a number of social outcomes that derive from the application of such a viewpoint on disability. He argues that individuals with disabilities are often regarded as 'invalid', or not valid, and as a consequence these individuals lose some degree of power or status. As such, it is perhaps not surprising that people with disabilities have been largely relegated to peripheral positions and excluded from valued positions in mainstream society (Nixon 1984; Thompson 1998). Nixon (1984) argues that such a state of affairs may be attributed to the misplaced sympathy and over-protectiveness of the able-bodied majority, who are reluctant to provide persons with disabilities with access to risky, demanding, and valued roles. However, he also suggests that expressions of sympathy and public concern 'may be a convenient excuse for the reluctance of those in power to meet the demands of the disabled minority for fuller participation in society and greater access to its rewards' (Nixon 1984: 185). He goes on to say that the situation could also 'mask a more fundamental unwillingness among those in power to share some of their resources with their less privileged and less powerful disabled counterparts' (Nixon 1984: 185).

In the context of sports coaching, we consider the uncritical adoption of such a perspective on disability to be problematic. One of the consequences of unquestioningly accepting the medical model is that some coaches may consider the content of sport and physical activity to be unsuitable for athletes with disability due to their frailness (Miller 1994). In addition, coaches working with athletes with a disability may place a greater emphasis on what these athletes cannot do, as opposed to what they can do. In this respect, coaches may develop particularly low expectations in terms of the content to be delivered and the performances that athletes with disabilities are capable of achieving. In a similar vein, the acceptance of the medical model view of disability may lead coaches to view athletes with disabilities as victims to be pitied or, alternatively, as brave heroes. According to Thompson (1998: 92), such practices may be regarded 'as a form of infantilization, a patronising approach that overemphasises the amount of personal care needed and underemphasises the importance of rights and empowerment'. Consequently, in drawing upon the work of Thompson (1998), we invite coaches to recognize that their social response to an athlete with a disability may be as much 'disabling', if not more so, than the impairment itself.

Despite the predominance of the medical discourse, DePauw (2000) argues that, in recent years, there has been a trend towards the progressive inclusion and acceptance of individuals with a disability in the wider society. This trend has been mirrored in the context of sport, where DePauw and Gavron (1995: 9) note that 'while there are still some contraindications for full, unrestricted participation, they are decreasing as a result of changing attitudes about the frailty of persons with disabilities and a new acceptance of their abilities'. As indicated in the introduction to this chapter, this advancement may, in part, be attributed to the disability rights movement and the emerging field of disability studies, which 'has challenged professionals to reconceptualize disability in the context of social relationships (e.g. Chappell 1992; Davis 1995; Hanks and Poplin 1981; Linton 1998) and social theory (e.g. Oliver 1990)' (DePauw 2000: 360). In this respect, DePauw (2000) outlines how the reconceptualization of disability has resulted in people with disability being viewed in a variety of ways. For example, she highlights how the interdependence paradigm is concerned with promoting social change through the analysis of micro and macro systems.

Of particular relevance to sports coaching is the social minority model proposed by Sherrill (1993). Rather than focusing on biological and psychological deficit and anomaly, this perspective encourages coaches to view athletes with a disability to be simply different, rather than less than, or inferior to, their able-bodied counterparts (DePauw, 2000). Furthermore, this particular model of disability promotes the use of positive terminology, which tends to be person-first orientated, and discusses individual strengths and weaknesses rather than defects, problems, or characteristics in a quest to empower athletes with a disability (DePauw, 2000). Moreover, and perhaps more significantly, this model encourages practitioners to recognize that disabilities are socially constructed, and as such they may wish to consider how they could alter, adapt and change the social and physical environment in which they work so that individuals with disabilities are able to exercise their capabilities in full (Ballard 1993). Such critical thinking may result in coaches choosing to combine athletes with and without disabilities in their coaching sessions. It is this issue that will be explored in the following section.

INTEGRATING ATHLETES WITH AND WITHOUT A DISABILITY

For coaches who choose to work with athletes with a disability or who work in educational settings, where the integration of athletes with and without a disability may be a legal requirement, a critical understanding of integrative practice could prove to be valuable to their professional practice. In recent years, there has been a worldwide trend toward the integration of athletes with disabilities into situations where they participate with athletes without disabilities (see DePauw and Doll-Tepper 2000; Downs 1995; Hutzler *et al.* 2002). While sports programmes designed specifically for athletes with a disability still exist (e.g. ParaOlympics), DePauw (2000) argues that inclusive and integrative sports programmes are an important means of promoting healthy and active lifestyles for all individuals. For athletes with a disability, she suggests that the following benefits might accrue:

- Opportunity to develop social skills necessary for interaction with others;
- Opportunity to develop friendships with peers with and without disabilities;
- Opportunities to interact with age-appropriate role models among able-bodied peers;
- Decreased isolation;
- Increased expectations and challenge;
- Attitude changes among peers and consequently acceptance;

- Increased appreciation of difference;
- Greater understanding of disability rights and equity

(DePauw 2000: 363)

In a similar vein, Nixon (1984) suggests that integrated sport provides athletes with a disability a valuable arena for challenging the societal stereotypes, as well as overcoming the social isolation and stigma that is traditionally associated with persons with disability. For athletes without a disability, Goodman (1995) suggests that integrated sports have the potential to provide individuals with the opportunity to not only learn about disabilities but also to better appreciate individual differences.

While there are many benefits associated with integration, it would be unrealistic to assume that it is the best option for all athletes with a disability in all circumstances (Goodman 1995). Indeed, there has been considerable debate in the physical education and coaching literature regarding the nature and extent of appropriate integration. For example, Winnick (2000) outlines a continuum of integrated sports participation, ranging from total inclusion to segregated sport and physical activity, and discusses the appropriateness of each strategy. Perhaps the key point for coaches here is that they need to recognize that successful integration requires more than simply placing athletes with, and without, disability together. Instead, Goodman (1995) suggests that coaches need to be sensitive to contextual and situational variables such as the personal background, motivation, the sporting and social skills of an athlete with a disability, the nature of the sport itself (i.e. team or individual), and the available equipment and facilities.

According to Nixon (1984), successful integration, or 'genuine integration' as he terms it, requires interaction between athletes, with and without a disability, in which the disability stigma and minority status of individuals with a disability has been removed. Here, he contends that genuine integration is unlikely to occur if the sport setting overtaxes or under-utilizes the abilities of either group of athletes. By way of an example, Nixon (1984) suggests that the integration of visually impaired athletes may be more successful in individual sports such as swimming and track and field athletics, where an athlete may use the abilities in which he or she is confident. In addition, he contends that the genuine integration of athletes with a visual impairment could be less successful in team sports such as soccer. In this context, athletes without a disability might experience feelings of frustration or resentment toward those athletes with a disability, while athletes with a disability may come to feel inadequate or frustrated with the situation or themselves. In order to minimize the frequent occurrence of the latter, Nixon (1984) provides a potentially useful framework for coaches to utilize when considering implementing an integrated programme in their particular sporting context. Specifically, this framework considers the personal attributes of the athlete, the level of adaptation required for integration, and the level of competition in which athletes are competing. The remainder of this chapter will focus upon these three components and their implications for coaching practice.

With regard to the personal attributes of the athlete, Nixon (1984) states that it is first necessary for coaches to recognize the abilities of an athlete with a disability. This process also requires the coach to critically interrogate his or her own beliefs so as to avoid inaccurate, or oversimplified, conceptions of athletes with a disability. Another feature that coaches may also wish to consider is the background of an athlete with disability, that is, does he or she have the necessary background (i.e. experience, physical skills, social skills) to participate in the essential aspects and features of the particular sport? In this respect, Nixon (1984) suggests that coaches may wish to consider the degree to which the skills and experiences of the athletes with and without a disability are equivalent. We believe that such considerations are important factors in determining the content to be delivered to athletes in integrated sports settings and, accordingly, the nature of the sporting experience for the athletes.

In addition to considering the personal attributes and background parameters of the athlete, Nixon (1984) also suggests that the level of adaptation required to integrate athletes with and without a disability is an important consideration if genuine integration is to occur. Here, he suggests that when the integration of athletes with a disability is dependent upon extensive adaptations there may be some resentment and frustration on behalf of the athletes without a disability. Moreover, in keeping with the preceding discussion on the need for coaches to critically evaluate their beliefs regarding athletes with a disability, he contends that the degree of adaptation required may be influenced by coaches' attitudes rather than the actual needs of the athletes with a disability. As such, Nixon (1984: 188) notes that while adaptation can enable people with a disability to engage in activities previously denied to them, 'there may be consequences of adaptations in integrated settings that defeat the intentions of organizers [read coaches] wishing to promote integration'.

The final factor that Nixon (1984) contends coaches may wish to consider when deciding whether to integrate athletes with and without a disability is the level of competition in which the athletes are participating. Indeed, he suggests that in sports settings that include athletes with and without disabilities 'the degree of competition' may be a 'significant issue' that is possibly 'difficult to resolve' (Nixon 1984: 184). In the context of team sports, he argues that, rather than promoting positive and friendly interactions and relationships between athletes with and without a disability, highly competitive team sports settings may instead foster the development of tensions with an athlete's own team members, as well as members of opposing teams. For example, he notes that 'in highly competitive settings, losing could increase the stigmatisation and self-denigration' experienced by athletes with a disability (Nixon 1984: 190). However, while potentially negative experiences may be more likely to occur in team sport settings, they may be much less likely to transpire in other sporting contexts, such as individual sports (e.g. swimming, weightlifting). As such, coaches need to critically reflect upon the constraints and opportunities of their particular situation and the needs of all the athletes in their charge before making a decision regarding the nature of an integrative programme and the content to be delivered. In drawing upon the work of DePauw (2000), it would appear that genuine integrative experiences are more likely to occur in sports settings when coaches work towards achieving the following outcomes:

- All athletes are provided with the opportunity to learn and grow;
- Athletes are challenged individually as well as collectively;
- The working climate is affirming and open for all, and is conducive to learning;
- Activities are age-appropriate as well as ability-appropriate.

(DePauw 2000: 365).

CONCLUDING THOUGHTS

In an effort to facilitate positive sporting experiences for athletes with a disability, it would appear that critical reflection on behalf of the coaches is a valuable first step towards achieving this goal. In this respect, and in drawing on the existing physical-education literature, we suggest that coaches may not only choose to interrogate their beliefs regarding the abilities and capacities of athletes with a disability, but also their own professional knowledge base regarding the theory and practice of working with this diverse group of athletes (Lieberman *et al.* 2002; Schempp and Oliver 2000).

With regard to the integration of athletes, with and without a disability, we believe that Nixon's (1984) work provides coaches with a useful framework to critically examine their efforts to provide positive experiences for athletes with and without a disability alike. Indeed, Nixon (1984: 191) believes that the failure of coaches to take into account their own beliefs regarding athletes with a disability, the nature of the sport, the background and skills of the athletes themselves, the level of adaptation required, and the competitive level of the sport setting among other variables 'could damage genuine integration and reinforce the stigmatisation' of athletes with a disability. Perhaps the most important point to arise here is that coaches should, in the quest to provide all athletes with high quality sporting experiences, reflect upon the constraints and opportunities of their particular coaching situation in relation to integrative practice.

▼ END OF SECTION THREE: TASKS

TASK 1

Choose a particular activity with which you are familiar and then for each type of content knowledge (subject-matter content knowledge, pedagogical content knowledge, curriculum content knowledge) identify examples of declarative, procedural and conditional knowledge for that activity (see page 125 for guidance).

TASK 2

Read the following vignette (adapted and abridged from Tinning *et al*. 1993) and answer the questions below.

Georgia is the coach of an under-10 local school soccer team. She always finishes the skills part of the soccer practice with a relay, since the young people in the team appear to enjoy this activity, if the noise they make is anything to go by. Georgia chooses four team captains and asks them each to pick teams for relays. Once the four teams are arranged Georgia explains the rules of the relay race. Each child is required to dribble the soccer ball around the cones to the end, and back through the cones before passing the ball to the next child in the line. When the whistle signals the start of the relay two boys do not dribble around all of the cones. Georgia notices this and sends them back to repeat their run. Most children take the requirements seriously and dribble around the cones. One boy, who had previously got caught cheating, chastised one of the less physically able children in the team for taking too long. Throughout the relay, Georgia urges the children on with statements such as: 'Go as fast as you can', 'Hurry up, she's catching you', etc. The first team to have all its members complete the relay and be sitting down is declared the winner. Georgia completely overlooks the fact that the first team seated has one member less than the other teams. The other teams are at pains to point out this fact but their protests are in vain.

1   What are the overt messages of this relay activity?
2   What are the hidden messages of this relay activity?

TASK 3

Using the Game Performance Assessment Instrument (GPAI) (see example in Chapter 11), assess the performance of an athlete of your choice. You have to decide upon which component of the game performance you will assess, remember to identify all three aspects of performance, and develop the criteria. Once the data has been collected you must analyse the athlete's overall game involvement as well as performance in relation to the specific criteria.

SECTION FOUR
THE COACHING
CONTEXT

13 The discourses of coaching   151

14 Coaching ethics   162

15 Coaching holistically: why do it and how can we frame it?   174

16 Coaching holistically: a way forward for coach education   181

CHAPTER 13

▼ **THE DISCOURSES OF COACHING**

- Introduction   151
- What is discourse?   152
- Why study discourse in the coaching context?   152
- The dominant discourse of 'coaching science': performance,
  rationality and a hierarchical coach–athlete relationship   154
- The effect of power-dominated discourse on athletes   156
- An alternative coaching discourse   159
- Concluding thoughts   160

INTRODUCTION

This chapter explores the discourses of coaching; that is, the language used to describe and explain it. In particular, it examines how that language leads us to think about and perceive the coaching process and those involved in it in certain ways. Discourses are formed by beliefs, ideologies, and power arrangements, and consequently are reflective of those social constructions (Cherryholmes 1988). The study of discourse then is an examination of how influence is achieved in and through talk; that is, of what is said and the way it is said (Faulkener and Finlay 2002). It pays attention to the language-in-use and the power that such language has over perception and behaviour (McGannon and Mauws 2000).

This chapter investigates the representation of knowledge through language, as it relates to coaching. It examines the discourse used both by coach educators and practising coaches, and the influence this has on athletes. It thus explores the 'discourse of expertise' so apparent in sports coaching, which feeds a dominant rationality-based pedagogy. Within this current arrangement, coaches are viewed as knowledge givers and athletes as receivers who need this knowledge to improve their performances. It is a discourse that legitimizes the power-dominated means of preparing largely unquestioning and compliant athletes (Johns and Johns 2000). The chapter looks at how both coaches and athletes are situated within this dominant discourse and how their respective locations 'afford and limit how they speak, feel and behave' (McGannon and Mauws 2000: 148). After a discussion on the nature of discourse and the value of studying it within the coaching context, we examine both the discourse of 'coaching science' and its effect on athletes. Subsequently, a possible alternative coaching discourse is suggested (Johns and Johns 2000), one that is sensitive, considered, and which involves athletes in their development to a much greater degree (Tinning *et al.* 1993).

WHAT IS DISCOURSE?

Traditional perspectives of examining language have been defined as representationalist (McGannon and Mauws 2000), where the words we speak are unproblematically considered to represent that to which they refer. Words are thought to be 'merely labels with which we refer to things in the world' (McGannon and Mauws 2000: 151). However, a differing interpretation of talking, which rejects this assumption as 'simplistic', comes from the discursive perspective. This focuses not on what words might refer to, but on what can be accomplished by using words in the ways we do (Heritage 1984). Hence, where the primary consideration of the representative perspective is with verbal *content*, that of the discursive lies with the *outcome* of speaking. From the discursive perspective then, the task is to understand (i) how talk is produced by, and for, its particular audiences, (ii) the beliefs and motives that create the talk and (iii) the consequences of such talk (Faulkener and Finlay 2002; Wilkinson 2000). In line with the critical stance taken throughout this book, it is this perspective that is adopted within this chapter.

In delving deeper into its nature, we see that the discursive perspective is interested in the complex ways in which speakers construct and understand conversation, with all utterances being treated as 'meaningful social doings' (Wood and Kroger 2000: 12). Language is therefore considered not only as a tool for communication or description, but as a 'social practice . . . a way of doing things' (Wood and Kroger 2000: 12). It is viewed as a 'domain in which our knowledge of the world is actively shaped' (Tonkiss 1998: 246) as it provides the means that allows us to make sense of our own identities and circumstances (McGannon and Mauws 2000). Consequently, any meanings we construct from information given are likely to be greatly affected by the choice of descriptors, metaphors and analogies used by the speaker, as they 'frame' the activity for us. Such 'framing' has been described as having the ability to 'paint pictures in our heads' with all the resultant implications (Sabo and Jensen 1994). Language, thus, should never be viewed as neutral, but rather as a means of communication which is imbedded and riddled with 'overt and covert social biases, stereotypes and inequities' (Messner *et al.* 1993: 110). We might say that discourse does ideological work (Kirk 1992), as it both embodies and rationalizes a value-laden structure, which allows for the promotion and perpetuation of some interests and practices over and above others (Penney 2000). Discourse, then, according to Ball (1990: 17), is essentially about power; it is about 'who can speak where, when and with what authority'. In this way, it endorses certain possibilities for thought while dismissing others. Hence, it becomes not only about what is said and heard but also about what is not, as what is left out in addition to what is included will influence participants' views of 'necessary' knowledge (Penney 2000).

WHY STUDY DISCOURSE IN THE COACHING CONTEXT?

To answer this question we need only acknowledge the socially constructed nature of language. If we acknowledge that discourse is selective in terms of agenda, interests and values, we accept that it both privileges and legitimizes, and excludes and marginalizes. We need to study it therefore, primarily to acknowledge our roles in these processes, thus understanding how our ways of speaking influence our behaviour and the interactions we have with others (McGannon and Mauws 2000). In this respect, knowledge of its power can help us better manage and frame conversations towards preferred ends. The initial task here is to examine our everyday coaching language-in-use. This allows us to deconstruct the signifiers, behaviours and language of coaches in considering the 'logic' of their privileged positions, and why they come to define both themselves and their athletes in particular ways. It is an 'exercise in vigilance' in relation to 'imagined values' (Bromley 1995: 155), thus treating with considerable suspicion the seductive power of dominant discourses in simplifying, stereotyping and dulling individual experiences (McCarthy *et al.* 2003). Once we understand the micro workings of language and how these are linked to the cultural macro effect, we can then recognize our own positions and influence in relation to the discourse we use, so that we can consider prospects and potential for change. An examination of what we say and how we say it is also significant because our interactions are not characterized by infinite possibility, as, 'both what can be said and how it is said are constrained by the characteristics of the discourse within which it occurs' (McGannon and Mauws 2000: 156). We thus need to identify the boundaries of the discourse that we inhabit, as only then can we become aware of different sites within it (McGannon and Mauws 2000). Such awareness helps us to recognize that the current coaching discourse and the 'knowledge' which sustains it are reflective of vested interests, and of the need to treat it as such. In effect, we need to study discourse, so that we can, if desired, 'change our talk' and, because language is reflective of our realities, 'change our practice' (Wood and Kroger 2000).

However, we are very aware that the discourses within which we speak are enabling as well as limiting forces. Consequently we have no intention of 'throwing the baby out with the bathwater'. Discourses are enabling in that they allow us to speak of things in particular ways, thus increasing our 'sense making' capabilities. In essence, they allow us 'to understand, to think and [to] make sense' (Kirk 1992: 48). On the other hand, they are limiting in that, as outlined above, they proscribe other ways of thinking and speaking, hence, restricting these capabilities or 'conditions of possibility' (Foucault 1972). The point in highlighting the workings and influence of language is not to call for an 'objective' neutral substitute within which we can communicate, as such objectivity in a social world is not a credible option. Rather, acknowledging that we will always live within value-laden discourses, our interest here is in exploring the freedom to work creatively within the existing framework. In doing so, we can bring to the fore aspects of the current discourse that have previously remained in the background or at the periphery of our practice (Penney 2000). The value of critically examining coaching discourse then is multiple. First, through employing a deconstructive strategy to confront the current validity of coaching 'expertise', we can challenge conventional understandings of coaching theories and that which they purport to represent. Hence, we can examine and understand the status quo for what it is, and why it is as it is, before reflecting on other ways to possibly improve it. The least we can do here according to Kirk (1992) is to question definitions, purposes and current relevance. Secondly, studying talk allows us to beg the question of what are coaches doing with their words? That is, what is being transmitted and accomplished by their speaking as they do? (McGannon and Mauws 2000). This would enable us to credibly examine the legitimacy of such experts and the knowledges they espouse. Finally, through giving us the ability to uncover what determines actions and thoughts, it also gives us the freedom to explore other discursive coaching options, thus opening the search for ways to 'do it better'. Getting coaches to critically examine their discourse then leads to a better understanding of self and one's behaviour, whilst encouraging them to 'think outside the square' to creatively solve problems. It consequently offers the potential for coaches to be central to, and proactive in, shaping the future of coaching and coach education in particular ways.

THE DOMINANT DISCOURSE OF 'COACHING SCIENCE': PERFORMANCE, RATIONALITY AND A HIERARCHICAL COACH–ATHLETE RELATIONSHIP

According to Johns and Johns (2000) among others, the discourse of modern sport is embedded in a performance pedagogy, which is based on scientific functionalism. Here, the body is viewed as a 'machine', which can be developed and improved through appropriate exercises and training regimes (Prain and Hickey 1995). Similarly, much of the current coaching discourse is also biomedical in nature, which arguably has emanated from coaches and officials whose positions of power depend on its promotion (Johns and Johns 2000; Cherryholmes 1988; Tinning 1991; Schön 1993). It is a discourse that favours technical description and procedure, with value placed on the specialist 'factual' knowledge of coaches to provide direction and sequence (Prain and Hickey 1995). It is also a discourse which views the athlete's body as a 'biological object to be studied, manipulated and its movements minutely measured' (Wright 2000: 35). For example, witness the topics covered at the recently held UK Sports Institute (2002) sponsored conference entitled 'Leadership: World Class Coaching'. They included the biological and rationality dominated 'Optimising trunk muscle recruitment', 'Athens – Heat, humidity and pollution', 'The pose method running' and 'The performance enhancement team' among others, leaving delegates in no doubt as to what sort of knowledge 'expert' coaches should have.

Such an approach views coaching as unproblematic, thus assuming the establishment of a clear set of achievable, sequential goals. As a consequence, coaches have been encouraged to 'take charge' and control the coaching process, which includes their athletes, as much as possible (Seaborn *et al.* 1998). Indeed, the current coach–athlete relationship is characterized by rank and power, with one party perceived as having knowledge, and the other as needing it. This situation has, in turn, reaffirmed the hierarchical discourse often employed in coaching, as it takes for granted the structures of power that exist within the traditional coach–athlete relationship (Slack 2000). In this way, the discourse used tends to bolster the status quo, inclusive of the 'common sense' assumption that coaches should 'lead from the front'. Athletes, on the other hand, should subordinate themselves to those who can 'help' them achieve their objectives (Slack 2000). It is a presumed top-down structure of leadership, with strategy and expertise necessarily and legitimately viewed as being the domain of the coach. In addition to a subject-specific vocabulary, the discourse has also resulted in what can be described as a coach-initiation, athlete-response, coach-evaluation pattern of interaction (Prain and Hickey 1995). Such a structure can easily degenerate into being automatic 'recitations' (Cazden 1988) rather than opportunities for athletes to genuinely interact verbally and develop new understandings (Prain and Hickey 1995). Within such conversations, coaches inevitably control the turn-taking contributions, thus ensuring that a 'desired' agenda is maintained. A basic problem here, which is reflective of the rationality approach in general, is the frequent failure of coaches to account for individual diversity, leaving athletes unfulfilled and demotivated. As Alvesson and Willmott (1996) point out, in such orthodox manifestations of the coaching role, athletes only really have 'relevance' when the implementation of plans directly depends upon their conscious compliance. The issue for coaches then becomes how can the support of athletes and others be effectively 'engineered', rather than how best to appreciate and address their underlying concerns (Slack 2000). Alvesson and Willmott (1996) refer to such a situation as the use of 'strategy talk'. This works to restrain the involvement of certain groups (like athletes) in decision-making processes, in that the discourse used by those in positions of power 'frame issues in a way that privileges [their] reason', thus giving them the initiative in any interactions that take place (Alvesson and Willmott 1996: 136). Through using the dominant discourse and identifying with its practices, coaches are able to legitimize their positions and gain influence and credibility, thereby demonstrating the relevance of their role. Additionally, as a consequence of adhering to the discourse, they are well placed to receive both assistance from governing bodies and compliance from athletes to whom they act as unquestioning authorities in setting workloads and establishing ways of behaving (Johns and Johns 2000).

Not surprisingly, the prevailing rationalistic-performance coaching discourse has led to the development of language within the profession which is infused with the driving concepts of productivity, efficiency, prediction and accountability. This has led to binary thinking among coaches, which has not only profoundly influenced the nature of the coach–athlete relationship, but also the subsequent preparation of athletes (Johns and Johns 2000). Consequently, although one can easily assume that athletes are empowered by their own goal orientation and the self-chosen means to achieve it (Johns and Johns 2000), a more critical interrogation of coaches' discourse reveals a power-dominated control mechanism, which results in the 'production of docile bodies that monitor, guard and discipline themselves' (Eskes *et al.* 1998: 319). In this way, through continuing to speak and coach in rationalistic terms, coaches can be seen to influence the behaviour of their athletes as well as their own.

THE EFFECT OF POWER-DOMINATED DISCOURSE ON ATHLETES

A clear example of the current power-dominated discourse in action lies in the increasing emphasis placed on athlete conformity and compliance. Here, any 'conflict' in the coach–athlete relationship is considered as dysfunctional; a concept clearly at odds with the messy reality of coaching. It is also a stance that implies that individuality cannot be a force for positive change and progression. The result of the situation is that both coaches and athletes are encouraged to see the 'proper' coaching environment as one that is characterized by cooperation, consensus and conformity (Kirk 1992). It is a view that can lead to social oppression, both physically and cognitively; physically in terms of reproducing an acceptably formed athletic body, and cognitively in relation to inhibiting individual creativity (Apple 1979).

Before examining scenarios of both instances, it is worth noting that the success of this drive for conformity, although instigated by the coach and his/her discourse, is largely achieved through athlete self-regulation. Here, athletes are often seen to rigorously comply with, and strictly adhere to, coach-produced training regimes that include carefully controlled lifestyle and weight management programmes (Johns and Johns 2000). Such apparent voluntary actions have been referred to as the 'technologies of the self' (Foucault 1977), where athletes adopt the means by which they police their own preparation and appearance in line with coaches' expectations. This compliance is often ensured as athletes have limited discourses upon which to draw. Consequently, they 'take their cues' from their coaches in terms of how to think and speak of their preparation, performances and of themselves as athletes. Indeed, this is the crucial point here, that coaches 'frame' the sporting experience for their athletes. They talk in terms of efficiency, productivity and time, hence, athletes similarly come to think of themselves in mechanistic terms. In this way, discourse given from positions of power can be considered akin to the 'hidden curriculum' in education (Kirk 1992), which refers to the often subconscious learning of knowledge, attitudes and assumptions as a result of participation in an activity. These learned values become unwritten rules, etched in the mind, and come to significantly influence our behaviours, strategies and the people we become (Kirk 1992). Such readily adopted practices provide clear examples of how power is woven into the fabric of culture (Williams 1977).

The drive for physical conformity and its potential negative consequences has been particularly evident with regard to the female body image, in terms of what it visually means to be an athlete. It appears that the presentation of the sporting body, as viewed in 'subjective' women's sports such as gymnastics, synchronized swimming, figure skating and diving among others, has increasingly come to rely on the way in which it conforms to social trends and styles, in addition to how it athletically performs (Johns 1998). This has brought the visuality of the body and its preparation within sport, as a site for critical examination, to the fore. Not surprisingly, investigations have revealed paradoxes between the desired body 'look' and weight, and its optimum performance condition (Franklin 1996). They have also revealed a complex set of power and domination structures, which normalizes many practices in sport that might be considered harmful outside it (Birrell and Cole 1994; Chapman 1997).

In many ways, such a situation promotes an ethic of excess (Johns 1998) and is often played out along the thin edge of the body's natural limits (Franklin 1996). It is sustained by the politics of athlete self-surveillance, which, in turn, is made up of a sense of personal responsibility, obligation to constant practice, and continual self-regulation, and is often manifest through the keeping of training diaries. Such diaries ensure that training workloads become accepted by athletes as 'regimes of truth' (Chapman 1997), over which they have 'control'. Here, athletes believe they are subject to what Foucault (1977: 184–5) has termed a 'normalizing gaze' from coaches (and other athletes) to see if the training has been adhered to. It is a gaze that makes it 'possible to classify and to punish', and thus further encourages them to engage in disciplinary practices. Not surprisingly, such practices can have negative consequences for athletes, as witnessed by two participants from Johns and Johns' (2000) recent study who recalled how their self-esteem was eroded by similar technologies of power:

> One (gymnastic) coach would weigh us 4 times a day, that was ridiculous. We had to weigh in before each practice and that made us really self-conscious. And then she would say "You're fat, why do you weigh more than you weighed this morning? What did you eat this afternoon?" It was an interrogation and it was terrible.
>
> (Johns and Johns 2000: 228)

> Coaches in rhythmic gymnastics just love to control their athletes. They said I may as well quit coz I wasn't mentally ready to lose weight. It gave me insecurities about my body image and I remember thinking I looked like a whale. I came to realize that it was a question of respect. I don't think a lot of gymnasts are treated with respect, so you end up hating the sport [and] feeling bitter.
>
> (Johns and Johns 2000: 227)

To give another example of how the drive for productivity and conformity can result in negative experiences for athletes, consider a football player who has a tendency and ability to execute creative, individual tasks very well. Hence, she brings an imaginative dimension to team play. On the occasion when, in possession of the ball, she takes the riskier option to achieve greater penetration of opposing defences, which she is fully capable of doing, she feels a sense of fulfillment, adventure and actualization. However, if possession is lost as the consequence of the move, she receives criticisms from the coach, and possibly from the other players for losing the ball they worked so hard to gain. Despite some moves working, her colleagues are loath to support her play as they believe more-than-often the ball will be lost (i.e. her play lacks an 'end product'). Even if the move works, she is often isolated, as her colleagues do not support in enough numbers, as they are not confident that possession will be retained. With less support, this becomes a self-fulfilling prophecy as, indeed, the ball is lost on more occasions, which, in turn, leads to increased castigation by both colleagues and coach. Subsequently, even when opportunities to be creative present themselves, she begins to experience fear, both of losing the ball and of her team mates' and coach's reactions if she does. As a result, she ceases to try the difficult and innovative, preferring to adopt a safer, less imaginative passing option, thus sacrificing her talent and the unique contribution she brings to the team. In effect, she conforms to the norm.

This example illustrates the influence that a dominant 'product', collective discourse, can have over a young athlete's development. The starting point of analysis here is the player's position within the discourse; that is, how she is seen by others and how she sees herself as a player (McGannon and Mauws 2000). Here, the individual athlete is constantly positioned as a 'team player', a cog in a larger wheel. Hence, she has similar functions to other cogs who must contribute equally to a collective outcome, within an encompassing coach-dominated context. Furthermore, with respect to the socially constructed role of player, the 'good' player is thought of as one who listens to the coach and subsequently carries out instructions without question, trains hard, considers the efforts of team mates, and puts the team's needs ahead of her own. To reinforce such values, players are constantly bombarded with such dressing-room signs and sentiments relating to sacrificing the self for the good of the team (e.g. 'there is no I in team', 'teamwork works', etc). Consequently, there are a range of expectations, expressed through a particular discourse associated with the term 'player', or more accurately 'good player', that structures how players make sense of their situation and behaviours. The carrying out of these expectations dictate whether the player is regarded as a 'good' one or not, both by others and themselves (McGannon and Mauws 2000).

In our example, the contextual discourse established by the coach becomes too strong for our creative player to resist. To keep her place in the team she will have to conform, thus inhibiting her creative talent and enjoyment of the sport. Indeed, it appears that athletes in general aim for the achievement of an ideal representation of an unwritten subjective standard as set by the coach (Johns and Johns 2000). Furthermore, successful athletes are seen to apply a rigid technology

THE COACHING CONTEXT

of the self to comply with this 'coaches' view of the world', which is strengthened by the perceived constant gaze of coaches, peers and self.

AN ALTERNATIVE COACHING DISCOURSE

The critical analysis embarked upon in this chapter has highlighted the problematic nature of the coach–athlete relationship, particularly within high-performance sport. It is a relationship characterized by one side having knowledge and influence, while the other is defined by a 'need to know', a desire to conform and an inability to risk (Johns and Johns 2000). However, realistically, we are very aware that coach and athlete require much self-sacrifice and commitment to be successful in sport. Consequently, compliance and productivity are needed. Indeed, there is no need to reject all notions associated with the current discourse. Alternatively, the point here is to become aware of the relativity of what we hold true and how we express it, and to promote questioning about the consequences of these truths and practices before progressing to examine ways of improving (Wright 2000). Echoing the earlier call by Johns and Johns (2000) therefore, we are not suggesting a total change in the ways of competition preparation and talking about it but, rather, that the power arrangements upon which the highly rationalized sport discourse is based be removed, or, at the very least, amended.

Johns and Johns (2000) provide an interesting possible reformulation of the current sport performance-pedagogy discourse. They reject the current binary coach–athlete structure, and alternatively emphasize a greater respect for athletes through the establishment of more equitable relationships. This would include a discourse that is more 'symmetrical and non-dominated' and not 'distorted by power and ideology' (Cherryholmes 1988: 89). It thus reflects an altered performance pedagogy based on a structured freedom, which emphasizes the importance of the individual within the collective and the social responsibilities of athletes and coaches within the relationship both to themselves and to each other.

A concrete starting point for developing such a discourse could be to attach greater importance, as a coaching resource, to the personal knowledges of athletes, which is based on individual experiences and practices. Undoubtedly, athletes posses a wealth of knowledge about achievement and, in particular, what 'works' for them, which is not currently being effectively drawn upon in their preparation. The challenge here is to elevate and integrate this knowledge into good practice, as opposed to ignoring or downplaying it. Respecting and building on athletes' current knowledge would also alter the power dynamic in traditional coach–athlete relationships to a more equitable one. Such a change in thinking could then lead to a change in speaking; that is, to an altered coaching discourse characterized less by binary 'us' and 'them' thinking to one more defined by a collective 'we', within which the individual's unique and creative talents are valued. The altered relationships would be nondidactic in nature, with athletes actively contributing to their development through a deeper reflection of their own performances (Cazden

1988). Through such a process, they could experience greater success, pleasure and understanding of their sporting experience. Alternatively, coaches would be forced to develop flexible discursive practices to continually challenge their athletes at many levels, whilst allowing more time to better observe, analyse and creatively assess development (Prain and Hickey 1995). This would afford the coach further resources and experiences to develop athletes in more holistic ways, whilst allowing both coach and athlete new and different means to construct and understand their situations. This type of relationship is needed if athletes are to experience the true value of their commitment. We, therefore, need to educate coaches to 'gamble' less on the compliance of athletes through claims to expertise, and alternatively to engage in a joint process of knowledge generation involving both parties which could tap into and develop deeper levels of potential.

Discourse and language reflect our beliefs and values and, as such, attempts at change are often met with some resistance. This is because our utterances serve others, as well as ourselves, in understanding the differing roles each of us plays within the discourse. Consequently, attempts to alter our ways of speaking could encounter resistance from others, as, 'in addition to repositioning ourselves, [such changes] also serve to reposition those with whom we speak' (McGannon and Mauws 2000: 158). As both coaches and athletes have become socialized into accepting their complementary roles, they are bound to feel uncomfortable and uncertain when the boundaries change. Thus, a coach could experience resistance from athletes if he or she attempts to change the discourse to one that is unfamiliar. Indeed, evidence suggests this to be the case. Consequently, unless care and sensitivity are exercised, athletes may be unwilling to accept radical new strategies which are alien to them (Jones 2001). Similarly, an athlete who wants to reposition him- or herself within an empowerment discourse may encounter resistance from a coach, who is reluctant to view the athlete's behaviours in anything other than the traditional coach-dominated way. Changing the way we talk then takes patience, perseverance, effort and understanding. To make a lasting change we must be aware of how the conversations we have with others and ourselves affect how we feel, think and behave. This note of caution should not dampen the drive for improved change however, as to coach is to occupy a very privileged position, one that is accompanied by many social responsibilities (Penney 2000). Therefore, we have a duty to choose our words and our talk carefully, to be aware of their legacies, and to constantly be searching for ways to improve.

CONCLUDING THOUGHTS

The discourse that currently dominates sports coaching can be seen as providing boundaries that define the nature of the coach–athlete relationship and the roles of each party within it. It is a discourse driven by a scientific, performance pedagogy, emanating from a power-dominated hierarchical relationship where the coach is seen as knowledgeable and the athlete not. Although athletes willingly enter the activity, it is a pathway founded on deeply established practice (Johns

THE COACHING CONTEXT

and Johns 2000). Athletes generally accept and internalize the discourse present, which is espoused as 'truth' by hierarchically positioned coaches. Athletes on the other hand are the 'novice recipients of this authoritative expertise, [who] experience the discomforting effect of power as authority that legitimizes certain aspects of knowledge while trivializing others' (Johns and Johns 2000: 231).

Although some have argued for a radical overhaul of power arrangements in sport to counter the existing discourse (Shogan 1999), a more realistic goal would be to reposition ourselves within it. By doing so we could establish an amended coach–athlete relationship based on a more equitable power-sharing relationship. Indeed, athletes in Johns and Johns' (2000) study declared that they were willing to settle for such a power structure as long as they understood the reasons for it. This is not to say that such an amended discourse does not itself require close future scrutiny.

In concluding this chapter, we would like to echo the words of Penney (2000). She stated that one of the key things to realize in considering issues such as discourse is that 'we are not all going to agree upon what the focus of attention should be, what aims our energies should be directed to, and how these can be best achieved' (Penney 2000: 62). However, there is a need to be aware of the variety of discourses than can potentially, and perhaps should, find expression in coaching, whilst recognizing that these will have different implications for the interests of different groups. Before we decide on alternative discourses then, there are issues of whom and what coach education and coaches ought to promote and exclude, which merit consideration (Penney 2000). Whatever the outcome of such a process, it is worth remembering that the dominance of certain discourses can and should always be contested, and that perhaps the time is now right for such a challenge in coaching.

CHAPTER 14

▼ COACHING ETHICS

■ Introduction   162
■ Ethical codes and ethical issues in coaching   164
■ Problematizing ethics: moving toward virtues-based conduct
  (McNamee 1998)   166
■ Personalizing coaches' ethical behaviour   170
■ Concluding thoughts   173

INTRODUCTION

The notion that sport builds character has been a popular claim for decades, and rests on the taken-for-granted assumption that there is some sort of internal connection between the practice of sport and the development of moral qualities (Carr 1998). Despite its positive overtones, the belief has often led to a culture of not teaching or coaching in relation to moral values, as it is based on the perception that a coach's task is simply to organize sporting activities for children/athletes who learn ethical behaviours from simply participating in them. Regardless of this tendency towards passivity, coaches are also expected to be positive moral role models for children, being responsible for guiding them towards the adoption of desirable cultural values (McCallister *et al.* 2000). Despite the popularity of the notion of sport being a character builder, it has not been the subject of widespread critical examination. Indeed, it has not garnered anything approaching general consensus, let alone necessary operational definitions. This is particularly so in relation to what is meant by the term 'character', and how the context and/or the coach is meant to develop it (Sheilds and Bredemeier 1995). This lack of clarity has led to an inadequate conception of the professional responsibilities associated with the coaching role in terms of athletes' moral development (Carr 1998).

Before we enter the discussion in earnest, it is appropriate that we provide definitions of both ethical and moral actions, lest there should be similar confusion in the ensuing analysis. According to the *Concise Oxford Dictionary* (Oxford 1991), ethics 'relate to moral principles'; to be moral is to be 'concerned with the goodness or badness of human behaviour or with the distinction between right and wrong' (1991), whilst a moralist is a 'person who follows a system of ethics' (1991). The terms are plainly inter-related and, therefore, as has been done elsewhere (Kretchmar 1994), they will be used interchangeably in this chapter. It is worth noting however, that ethics and morals by themselves are value-neutral, therefore, the issue at hand is for coaches not just to have ethics, but to have 'good' ones and to be aware of how they are reflected in their actions.

In trying to debunk the myth of the character-building qualities of sport, Carr (1998) contends that involvement in it is no more morally or ethically educative than any other pursuit or school subject that involves children learning to work cooperatively with others. The important caveat here is that, although it cannot be assumed that ethical behaviour will be learnt through mere participation, the sporting environment may well be a place where it can happen. Perhaps the preliminary question to be addressed then is whether coaches should be regarded as moral educators.

Echoing our belief that coaches ought to be concerned with holistically educating athletes (for a further discussion here see Chapter 15), and in light of their often influential positions as 'significant others', we believe that coaches should qualify as agents of moral education. This, however, is a consequence of the particular professional role occupied and not because of the peculiar nature of physical activities. The ethical learning context then is one that is created and maintained by the coach, and not by virtue of it being defined as 'sport'. To fashion such an environment, coaches must first recognize that the ethical development of the athletes in their charge is a part of their role, and that, similar to other pedagogic professionals, they are 'employed to teach in a context of wider concerns about how to live and what to value in life' (Carr 1998: 131). They hold important positions (often being *in loco parentis*) with regard to caring for minors; a duty that, like it or not, carries significant ethical obligations and responsibilities.

Having declared our stance that a coach should act as a moral guide, the purpose of this chapter is to explore how he or she can go about becoming one. However, the aim is to go further than to merely document circumstances where ethical dilemmas could typically emerge for coaches, or to direct coaches to 'ready made' moral decisions as manifest in existing codes of conduct. Rather, it is to promote an understanding of the often complex and relative ethical dilemmas in sport, and how to better deal with them. In this respect, it builds on the earlier work of Sheilds and Bredemeier (1995) in seeking to extend current theory by discussing a framework useful for understanding, investigating and promoting ethical action in coaching. What informs our approach here is the need to avoid the individual–social dualism which has so far over-simplified much of the work into coaches' ethical dilemmas, and to emphasize that social interactions and the contexts in which they occur affect the moral behaviour of the individual. Moral dilemmas in coaching therefore are often better viewed as 'shades of grey', with the challenges to the fine line of distinction between ethical and unethical behaviour being complex and open to interpretation (Lyle 2002).

However, this is not to advocate a totally relativist stance, thus abdicating responsibility for trying to live a life founded on good ethics. Indeed, following a discussion on the purpose of an ethical code and current writings on ethical coaching issues, the work of McNamee (1998) and Fernandez-Balboa (2000) are used to provide a framework whereby coaches' ethical decisions are personalized and made accountable. Here, the case is made for a 'virtues' as opposed to a 'rules-based' code of conduct approach, in order to secure lasting change in the moral climate within which coaching occurs (McNamee 1998). This places the onus firmly on coaches to carefully consider courses of action and their consequences in relation to ethical behaviour. Finally, the significance of the chapter also lies in making the case for coaches to be professionally educated in relation to developing moral sensitivity in their practice whilst cultivating positive social values among their athletes (Carr 1998).

ETHICAL CODES AND ETHICAL ISSUES IN COACHING

Sport is often thought to mirror society and its prevailing value trends. Additionally, because of its popularity, it is often considered a primary medium through which many young people come to learn about the core values of their culture. Having the potential to convey social values however, also encompasses the transmission of undesirable as well as desirable ones (Sheilds and Bredemeier 1995). Consequently, some critics have claimed that sport impedes, as opposed to develops, 'good' value learning, and point to the many reports of unethical behaviour related to violence, parental brawls, aggressive nationalism, sexism, racism, homophobia, and illegal use of performance-enhancing drugs as evidence of their claim (Reddiford 1998). Such behaviour results from both adopting values that are counter to the norm, and of following desired social values too closely. This latter tendency has been termed 'positive deviance', which distorts ideals and leads to twisted value priorities where the ends are seen as justifying the means. Indeed, recent questions about the morality of sport have largely arisen from such deviance, as witnessed in the harsh competitive ethic driven by huge extrinsic rewards evident at many levels. It is a concern about the emphasis placed on the prize more than the process which tends to blur 'our vision of the human and humane potential of sport' (Sheilds and Bredemeier 1995: 2). According to Kretchmar (1994), it is through such a distorted focus that we develop 'moral callouses' which, in turn, keep us from engaging with ethical questions of right and wrong at any meaningful level.

Ethical issues then are very much a contemporary concern for coaches, with considerable attention having been given over recent years to appropriate and inappropriate coaching behaviour. This has been generated by a seemingly endless array of athletes failing drug tests, allied to several high-profile sexual harassment cases and allegations of child abuse (Lyle 2002). The range of ethical issues likely to concern coaches was recently categorized by Lyle (2002) into interpersonal relationships, power differentials, influencing outcomes or performance, social role (failure to maintain), and inappropriate goal setting. He expanded on this categorization by stating that ethical issues are likely to arise when a power differential exists in an interpersonal relationship, as is typical of the coaching context. Consequently, as many coach–athlete relationships are characterized by differences in age, experience, knowledge and gender, as well as close physical contact, psychological dependency and emotional intensity, they are a fruitful context within which unethical behaviour can occur. The resulting tension is heightened in elite sport where both coaches and athletes constantly stretch the boundaries of permissible action in order to maximize performance (Lyle 2002).

Despite the potential for sport to generate unethical behaviour, it can also serve as an important catalyst for moral growth, personal development and social justice. Hence, it can be seen as a moulder, as well as a mirror, of social values, as it is replete with opportunities to encounter, learn and live positive social principles (Sheilds and Bredemeier 1995). Indeed, Sheilds and Bredemeier (1995) argued that sport can be a particularly valuable context for moral education, as the 'ground rules' of the game are more generally accepted, assumed and respected as being fairer than those of society. Consequently, in providing a platform for the further development of ethical behaviour, the 'fair-play' assumption associated with participating in sport could work in its favour.

As a consequence of the potential to break the rules, and in response to those who have done so, many sport-specific and generic ethical codes of conduct have been established. For example, in 1979 Martens and Seefeldt proclaimed the Bill of Rights for Young Athletes, while in 1992 the Council of Europe created the European Sports Charter, both of which arose from unease regarding issues of over-competitiveness in youth sport. These were followed (in 1998) by the Brighton Declaration on Women and Sport in response to concerns over gender equity, and (in 1996) by the National Coaching Foundation's wide-ranging guide to ethical practice which was a further attempt to regulate the behaviour of coaches (Kidd and Donnelly 2000). Their value has been justified by the premise that by giving an outline of what is permissible and what is not, they demonstrate to everyone concerned what behaviours can be expected from professionals (Lyle 2002).

Such codes are considered to be 'issues-led' with general concerns related to cheating, drug taking and child abuse dominating the agenda. Additionally, despite their potential for developing positive virtuous practice, they have traditionally been presented in negative terms. That is, such codes have focused on apparently inappropriate behaviour. Thus, they remind us of the social rules by which we should live, of what 'ought to be', by emphasizing what we should not do. Similarly, the rationales for writing such codes have been couched in negative terms; for example, 'to avoid arbitrariness', 'to highlight impermissible conduct', 'to impose clarity and simplicity in a confusing world', 'to set out standards and criteria by illustrating the need for them' and 'to provide a framework for resolving conflict' by confirming what is not allowable (McNamee 1998). It is a common-sense view of morality, expressed as a set of rules, which are designed to stop people from acting unfairly in the pursuit of their own interests to the detriment of others.

PROBLEMATIZING ETHICS: MOVING TOWARD VIRTUES-BASED CONDUCT (MCNAMEE 1998)

Despite the fact that existing codes of professional practice are generally accepted to be necessary documents, some scholars have recently questioned whether they are entirely relevant (Carr 1998; McNamee 1998; Reddiford 1998). The concerns relate, not to the aims of such codes, but to their inadequacy in dealing with the ethically complex coaching environment, and to their view of morality as a set of clear regulations to be unproblematically followed. The absolutist lines they draw have been criticized for leading us to 'right–wrong' binary thinking, and to the false belief that we are successfully addressing moral difficulties when we are not (McNamee 1998). Consequently, although their clarity is often unquestioned in terms of outlining 'proper' human relationships in the coaching environment, such codes have been accused of inviting us to think of ethical life in terms of a series of rigid obligations. McNamee (1998: 148) views them as being reflective of moral conservatism, 'a flight back to the language of moral certainty, of duties, and rules', and to a 'culture of blame and punishment for perceived wrongdoing' (1998: 151). Such regulations maintain that rule adherence is at the heart of ethical conduct, and imply that if coaches follow rules then they must have a sense of moral maturity. Although such codes have been useful in identifying those who are unethical in their practice thus enabling punishment, needless to say, we believe there is more to the development of moral maturity than that. Indeed, Reddiford (1998) considered such codes as having had little, if any, effect on the moral motivation of those who seek to make unjust gains, and that their existence merely leads to more sophisticated ways of cheating. McNamee (1998) also questioned the need for rules which outline obvious wrongdoings. For example, he asks

> why do we need a rule concerning sexual harassment in a code of conduct?
> Is it not clear that such actions are wrong, so why do we need a code to
> tell us this? We can no more sexually harass our colleagues or athletes
> than any other person in the street. The rule tells us nothing new.
>
> (McNamee 1998: 158)

Alternatively, he believes that the psychology of the situation that produces such unacceptable behaviour needs to be understood in order to ensure (as best we can) that it does not happen. To secure such adherence, we should work towards a climate of conduct that precludes such actions because we sincerely believe them to be inherently wrong and not just because a rule-book tells us they are.

Finally, McNamee (1998) criticizes the rule-based approach as being, by its very nature, underdetermined. That is, he questions how a set of regulations can anticipate or describe all the actions that may be considered unethical, or tell everyone what to do and what not to do in all circumstances. Plainly, it cannot. Such codes appear to leave many questions unanswered as they are simply unable to write out the 'particularity of quandary' (McNamee 1998) or to assist coaches in addressing the infinite variety of moral issues they constantly face once they have avoided obvious wrongdoings. Even when attempts have been made to achieve absolute rule clarity and precision in terms of a certain act, judgement is often still needed in interpreting a possible unethical behaviour as fitting a given category (Reddiford 1998). Such codes then are regarded as being too simplified to have much impact on behaviour, whilst being inadequate in preparing coaches to answer the morally fundamental recurring question of 'what will I do here in the light of what I consider myself to be?' (McNamee 1998).

To further illustrate the problematic nature of ethical decision making in coaching, consider the following scenario which has been adapted from the work of McNamee (1998). I am the coach of a middle-distance 16-year-old athlete, Rhys, who shows great promise. His parents are keen and supportive, both of his involvement in sport and of me as a coach. They want him to be pushed to fulfil his potential. However, at present, he is struggling with his interval training and just can't reach the agreed targets set ('agreed' in terms of me suggesting a training schedule, and him just nodding!). In all probability, this is because he has not kept to the strict training regime laid out for him. This afternoon, he is tired after the morning run and looks distinctly unenthusiastic about the session ahead. How should I react, what should I do? A multitude of questions run through my mind. Should I make him run more intervals on the track? Is he too tired to do them properly? Is he self-motivated enough to do them properly? Have I done enough to prepare him for the forthcoming championships? Has he achieved the 'agreed' goals? Were they really agreed goals? Have I pushed him too hard? Do I have to toughen him up? These are everyday, ethically tinged questions for a coach that fall well outside the rule-governed jurisdiction of proclaimed codes of conduct. There are no rules to guide me here. After a minute's consideration, I decide that the only way to get Rhys to succeed is to push him harder; after all, that is what his parents want. I warn him that if the next set of sprints is not completed within a certain time, 'we'll be here all night till they are' or 'I'll withdraw you from the championships'. I tell him to 'harden up' and to 'tough it out'. In response, through great effort, he completes the set satisfactorily. I feel vindicated. I have proven to him what he's capable of, if he is only prepared to work hard enough. I chastise him for his lack of will power and remind him of others' sacrifices that allow him this opportunity to explore and exploit his talent. Rhys walks away in an angry sulk, his animosity towards me obvious. To a degree, I understand his reaction. However, I am comforted in the knowledge that I have simply complied with the wishes of his parents, whilst demonstrating to him what he is capable of. I have engaged in no obvious wrongdoing, and merely kept to the agreed training schedule.

Although no rules as enshrined in a code of conduct were broken in the scenario described, it could be argued that the trust between the athlete and the coach has been violated, or at the very least been placed under considerable strain. On the other hand, perhaps it was exactly what Rhys needed to make him value his talent. Such dilemmas highlight the complexity of the ethical dimension in coaching and the inadequacy of rules-based codes of conduct in helping coaches to deal with it. As there are no rules here, such an issue as how hard should young athletes be pushed must be left to the discretion of the coach. In short, we just have to trust the coach to make the right decisions. To help them in this regard, coach education programmes should include a personal ethical component grounded in such real issues as described above. For McNamee (1998), the main consideration within such a situation should not be 'whether I have broken any rules', but 'what should I do in light of what's best for my athlete and the claims I make for myself as a good person'. The immediate issue for coaches then becomes how to determine what is right from wrong; that is, 'What do I believe qualifies as ethical behaviour and what does not?' and 'What is this decision based on?'

In relation to the wider issue of what qualifies as ethical behaviour, a common view in Western culture is to believe that moral perspectives are strictly a matter of preference (Sheilds and Bredemeier 1995). Although we acknowledge the role of context in deciding the most appropriate course of action, to abandon the debate to total relativity would leave coaches with no pilot or rudder by which to charter rough and dangerous seas. The perspective of the cognitivists on the other hand appears a little more convincing in providing such assistance (Sheilds and Bredemeier 1995). They consider that behaviour is ethical only if it is motivated, at least in part, by such reasons. For example, if a coach passes on some knowledge to another coach because he or she thinks that doing so will give him or her an emotional edge that can later be exploited, while a second coach does the same act for purely altruistic reasons (i.e. just to help the other coach), we would say that only the second coach acted morally. Such a stance echoes the classic work of Rokeach (1973) in psychology, who equated morality with altruism or 'other-regard' (i.e. regard to the 'other'), considering selfishness a threat to it. Although this might provide a good guide to moral action, to parcel and leave it so neatly is unrealistic, as such a stance can be countered by the argument that often a concern of the moral agent is to cultivate his or her own morality by virtue of acting morally. This inevitably involves a focus on the self and can be termed selfish. Others meanwhile have disagreed with the altruistic thesis from the viewpoint that 'what is required to be fair and just is not self-denial but a balancing or coordination of self interest with the interests of others' (Sheilds and Bredemeier 1995: 19). Again, the thoughts of the self have a place.

Similarly, when searching for the meaning of morality the philosopher Habermas attempted to explain ethical action in terms of its relationship to the general 'norm' (Sheilds and Bredemeier 1995). Consequently, 'truth' was defined as the consensus reached through dialogue. Critics, however, have contended that not every such agreement leads to good ethical actions, for example, witness the positively deviant yet accepted sub-culture of many sports which often lead to brutalizing training regimes. Additionally, within contests, there frequently appears to be a shared limited appreciation of the 'spirit of the rules', as there is general agreement on pursuing every advantage possible to secure on-field victories (Reddiford 1998). Such a sentiment was even expressed by that model of traditional English sporting excellence and sportsmanship C. B. Fry, who believed that 'if both sides agree to cheat, then cheating is fair' (Reddiford 1998: 225). Indeed, many actions carried out under the guise of sport would be considered unacceptable in wider society but are tolerated in context by all concerned as they are considered 'part of the game'. Defining moral actions in the sporting context then is elusive in itself. Despite the seemingly problematic and often contextual nature of ethical actions however, we do believe that some moral principles should be virtually unassailable. These include concepts such as respect, integrity, equity and fairness. The difficulty, of course, comes in interpreting and implementing them, in a social environment that is forever changing, so that they are consistently upheld. Perhaps a way forward in this regard is to accept that while such principles form the core of ethical action they can, and should, remain flexible. Rokeach's (1968) work on values can help our understanding here, as he believed there were different kinds of values which could be classified by what he termed the 'regions of the person'. The metaphoric language was used to highlight that some beliefs are more critical and more central to self-identity than others. This is a view supported by Blasi and Oresick (1987) who concluded that

> not all beliefs have the same value and the same effects. Some are only peripherally related to our identity. If one acts against such beliefs, one is inconsistent, but only in a weak sense. On the other hand, certain beliefs are so central to one's identity that one is compelled to act in accordance with them by psychological necessity; if one fails to do so, one is inconsistent in a strong sense.
>
> (Blasi and Oresick 1987: 72)

Consequently, it appears that we are able to have principles and to treat them flexibly, particularly the more weakly held ones, without being considered inconsistent. In this way, we can be adaptable whilst constantly upholding certain moral standards (this is similar to the discussion in Chapter 5 on the development of functional coaching philosophies). Sheilds and Bredemeier (1995: 13) liken it to a 'belief tree', where the roots equate to core beliefs, the branches are the intermediate beliefs, while the 'peripheral beliefs, like leaves, drop off easily in response to the shifting winds of life'.

The ethical flexibility implied in the metaphorical belief tree was recently found in the behaviour of expert coaches (Jones et al. 2004; Saury and Durand 1998). It also falls broadly in line with the call of McNamee (1998) to educate coaches through a 'virtues' as opposed to a rule-based approach, thus ensuring that contextual decision making takes place as opposed to rigid rule-adherence. For him,

COACHING ETHICS

ethics and ethical conduct cannot simply be reduced to the idea of rule responsibility, hence, what is important is to develop coaches who genuinely follow the spirit of the rules and not those whose behaviour merely equates to rule-observance where this means the avoidance of rule-breaking actions (McNamee 1998). Such a stance builds on the work of Kohen (1994) who believed that the professional must be given discretion, grounded in a highly internalized sense of responsibility, in order to effect context-sensitive ethical action. This sense of responsibility is crucial to answer the earlier cited recurring internal questions of 'in what do we ground our interpretations of what is right?', and 'What makes us confident of the rightness of our decisions?'

According to McNamee (1998), the answer is in developing a deeper moral code to live by, one based on personal virtue. Such a code seems particularly applicable to the sporting domain where coaches' goals, and the accompanying decisions they take, are both relative and absolutist, and almost always complex. Unavoidably then, due to the inability of rules-based codes of conduct to cover all eventualities, the coach becomes someone in whom an element of trust and discretion is invested. The least athletes and parents can expect is that decisions affecting them are taken within a good ethical framework of responsibility to performer, self, and sport (McNamee 1998). Hence, we need to develop coaches who respect the rules to ensure that the contest is a fair and enjoyable one, as opposed to not breaking them from a fear of being caught and punished (McNamee 1998). We need coaches who adhere to the spirit of the game and do not bend the rules as much as possible, who do not substitute codes of conduct in place of their own virtuous development, or who fear creatively engaging with the range of options open to them over and above the rules laid out. The following section outlines a suggested strategy for how this can be achieved.

PERSONALIZING COACHES' ETHICAL BEHAVIOUR

Despite much having been written about morality (or the lack of it) in sport and the widespread production of rules-based codes, most coach education programmes continue to devote minimal or very superficial attention to ethical issues (Fernandez-Balboa 2000). Consequently, the coaches who pass through such programmes are unaware of the complexity or even of the existence of much unethical behaviour, nor are they mindful of how to deal with it. What is more, because they are not encouraged to critically think about such issues, many do not see the relevance of doing so when asked. Fernandez-Balboa (2000) neatly encapsulates the prevailing attitude in this regard:

> Spending a lot of time on ethics does not really apply to me. You see, I am (or am going to be) a coach, and my role is to teach physical skills to help athletes improve. I will help many people this way, and that is a good thing, isn't it? Besides, I think I am a pretty good person. I get on

well with people and some of my friends are from different ethnic backgrounds.

(Fernandez-Balboa 2000: 134)

He goes on to say that such a line of argument denotes great naivety with regard to unethical behaviour and its damaging consequences. While we may think ourselves to be basically good and try to do what we consider to be the right thing, unless we critically examine our beliefs and actions, we could be teaching and practising unethical behaviours without being aware of it (Dodds 1993). This is because coaching does not exist in an inter-personal vacuum, but in 'socio-cultural systems which have inherent discriminations and values attached to them' (Fernandez-Balboa 2000: 135). It is through the subsequent process of socialization that we acquire certain beliefs about others and ourselves and what is considered appropriate behaviour. It is also a process from which we invariably learn concepts such as 'us' and 'them'; that is, a dichotomous (i.e. either/or) way of thinking and how to manifest such notions in actions of acceptance or rejection (Eckert 1989). The resulting behaviour often leads to stereotyping, stigmatization and the humiliation of others (Fernandez-Balboa 2000). Despite good intentions then, without critically reflecting upon knowledges and actions, we always run the risk of perpetuating what is damaging and degrading (Fernandez-Balboa 2000; Jones 2000). This is precisely why it is not enough to simply list ethical issues, and consider the work of morally educating coaches to be done. Rather, we must critically engage with such issues at the personal level, so that we can deal with them as they appear in practice. It is through such engagement that we can aspire to base our coaching on virtuous, good ethical practice which we sincerely believe to be right, as opposed to given rules.

Despite ample evidence that the traditional coaching model does little to develop the moral characteristics of participants, there continues to be a disproportionate emphasis placed within it on physical development as opposed to the ethical and social aspects of the person. Hence, the enhancement of skills appear more important than matters of bigotry, discrimination and abuse (Fernandez-Balboa 2000). This is evident in both coach education programmes and coaching practice. For example, how often in coach education programmes do we encourage coaches to critique and deconstruct the assumptions that they live by in their coaching? How often do we ask them to question the myths that surround sport (e.g. 'participation builds character') with regard to the unethical behaviours that such an assumption could engender? Indeed, do not the traits that appear so valued in competitive sport (e.g. prowess, dominance, aggressiveness) go against much moral reasoning and social responsibility? Similarly, does not the presumed meritocratic nature of sport encourage coaches to treat their athletes as convenient commodities that can easily be disposed of once they no longer fulfil their purpose? To address such issues, we need to examine and question how illogical our logic can be, and recognize that even when it is well-intentioned, uncritical coaching has problematic and dangerous implications (Fernandez-Balboa 2000). This is precisely why it is important to consider our actions in the light of what we deem to be virtuous behaviour. Such behaviour should be based on the well-being and development of the 'other', in balance with a degree of self-respect and a strong awareness of the consequences that actions bring. The reflection that takes place is important as it keeps us vigilant in relation to our sentiments and practices, and encourages us to constantly ask if what we do denies the rights, choices and potentialities of others in any way (Dodds 1993).

According to Fernandez-Balboa (2000) a direct way to address the potential that we have to act unethically, and thus to develop a more virtuous approach, is to follow the systematic steps devised by Johnson (1996). These involve:

- Admiting the possibility that we have prejudices;
- Making honest attempts to identify what they are;
- Identifying specific actions that reflect those prejudices;
- Seeking support from others who may be able to help us in overcoming them.

Such a process is aimed at making us realize the limitations of our thinking and to help us recognize that our view of 'truth' is only one such version where many exist. To contextualize the process into the coaching context, the questions that we should ask ourselves relate to those ethical issues that are important to us. For example:

- Do I give athletes a real range of choices that are agreeable to them?
- Are my comments and actions considerate of others' beliefs and life experiences?
- Do the athletes I work with fear me? Why?
- Do they respect me? Why?
- How well do I actually know the athletes I work with as people? What evidence do I have on which to base that belief?
- What is my first reaction when an athlete makes a mistake?
- Do I include athletes in the decision-making process? If so, how? If not, should I?
- Do I take the time to learn the perspectives of others?
- 'Does my physical presence confer dominance?' (Fernandez-Balboa 2000: 140)
- How much power do I have over the athletes I work with?

By critically engaging with such questions, we can expose some of the common-sense, everyday actions of normal life which can lead to unethical behaviour, and so aspire to develop a virtues-based framework through which more moral coaching can occur. The above list is by no means definitive; coaches should expand on it in ways they deem appropriate to their context and circumstance.

CONCLUDING THOUGHTS

In relation to fighting unethical issues in coaching, we agree with Fernandez-Balboa (2000) who concluded that the battle can never be considered over. This is because, not only is there a great deal to confront in the outside world, but much also remains embedded and embodied in ourselves. Consequently, it is a process that is both private and public. As coaches, we have numerous opportunities to deal with many and varied ethical issues on a daily basis. Therefore, it is important that we learn to recognize such issues both in others and within ourselves, and be able to deal with them. If we accept that unethical behaviours are not natural but learned and can permeate many areas of our lives, we can accept that, through critical vigilance and reflection, there are ways to break the cycle and the 'traps of our own reasoning and conditioning' (Fernandez-Balboa 2000: 142). Through such engagement we can better aspire to a virtues-based as opposed to rule-based coaching, thus better ensuring sincere ethical behaviour in our practice.

CHAPTER 15

▼ **COACHING HOLISTICALLY: WHY DO IT AND HOW CAN WE FRAME IT?**

- Introduction 174
- The traditional model of multi-disciplinary coaching and coach education 175
- The case for coaching holistically 177
- Conceptualizing a holistic approach 179

INTRODUCTION

Although the value of holistic coaching has been increasingly recognized in recent times, this has tended to remain at the level of abstract thought and generalized support. The ambiguity surrounding what the concept actually means has, not surprisingly, been accompanied by a lack of suggestions about what holistic strategies look like and how one could be implemented. To avoid a similar oversight, we begin this chapter by defining what we mean by the term 'holistic coaching'. A dictionary definition of the term 'holistic' is a 'consideration of the complete person, both physically and mentally' (Collins 2003). Even though this sets us on our way, we would like to be more wide-ranging in our definition in asserting that the person is more than just the aggregate of mental and physical attributes, as he or she is also an emotional, political, social, spiritual and cultural being. To coach holistically then, is to coach with all of these considerations in mind. Although this inevitably leads to discussion about appropriate and workable boundaries for the coaching role, we consider that if such factors affect athletic performance and enjoyment then they should warrant consideration within the coaching remit.

We also believe that the essence of coaching holistically is to do so contextually. What we mean by this is that a coach needs to treat each situation, inclusive of its many variables, on its merits, to assess it, to carefully weigh the options and to choose the most appropriate course of action. To do this, he or she must draw on many knowledge sources and decide, with insight, how to amalgamate and utilize them in what fashion, when and where. Indeed, the hallmark of a holistic coach is one who has the ability to integrate various knowledge strands, including those that refer to the personal, emotional, cultural and social identity of the athlete. In short, he or she has the capacity to treat coaching knowledge as an assimilated, blended whole, acknowledging that it is considerably more than the sum of its constituent parts.

The main purpose of this chapter is to present the case for coaching holistically. It questions current assumptions surrounding the extent and nature of the coaching role, and how we prepare coaches for it. Hence, it aims to redefine and extend what it means to coach. This redefinition is based on recognizing the centrality of cultural and social relationships within the coaching process (Jarvie 1991; Jones 2000; Schempp 1998). Since such relationships are influenced by factors that are situational, political, ideological and moral in nature, we argue that coaches should carefully consider these factors and, therefore, take a holistic approach to coaching in order to realize the full potential of their athletes. The goal then is to increase coaches' sensitivities to individual athlete biographies, needs and identities, allowing them to better manage the relationship between the individual and the social context which, in turn, supports learning (Langley 1997).

In many ways, this penultimate chapter serves to encapsulate much of the book's central theme; that is, coaches' pedagogy must take account of complex contextual factors to fully develop the sporting experience for, and potential of, their athletes. It draws together the strands of thought developed throughout the book highlighting that coaching is, above all, a dynamic human activity with all the associated problems related to multiple goals, realities and needs. The chapter is also directly linked to the next (final) one in suggesting a framework within which we could locate a holistic approach. It thus allows the final chapter to explore the specific ways through which we can educate our coaches to adopt and deliver such a strategy. With regard to the content of this chapter, following a discussion about the traditional, compartmentalized approach to coaching and coach education and its innate limitations, the merits of coaching holistically are presented. Finally, health models from the World Health Organisation and from the indigenous Mäori peoples of Aotearoa/New Zealand are provided as examples of holistic frameworks.

THE TRADITIONAL MODEL OF MULTI-DISCIPLINARY COACHING AND COACH EDUCATION

Without re-stating the case made in earlier work (Potrac *et al.* 2000; Jones 2000), and in previous chapters of this book, suffice to say that traditional views of coaching have located it within a bio-scientific, product-orientated discourse. Consequently, coaching knowledge has been seen as unproblematic, with coaches viewed as mere technicians involved in its transfer (Macdonald and Tinning 1995). The discourse has been one related to 'processing' and 'packaging' athletes, in attempts to attain ever higher levels of 'output' (Bale and Sang 1996). According to Bale and Sang (1996: 21), such terminology, and the behaviour it engenders, has resulted in reducing athletes 'to inanimate objects, as things, to be recorded and ranked'. The implication is that the power to succeed is vested firmly in the individual (as long as they have the potential) if only they are prepared to train hard enough.

A principal contributor to this picture of athlete as 'machine' has been the education programmes set up for, and attended by, coaches. Here, conceptual views about the coaching role are shaped, as are perceptions about the 'valuable' knowledges needed to coach successfully. Such programmes have been almost exclusively multi-disciplinary in nature, containing discrete units within detached and parallel disciplines devoted to certain aspects of coaching knowledge (e.g. physiology, nutrition, psychology). Although much useful information has been contained within the structure, attending coaches have been left to make the cross-subject connections for themselves, which, recent research suggests, they have consistently failed to do (Saury and Durand 1998; Jones *et al.* 2004). Such findings give support to the claim that the current structure remains fragmented and disjointed (Jones 2000). Indeed, we can liken it to a 'smorgasbord of discon-nected facts and experiences' (Locke 1985: 10), which is hardly likely to produce consistent excellence in such a complex area of human relations as coaching. Additionally, for many, it appears that such programmes lack credibility, since by separating theory from practice, they routinize and simplify high level tasks (Macdonald and Tinning 1995). There has been a tendency in coach education programmes towards de-skilling the practitioner, both in terms of human and cognitive interaction as it assumes that knowledge is 'clean', sequential and given (Jones 2000). Connell (1985) refers to such a propensity as dehumanizing a most human of jobs.

An inherent problem with the above compartmentalized approach to knowledge is that the learning contained within it is often decontexualized. Without a contextual frame of reference, the learning has little relevance for coaches, since it does not reflect the integrated and complex nature of their practice. The learning also takes place in an expressive climate that is placid and neutral, causing coaches to suffer from 'reality shock' when they actually start working. Such programmes have the potential to produce limited two-dimensional, 'cardboard cut-out' type coaches (Sparkes and Templin 1992), who, driven by piecemeal mechanistic considerations, are unable to comprehend and thus adapt to the multifaceted and wide-ranging human context (Jones 2000). This focus has created a distorted framework that has failed to consider the full potential of the athlete, and more often than not ignored the social and pedagogical context. Indeed, such an approach is unable to take account of, and therefore clashes with, the unique and 'hybrid' nature of athletes (Shogan 1999) whose distinctive identities are created from many different practices and positions (Hall 1996). As such, we argue that there is a need for greater balance within a more integrated framework to better prepare coaches for the complexities of their role.

This issue was neatly conceptualized in a recent article by Burt (1998), albeit in the wider context of the contribution of 'kinesiology' as a subject for solving social problems. It was suggested that kinesiology was too narrowly conceived in rigidly separated sub-disciplines and too divorced from its central reality-based mission to properly deal with its stated aims. It was urged, instead, to focus on the quality of practitioners it produces and, hence, to fulfil its potential in dealing with and overcoming real-life problems. We issue a similar rallying call to coaching 'science'; indeed, the time may well be right to either better 'contribute or fall back' (Burt 1998: 80).

THE CASE FOR COACHING HOLISTICALLY

The argument here is based on recognizing coaching as intellectual as opposed to technical work, requiring higher order thinking skills to deal with the humanistic, problematic and dynamic nature of the tasks involved. Central to this is the integration and synthesis of the various knowledge strands that inform coaching, in an effort to reflect its multifaceted reality. The case for coaching holistically has been summarized around three principal issues. These include the need for coaches to consider (1) cultural factors, (2) the development of social competencies, and (3) the contexualization of practice, if lasting improvement is to occur.

In making the case that Kenyan middle-distance athletes are culturally, as opposed to naturally, produced, Bale and Sang (1996: 17) stated that 'running can mean different things to different cultures'. They argued that sport participation and achievement should be firmly placed within the context of culture if they are to be properly explained. The same could be said of coaching. Douge and Hastie (1993: 20) agreed that 'effective leadership qualities may be unique to a social fabric', while Schempp's (1998) declaration that 'our social worlds offer no immunity to sports fields or gymnasia', provide further evidence of the belief that knowledge of culture and related social factors should be prime considerations for coaches. Such a stance supports Cheffers' (1997: 4) philosophical lament that 'no individual is an island', and further emphasizes the need to coach holistically and contextually for meaningful progress to occur. For instance, in a New Zealand context, expecting a Mäori athlete to engage in direct eye-to-eye contact is problematic, since for Mäori looking an older person in the eye is a sign of disrespect (Durie 1998). Alternatively, Mäori are often more impressed by the unspoken signals conveyed through subtle gesture (e.g. a raised eyebrow), with words in some situations being regarded as superfluous and even demeaning (Durie 1998). For Mäori, 'emotional [covert] communication can assume an importance which is as meaningful as a [verbal] exchange and valued just as much' (Durie 1998: 71). Within the cultural context then, learning is considered both an individual and a social process, with meanings being constructed both in the mind of the learner and through his/her community of practice (Langley 1997). Consequently, we need to be culturally sensitive when coaching, as culture exerts a considerable influence over identities, motivations and behaviours.

To deal with the plethora of issues that the many and varied factors that influence the coaching process generate, the coach must assume a multitude of roles. Each role, in turn, demands certain knowledges, competencies and skills. For example, according to Martens (1996), not only do coaches need expansive technological know-how of their sport but also the pedagogical skills of a teacher, the counselling wisdom of a psychologist, the training expertise of a physiologist and the administrative leadership of a business executive. Indeed, we have often heard coaches compare themselves to social workers by stating that 'some athletes need an arm round them', or psychologists because they need to 'get inside athletes' heads', or negotiators when issues of athlete contracts, sponsor deals or any conflict-resolution issues need to be addressed. Others have expanded this duty list to include responsibility over the general well-being of athletes (Borrie 1998), the universal management of the coaching process (Lyle 2002), the quality and direction of each athlete's individual sporting experience, in addition to the overall success or failure of team performance (DeMarco *et al.* 1993). This breadth of duty and range of task leads us to question the traditionally assumed boundaries of the coaching role, and how we prepare coaches to fulfil the expectations placed upon them. For example, although we count on coaches to act in emotionally sensitive 'counselling' ways when appropriate, do we give them adequate training to successfully deal with others' intricate personal issues? In general, the answer is no.

Clearly, in a craft that incorporates a multiplicity of social roles, coaches need to be aware of the nuances, fine distinctions and consequences of behaviour, so that they can better achieve desired results. In order to deal with the fundamental nature of their work, Schempp (1998) advocated that coaches should centrally focus on the problems and realities of human interaction above other concerns of content. This would sensitize them to the unique dynamics of the local situation, enable them to act accordingly (Jones 2000) and enhance their social competencies. To improve such competencies, we need to think and move beyond the obvious, and insightfully consider why our 'coaching fortunes' are as they are. The process involves carefully considering the reasons behind the behaviour of ourselves as coaches and the athletes in our care, in the constant search for alternative, improved options.

Recent research (Jones *et al.* 2003; Jones *et al.* 2004; Saury and Durand 1998) has suggested that elite coaches, although not educated to do so, have a tendency to coach contextually. That is, they appear to utilize flexible planning strategies within detailed set routines that permit improvised adaptation to the evolving situation at hand. Such practice is based on the belief that definitive standards can not be applied outright, as they often conflict with other structural constraints within the coaching situation, and are often witnessed in relation to reacting to athletes' particular needs (Saury and Durand 1998). Consequently, in what clearly can be seen as a holistic approach, such coaches were aware of the need to care for their athletes' well-being beyond the sporting arena, and of exercising social competencies to ensure the continuance of positive working relationships (Jones *et al.* 2003, 2004; Saury and Durand 1998). The message here is that coach–athlete relationships need to be carefully nurtured, and be flexible enough to deal with the multiple realities and needs that exist within the coaching process if athletes are going to reach their potential and success is to be achieved. What is more, such relationships should extend far beyond the immediate sports field or gym to encompass the whole person. Current practice then suggests that the coach is much more than a subject-matter specialist and a method applier (Squires 1999), rather he or she is a person with multiple dimensions operating within given structural constraints in a dynamic social environment. From this perspective, coaching is fundamentally about making a myriad of connections between subject, method and other people to overcome the many and varied problems faced.

Despite such a reality, many coach education programmes continue to teach universal course content in a fragmented, sequential form (Gilbert and Trudel 1999). Consequently, coaches learn little of the types of unique problems they will encounter in practice, which are often social and emotive in character. To avoid the oversimplification of a very complex process, and of coaches feeling ill-prepared to deal with the cognitive demands of the role, coach education programmes should engage with, and reflect, the multifaceted, intricate and personal nature of practice. Geertz's (1973) reminder seems particularly apt here, in that there can be no ascent to 'truth' with a descent to individual cases. Indeed, some coaching scholars are now turning to more experiential, subjective, non-linear and hence holistic perspectives of knowledge to guide action, as they have the potential to give a deeper, richer understanding of the totality of coaching (Langley 1997).

CONCEPTUALIZING A HOLISTIC APPROACH

Modern sport, as it is organized and experienced, is essentially a Western phenomenon radiating outwards from the European core (Bale and Sang 1996). Taking its roots into account, it is not surprising that 'sport knowledge' is generally atomized and compartmentalized within a rationalistic discourse, while the deeper emotional and spiritual dimensions are often discounted (see Chapter 13 for a fuller discussion on the rationalistic discourse of sport). Although such knowledge continues to exist as a natural assumption of 'the way it should be' (Paraschak 2000), it is by no means the only way of knowing or of framing experiences in sport. Indeed, we contend that athletes' well-being and performance are linked to their historical, social, cultural, economic, political and environmental circumstance. Underlying this view is the theme of integration, where the divisions between temporal and spiritual, thoughts and feelings, mental and physical are inter-connected and inter-dependent. When applied to coaching, this view reminds us that there is more to it, and subsequent sports performance, than an athlete's biological function or dysfunction. There is also an ecological and caring dimension through which a sense of personal harmony can be achieved.

An example of a holistic philosophy in operation, albeit in relation to health, is that used by the World Health Organisation (WHO). Here, health is defined as involving the 'complete physical, mental and social well-being' of an individual and/or community (Seedhouse 1997: 36). Hence, if aspirations and needs are to be met within contextual constraints, social, physical and mental aspects of lives need to be in balance (Seedhouse 1997). Like most definitions, the WHO interpretation of health is not without its limitations (see Seedhouse 1997). Nonetheless, if coaches wish athletes to realize their full potentialities, it may be a useful framework from which to begin to develop a holistic framework for use in coaching.

A second example of a culturally specific holistic framework, similar to that used by the WHO, is Hauora, a concept of health conceptualized and defined by the Mäori of Aotearoa/New Zealand. Hauora has been explained by Mäori as a holistic philosophy of health that recognizes the integration and connectivity of four critical dimensions; the physical, the mental and emotional, the social and the spiritual. Mäori recognize that all four dimensions are inter-related and need to be in balance if a person is to achieve a sense of well-being. A common metaphor used by Mäori to explain Hauora is the whare tapa wha (the four walls of a house) (Durie 1998). Each wall represents a different dimension (i.e. physical, mental and emotional, social and spiritual) with all four being necessary to ensure strength and symmetry, while the overarching roof represents overall hauora. The four walls are portrayed as a set of inter-connecting and inter-dependent variables, thus promoting an understanding of the links between the human and the environment. Another metaphor used to explain Hauora is te wheke (the octopus), which contains eight, as opposed to four, variables (Pere 1991). Each of the octopus's eight tentacles symbolizes a particular dimension of health, with the body and head representing the whole family or social support unit that oversees them. The tentacles intertwine, indicating the close and dynamic relationship between all of the dimensions (Pere 1991).

While the whare tapa wha and te wheke are useful metaphoric frameworks to develop a holistic approach to coaching in Aotearoa/New Zealand, the challenge for coaches outside of this context is to develop their own culturally specific frameworks. In doing so, coaches need to explicitly acknowledge the relationship that exists between athletes' well-being and performance. In comparison to current conceptualizations of the coaching process, adopting a holistic approach is definitely different.

CHAPTER 16

▼ **COACHING HOLISTICALLY:
A WAY FORWARD FOR
COACH EDUCATION**

- Introduction   181
- A critical task-based approach   183
- A narrative approach   184
- A problem-based learning (PBL) strategy   186
- A mentorship scheme   187
- Concluding thoughts   189

INTRODUCTION

AND FINALLY . . . with greater recognition of the benefits that working in a more holistic manner brings, increased innovation and risk-taking are creeping into coaching practice in the search for methods that deliver such outcomes. These developments, however, remain few and far between, as, although awareness of the value to coach 'in the round' is growing, the knowledge of how to do it remains scant. In this final chapter, we go some way to address this neglect by directly progressing from the abstract conceptual metaphors discussed previously to proposing some definitive principles and subsequent pedagogical strategies through which the goals of coaching holistically can be realized. It reflects our belief that coach education should be located in, or replicate as nearby as possible, the 'swampy lowland of practice' (Schön 1987: 3), as only there can it be tailored to address the thorny questions which equate to its holistic complex reality. Such strategies include the use of critical tasks, narratives, problem-based learning scenarios (PBL) and mentoring schemes. Finally, in view of their direct connection, a conclusion summarizes the basic contentions discussed both in this chapter and the previous one.

A good place to start, in relation to these strategies as with most curriculum development exercises, is with the aims and desired learning outcomes. We therefore need to ask the basic questions of specifically what knowledges and attributes would we like coaches to possess so that they can work in a holistic manner and, more importantly, how can we develop them? Similar to the argument posited by Culpan (2000) in a physical education context, we believe that, in addition to information related to physiology, psychology, human movement and the technical and tactical specifics of particular sports, coaches should also be required to learn about the socio-pedagogical factors associated with sports. In particular, the impact these factors have on (1) athlete self-actualization (which refers to the identity and personal worth of the athlete within the cultural/social context); (2) athlete learning processes (which equate to how individual athletes learn and prefer to learn); and (3) social competencies (which focus on their abilities to develop socially respon-sible behaviours towards the self and others). Some of the other forms of knowledge that we consider useful for a coach to possess are discussed in Chapter 10 on content knowledge.

Having identified the cornerstones of the content knowledge, the next question to be addressed is how to treat and use them within a coach education programme. The emphasis here should be on balance, critical examination and what Burbules (1995) terms 'reasonableness', which, in turn, possesses three interrelated aspects. The first of these is avoiding distorting tendencies by learning to deconstruct socially imposed patterns and allowing informed reason to take their place (Fernandez-Balboa 2000). The second is that of pragmatism. This differs from practicality in that where the latter often contributes to choosing the easier, more comfortable path, pragmatism 'forces us to be sensitive, to deal with uncertainty, to acknowledge our limitations and to be flexible' (Fernandez-Balboa 2000: 139). The third aspect is that of judiciousness, which equates to a capacity for moder-ation, 'even in the exercise of reasonableness itself' (Burbules 1995: 96). This is considered crucial, as it makes the others accountable (Fernandez-Balboa 2000). It also enables us to consider evidence and consequences, and to deal better with paradoxes and contradictions while remaining principled. In other words, it gives us the ability to make judgements 'about whether a given state of affairs is just or not' (Evans and Davies 1993: 23).

Through engaging with coaching knowledge in this way we can better approximate developing the cognitive 'quality of mind' essential for success in a dynamic envi-ronment (Jones 2000; Potrac *et al.* 2000). 'Quality of mind' here equates to certain well-honed 'mind traits' as identified by Fernandez-Balboa (2000) from the work of Paul (1993). These include:

- *Intellectual humility*, which relates to engaging with such self-addressed questions as 'Do I understand why I believe in what I do?' 'Do I have a holistic perspective about what and how I coach?' and 'Do I accept that my views are limited and how they are limited?
- *Intellectual courage*, where further self-confrontational questions could include 'Can I be more open-minded?' 'How do I react when confronted with opposing points of view?' and 'Can I explore ideas with which I usually do not conform?'
- *Intellectual integrity*, where we may wonder 'Are my actions congruent with my declared moral principles?' 'Do I know what my principles are?' 'Are my prin-ciples and hence my coaching methods ill-conceived or inadequately informed?'

THE COACHING CONTEXT

- *Intellectual perseverance*, where we may ask 'Have I invested enough time in reflecting on this aspect of my practice and deciding on what is the right thing to do here?' 'Once I discover a potential danger, do I follow it through by ensuring my athletes' safety?'
- *Intellectual caution*, which refers to the ability to discern false paths and premises. Here, possible self-questions could be 'Do I really know why I coach as I do?' 'Are my methods the result of habit?' 'Can I devise more empowering, holistic methods of coaching?'

Before it can be placed within an education programme, this process of personal and cognitive development needs to be encased within more definitive coaching scenarios for it to have contextual relevance. Furthermore, to remain true to the holistic definition given at the beginning of the previous chapter, it needs to be delivered in an integrated, as opposed to a compartmentalized, manner. Four ways in which this may occur are through the use of critical tasks, narratives, problem-based learning (PBL) and a mentorship scheme.

A CRITICAL TASK-BASED APPROACH

As presented here, a critical task-based approach has been adapted from the work of Kirk (2000). Central to it is the notion of caring for, and about, the needs of athletes, with the term signalling an attempt to actively engage coaches in their learning. Learning is also viewed as being situated and multidimensional in that 'individuals typically learn more than one thing at a time' (Kirk 2000: 204). The coach educator's role within the task-based approach is that of facilitator. His or her principal duty is to structure the learning environment in ways that encourage and assist coaches to acquire the needed information, skills and understanding. This can be done in a number of ways, including conducting a situation analysis, continuously setting progressively challenging and interesting tasks, using and discussing a range of pedagogical styles, providing a positive and supportive learning environment, and giving timely, detailed and appropriate feedback on student progress (Kirk 2000). For example, coaches can be given written tasks that require them to extract information from a range of relevant sources, including video, written texts or tutor explanations, thus acknowledging that individuals learn in different ways. In common with the other strategies discussed below, the approach is informed by the belief that students (in this case coaches) will develop a better understanding of concepts and information if they seek out the materials for themselves as opposed to being given them (Kirk 2000). It also allows the coaches to work at their own pace, acknowledging that on any given course there will be a range of capability levels. Further, it recognizes experience as a resource to be used to make sense of new information (Kirk 2000). While a degree of discomfort among the coaches is inevitable and perhaps desirable when using a task-based approach, a function of the facilitator is not to allow the discomfort to degenerate into defensive or dismissive responses (Kirk 2000).

A possible topic for a task could relate to the nature of power within coaching. With regard to the structure of the exercise, coaches would initially be required to read a number of texts both supporting and opposing a power-dominated leadership style and to note the key issues raised. This is intended to act as a 'primer' (Kirk 2000) for discussing such questions as

> *Should the coach–athlete relationship inherently be a power-dominated one? Justify your answer.*

The coaches would be encouraged to respond and justify their answers in light of the texts and of their experiences, noting the nature of the discussion and the points made. They would then view two contrasting video clips of top team-sport coaches in 'action'. Both clips depict coaches addressing their players in the dressing room before and after games. One coach is seen as chastising, yelling and verbally abusing his or her players, while the other talks in a calm and measured manner. Students would then be asked to consider the merits and drawbacks of each approach, and of their effects on the players and the ongoing coach–athlete relationship. The discussion could be given direction through the posing of key focus questions, for example:

- To what extent is the hierarchical nature of the coach–athlete relationship problematical?
- Where does the power lie in this relationship?
- How is the power exercised and what are the consequences (for both parties) of using it?
- How do such behaviours influence the creation of a learning environment?

The video clips and questions are aimed at challenging the coaches' personal perceptions of such issues as leadership, communication, philosophy, appropriate behaviour, coaching knowledge, pedagogy and the nature of the coach–athlete relationship. Hence, they are expected to draw together many aspects of practice into an integrated and holistic examination of the coaching role. The assessment could be either based on a verbal presentation or a piece of written work (or both) depending on the stated learning outcomes. Finally, an opportunity to follow up and discuss adopted initiatives should be built into subsequent sessions.

A NARRATIVE APPROACH

Narrative is a pervasive mode of organizing human experience that draws upon a variety of data sources to understand the individual (Connelly and Clandinin 1990). Hence, it would appear a very appropriate strategy to draw on, develop and represent holistic knowledge. It can be looked upon as a 'universal form of knowing the world' (Langley 1997: 149), as not only do the narrative 'tales' produced resonate with contextual lived experience and inner sense-making, but they can also facilitate reader understanding and engagement (Denison and Rinehart 2000). Such stories then, have the potential to capture, perhaps more than scientific formulae ever can, the richness and imprecision of the coaching experience, and our under-standing of what coaching is (Carter 1993; Jones *et al.* 2003; Jones *et al.* 2004). They are able to do so as they are more-than-often typified by a framework involving a set of characters, a situation involving a dilemma or struggle, events which attempt to resolve the conflict, and the temporal relationship between them (Langley 1997). Through such a framework, experience and how to deal with complex problems (as frequently witnessed in coaching) are organized into a coherent whole. Consequently, the narrative approach is able to link personal to much wider cultural and social issues through getting coaches to reflect on what they know, why they know it and how they use that knowledge in practical settings to achieve desired ends. This potential to develop connections between knowledge and action is a particularly useful quality (Langley 1997). The learning that takes place then is both personal and holistic, as it takes account of individuals' complex and unique circumstances and what makes them what they are.

Regarding the use of narratives on coach education programmes, coaches could first write and then deconstruct their own narratives in relation to particular issues; for example, the nature of the coach–athlete relationship. Such a process would highlight the interconnected and holistic nature of the coaching process, focusing on the many factors that influence the relationship and how individual coaches try to best manage them. These could include the use of power and empowerment, interpersonal skills, leadership, organization, pedagogy, motivation, cohesion and athlete expectations, among others. Focus questions around which such narratives could be constructed include:

- Which issues in the coach–athlete relationship do you consider significant, and how do you think they are connected, if at all?
- How has your personal biography influenced the way you coach and why?
- What are the contextual constraints on coaching practice, and how do they affect the way that you coach?
- What knowledges are vital for a coach to have, and why? Where do you get these knowledges?

The coaches could then be given a set of readings related to contextual influences on practice, and asked to further identify, through the production of a second written piece, with the issues raised. This would solidify the relationship between the social and the personal in getting coaches to better reflect upon and understand why they coach as they do. Once limitations have been identified, options of 'how to do it better' could be examined. Finally, these, if implemented, could be discussed and shared at subsequent follow-up sessions. Again, the role of the coach educator is one of facilitator, to assist coaches explore and express, both orally and through the written word, their subjective realities in a structured manner. It is also to highlight the multi- and inter-dimensionality of coaching, and to suggest ways of how eventual declarations and insights can be directly useful to practice.

A PROBLEM-BASED LEARNING (PBL) STRATEGY

Within a PBL framework, the 'curriculum' would be constructed around a set of carefully designed coaching issues or scenarios. The aim is to develop an integrated and holistic knowledge base in coaches founded on real-life problems that are typically cluttered and multidimensional. This would demand that coaches construct personal solutions drawn from a variety of sources. The strategy also requires them to take an active part in planning, organizing and conducting their own learning. Once the problem is set, coaches would typically engage with the knowledge they need to solve it, before applying a solution. Consequently, a PBL strategy aims to encourage and develop coaches' creativity and problem-solving cognitive skills by engaging them in challenging learning activities.

Within the wider PBL concept, there are many possible approaches or methods that could be adopted, ranging from the more prescriptive to the facilitative (Barrows 1986). A starting point, as suggested earlier in relation to all these strategies, could be to decide on the objectives in terms of what coach educators want coaches to learn. For example, and borrowing from the work of Bridges and Hallinger (1996) in leadership, if it is believed that the essence of coaching has much to do with 'improving performance through realizing the potential of others', the objectives would derive from this. Hence, they could emphasize the development of skills related to facilitating group problem-solving, communicating ideas, dealing with conflict, implementing solutions to identified problems and motivating the individual within the collective. More specifically, it is the precise problem that drives choices in relation to the content investigated towards its proposed solution. Such problems could involve a forthright and disruptive group of parents; inheriting a team created by, and still loyal to, a sacked predecessor; coaching a team with opinionated veteran players, and dealing with discipline and relationship breakdown, to name but a few. The problems could be presented in a number of forms, including highly contextualized written cases, via videotape or role play (Bridges and Hallinger 1996). However, they should always be bound by a time frame and have an end product (e.g. a written declaration or document about how the problem could be tackled). This provides a focus for the problem's solution and how to reach it, both of which should relate to the learning aims. Additionally, a number of unannounced interruptions can be built into the larger problem that demand immediate attention, to be solved within a given time limit of their own. This combination of general set problems, allied to on-the-spot surprises, mirrors several characteristics of coaching practice; that is, 'unpredictability, ambiguity and working on several problems at once' (Bridges and Hallinger 1996: 56).

The knowledge needed to address each PBL scenario would be drawn from relevant disciplines and the individual craft knowledge of the coaches, upon which they are encouraged to reflect. It can be gathered through a number of means, for example, set readings, class discussions and personal reflections. The content unearthed is meant to provide insight into the problem and its solution. For example, as coaches work through the conflict-resolution issue with athletes' parents, they learn about

THE COACHING CONTEXT

the legal aspects and the extent to which they can discipline athletes, the need to develop and appropriately publicize a functional coaching philosophy, the theory of how to 'diffuse' a potentially difficult situation, and current research related to constructively channelling aggression and of (re)integrating the individual into the team. This interdisciplinary approach mirrors the way that knowledge application occurs in the workplace, thus highlighting its relevance for a reality-based holistic coach education programme.

With regard to the teaching process, it can be done in a number of ways. For instance, coaches could be arranged into groups, within which they organize themselves into the separate but rotating roles of leader, recorder, researcher and so on. Initial reading lists could be provided, but only as guides, thus encouraging the coaches to research independently and creatively for solutions. The unannounced interruptions would take place when all the coaches are together, and would be required to be addressed immediately within a given time frame of, for example, thirty minutes. Discussion, reflection upon experience and researched knowledge provide the basis for the reasoning here. Similar to the earlier examples discussed, the role of the tutor is that of initial organizer and facilitator, with his or her behaviour being driven by the objective of allowing the coaches to manage as much of the problem-solving process as possible.

A MENTORSHIP SCHEME

A final method to be discussed in relation to delivering a holistic coach education programme is that of mentoring. Although many in the field agree on its value, mentoring, in the coaching context at least, seems to lack a clear conceptual definition (Bloom *et al.* 1998). According to Alleman *et al.* (1984: 327) mentoring refers to a 'relationship in which a person of greater rank, experience or expertise teaches, guides and develops a novice in a profession'. Similarly, Merriam (1983) defines a mentor as a supporter, counsel and guide to a protégé, while for Fletcher (2000) mentoring is synonymous with guiding and supporting a trainee through difficult transitions. Although these are only three amongst many, we would like to emphasize the common 'guidance' function which dovetails with the belief that real development in terms of professional expertise can not come from cloning but through reflection on interaction, researched knowledge and practice (Fletcher 2000). Mentoring then involves doing something *with* as opposed *to* a trainee; it is seen as an investment in the total personal growth of the individual. It is also, by nature, heavily contextualized, and therefore takes Schön's (1987) call to work in the 'swamp of practice' further than the previous suggestions of holistic pedagogical strategies. In this respect, it has increased potential relevance for coaches. Indeed, when carried out in a considered and formal manner, coaches could view it as a crucial means of professional development (Bloom *et al.* 1995; Bloom *et al.* 1998). However, recent research has indicated that mentoring is already very much in operation within coaching, without much success (Cushion 2001). This is because in its current unstructured and uncritical form it only serves to reproduce the existing coaching culture and practice (Cushion 2001). The key here then, as with all the concepts discussed in this book, is to reflect and engage with the process at critical, as well as practical and technical, levels.

The challenge within mentoring is not to ignore, or play down, the personal knowledge and experience of the trainee (or perceived lack of it) but to elevate and build upon it (Snow 2001). By doing this, coaches are given the opportunity to integrate information 'relevant to crystallizing their own philosophies and unique coaching styles' (Bloom *et al.* 1998: 278). Such a strategy is based on the need to situate coaches' learning in practical experience within a supportive framework. It would also enable coach education to get its 'hands dirty' by extending its thinking into practice. Thus, coach education programmes should include supervised field experiences, in a variety of contexts, to enable coaches to consider differences, make mistakes, learn from them and try again. This would provide coaches with multiple opportunities to test and refine knowledge and skills, make coaching judgements that are situationally meaningful, and understand the pragmatic constraints of coaching contexts (Cushion *et al.* 2003).

Although we have stated that the process is akin to guiding, the role of the mentor needs further clarification. According to Fletcher (2000) the mentor's remit is substantial and should extend into:

- exploring the personal dimensions and related anxieties of the novice in beginning a new post;
- assisting with integrating the coach into the club or institution;
- providing guidance in relation to where helpful coaching resources can be gleaned;
- assisting with the preparation and delivery of coaching sessions;
- guiding the coach's practical coaching and indicating alternative appropriate strategies within a supportive framework.

Although the above list could well appear on a mentor's job description, for a full appreciation of the depth of engagement needed to be successful, a more critical stance needs to be taken. For example, we believe that a mentor should empathize with the coach as the latter experiences the various stages of professional development, namely 'early idealism', 'personal survival', 'hitting the plateau', and finally 'moving on' (Furlong and Maynard 1995). He or she should also systematically challenge novice coaches as they progress through these stages with the intention of encouraging them to constantly evaluate their understanding of the coaching role and their performance within it (Fletcher 2000). What is key here is the posing of insightful open-ended exploratory questions by the mentor to de-mystify the coaching process, thus supplying coaches with the confidence that they can survive and thrive in a complex environment. The value of mentoring then involves considerably more than merely passing on 'survival tips' or 'the tricks of the trade' or even caring about coaches' well-being. Rather, its promise lies in 'its capacity to foster an inquiring stance' (Field and Field 1994: 67), which has the potential to inform insightful learning, particularly in relation to under-standing the holistic and complex nature of coaching.

CONCLUDING THOUGHTS

In many ways, the final two chapters, which are inherently interlinked, could be viewed as encapsulating the primary message of the book. They contain the summarized case for coaching holistically, calling for the inclusion of sociological and pedagogical principles within more reality-based coach education programmes as a means of realizing such a practice. The argument is based on the premise that we should coach with the contextual totality of humans in mind if athletic potential is to be fully realized (Rothig 1985). The penultimate chapter contains examples of frameworks within which a holistic approach to coaching could be located, whilst the final chapter contains some examples of pedagogical strategies through which a holistic coach education programme could be realized. The strategies are underpinned by the belief that it would be useful for coaches to consider and synthesize all their knowledge sources and to rationalize their actions; to help them to 'see beyond the obvious' and to think critically about their practice. The aim is to get coaches to think cognitively and creatively about alternative ways to coach, thus pushing back the boundaries of both coaching theory and practice. It is important to note that these only comprise a limited number of ways in which a holistic approach could be delivered, none of which are without their unique contradictions and problems. Despite their shortcomings however, we believe that getting coaches to coach holistically through imaginative and innovative professional preparation programmes holds the key for future excellence in coaching.

▼ END OF SECTION FOUR: TASKS

TASK 1

The aim of this exercise is to explore the responsibility coaches have to act in ethical ways, and to consider how they can do so better. Address the following questions:

1   Why do you think that parents trust coaches so much that they leave their children with them?
2   How are coaches qualified to have earned that trust?
3   What are the virtues of a good coach? Why did you identify these particular virtues?
4   How could the virtues be practised so that they can be improved?

Consider how your responses to the above questions relate to the consequences of any action or inaction. Additionally, discuss how they relate to what you consider to be your ethical 'conduct guide'. Finally, debate how to accommodate apparently contradictory ethical behaviour with stated conduct goals, and if such a 'contradiction' is ethical in itself.

TASK 2

To complete the following task select one coach to observe. To make the task more meaningful it would be useful if the coach was involved in a sport or activity in which you are involved. Preferably the coach will be working with more than one athlete. You MUST ask their permission to observe them. Analyse the language the coach uses by addressing the following questions:

1   What terms does the coach commonly use when providing instruction? Why do you think this is?
2   How do you think this makes athletes feel, and what do you think it says about the way the coach feels about the athletes?
3   How do you think the coach could better involve athletes' internal knowledge, feelings and experiences about their respective performances?

4   How do you think the coach could get athletes to meaningfully articulate their feelings about their own performances? Illustrate a possible line of questioning here.
5   What are the implications for coaches changing the language they use when coaching with regard to the relationship they have with athletes? How should they deal with the consequences of such a change?

TASK 3

To answer the following questions you are required to draw on a sporting context with which you are familiar. If you are not currently being coached, or hold a coaching position, reflect back to when you were in either of these situations. The process of answering the questions will provide insight into how holistic the coaching practices are or were.

1   How well do you think the coach knows his or her athletes? (e.g. do you think they are aware of athletes' respective family backgrounds?) Justify your answer.
2   How comfortable do you think the coach is when dealing with athletes' emotional or social issues? Justify your answer.
3   How could the coach be supported to handle athletes' social and emotional issues? Justify why you think the coach should, or should not, have to deal with the issues.
4   How do you think a coach can reconcile player independence within a team structure? Should he or she formulate a strategy to do so? Why, or why not?
5   What are the boundaries of the coaching role? Justify your answer.

TASK 4

You are a coach who has just taken over a school basketball team of 16–17-year-old boys. They possess a reputation for aggressive on-court conduct, which has begun to spill into their off-court behaviour. Consequently, complaints from both staff and other students in the school have increased. It is a situation that has become known to the school's governors. As the current coach, you have been asked by the Principal of the school to produce a fully referenced report detailing what you consider to be the principal causes of such behaviour and, more importantly, how you will deal with them. The report is to be presented at a forthcoming meeting with the governors.

Whilst working out how to address this wider problem, you are faced by a number of unforeseen interruptions which demand your immediate attention. Each of the following interruptions requires a written or verbal response, with every subsequent action being justified:

Interruption A

Two players are sent to your office for fighting during a training session which was being taken by an inexperienced assistant. You have a limited amount of time to ascertain what happened, why it happened, and decide what to do about it.

You need to understand the issues at stake and ask questions so that you can: understand the underlying cause of the fight; decide upon the punishment to be given (if any); and decide upon a relevant course of action for the rest of the team and coaching staff.

Interruption B

The parents of the two players disciplined believe that the punishment is too harsh and are demanding that a reprimand is all that is needed. Their manner is bordering on aggressive.

Interruption C

The Principal of the school becomes involved in 'trying to smooth things over'. He doesn't really like the basketball programme anyway and certainly doesn't want any negative publicity for the school. He questions the value of the programme for the school, and the players involved, if fighting is the result.

▼ BIBLIOGRAPHY

Adams, R., Turns, J. and Atman, C. (2003) 'Educating effective engineering designers: the role of reflective practice', *Design Studies*, 24(3): 275–294.

Alleman, E., Cochran, J., Doverspike, J. and Newman, I. (1984) 'Enriching mentoring relationships', *The Personnel and Guidance Journal*, 62: 329–332.

Allen, J. and Howe, B. (1998) 'Player ability, coach feedback, and female adolescent athletes' perceived competence and satisfaction', *Journal of Sport and Exercise Psychology*, 20(3): 280–299.

Alvesson, M. and Willmott, H. (1996) *Making Sense of Management: A Critical Analysis*, London: Sage.

Amorose, A. and Weiss, M. (1998) 'Coaching feedback as a source of information about perceptions of ability: a developmental examination', *Journal of Sport and Exercise Psychology*, 20(4): 395–420.

Anderson, A. (1994) 'How constructivism and behaviourism can complement each other in the preparation of physical education professionals', *CAHPERD Journal*, Fall: 13–18.

Apple, M.W. (1979) *Ideology and Curriculum*, London: Routledge & Kegan Paul.

Aries, P. (1962) *Centuries of Childhood: A Social History of Family Life*, London: Johnathan Cape.

Armour, K. and Fernandez-Balboa, J.M. (2000) 'Connections, pedagogy, and professional learning', paper presented at CEDAR 8th International Conference, University of Warwick.

Armour, K.M. and Jones, R.L. (2000) 'The practical heart within: the value of sociology of sport', in R.L. Jones and K.M. Armour (eds) *The Sociology of Sport: Theory and Practice*, London: Addison Wesley Longman.

Australian Film Institute Distribution Ltd (year unknown) *Kick to Kick*, (video recording), Melbourne.

Baker, B. (2001) 'Moving on (part 2): power and the child in curriculum history', *Journal of Curriculum Studies*, 33: 277–302.

Bale, J. and Sang, J. (1996) *Kenyan Running: Movement Culture, Geography and Global Change*, London: Frank Cass.

Ball, S.J. (1990) *Politics and Policy-Making in Education: Explorations in Policy Sociology*, London: Routledge.

Ballard, K. (1993) 'A socio-political perspective on disability: research and institutional disabilism', *New Zealand Journal of Educational Studies*, 28: 89–104.

Barnes, C. (1990) *Cabbage Syndrome: The Social Construction of Dependence*, Basingstoke: Falmer Press.

Barrows, H.S. (1986) 'A taxonomy of problem-based learning methods', *Medical Education*, 20: 481–486.

Bean, D. (1976) 'Coaching grid: a simple way to increase effectiveness in teaching games', *HPECR runner* 14 (3): 16–20.

Bengtsson, J. (1995) 'What is reflection? On reflection in the teaching profession and teacher education', *Teachers and teaching: Theory and Practice,* 1 (1): 23–32.

Benson, R. and Taub, D. (1993) 'Using the PRECEDE model for causal analysis of bulimic tendencies among elite women swimmers', *Journal of Health Education,* 24(6): 360–368.

Bergmann Drewe, S. (2000) 'An examiniation of the relationship between coaching and teaching', *Quest,* 52: 79–88.

Birrell, S. and Cole, C. (1994) *Women, Sport and Culture.* Champaign, IL: Human Kinetics.

Blasi, A. and Oresick, R. (1987) 'Self-inconsistency and the development of self', in P. Young-Nisdendrafth and J. Hall (eds) *The Book of the Self: Person, Pretext and Process,* New York: University Press.

Bloom, G.A., Salmela, J.H. and Schinke, R.J. (1995) 'Expert coaches' views on the training of developing coaches', in R. Vanfraechem-Raway and Y. Vanden Auweele (eds) *Proceedings of the Ninth European Congress on Sport Psychology,* Brussels: Free University of Brussels.

Bloom, G.A., Durand-Bush, N., Schinke, R.J. and Salmela, J.H. (1998) 'The importance of mentoring in the development of coaches and athletes', *International Journal of Sport Psychology,* 29: 267–281.

Borrie, A. (1998) 'Coaching: art or science?', *Insight,* 1(1): 5.

Bourdieu, P. (1977) *Outline of a Theory of Practice,* London: Cambridge University Press.

Bradley, H. (1997) *Fractured Identities: Changing Patterns of Inequality,* Cambridge: Polity Press.

Brettschneider, W.-D. and Heim, R. (1997) 'Identity, sport, and youth development', in K. Fox (ed.) *The Physical Self: From Motivation to Well Being,* Champaign, IL: Human Kinetics.

Bridges, E.M. and Hallinger, P. (1996) 'Problem-based learning in leadership education', in L. Wilkerson and W.H. Gijselaers (eds) *Bringing Problem-based Learning to Higher Education Theory and Practice,* San Francisco: Jossey-Bass.

Bromley, R. (1995) 'Richard Hoggart: the real world of people: illustrations from popular art – Peg's paper', in J. Munns and G. Rajan (eds) *A Cultural Studies Reader: History, Theory and Practice,* London: Longman.

Broughton, J. (ed.) (1987) *Critical Theories of Psychological Development,* New York: Plenum.

Brustad, R.J. and Weiss, M.R. (1992) 'Psychological dimensions of children's physical activity: theoretical and measurement issues', paper presented at the meeting of the Association for the Advancement of Applied Sport Psychology, Colorado Springs, CO.

Buck, R. (2003) 'Teachers and dance in the classroom: "So, do I need my tutu?"', unpublished doctoral thesis, University of Otago.

Bump, L. (1987) *Coaching Young Athletes,* (video recording), Champaign, IL: Human Kinetics.

Bunker, D. and Thorpe, R. (1982) 'A model for the teaching of games in secondary schools', *Bulletin of Physical Education,* 18 (1): 5–8.

Burbules, N.C. (1995) 'Reasonable doubt: toward a post-modern defence of reason as an educational aim', in W. Kholi (ed.) *Critical Conversations in Philosophy of Education,* New York: Routledge.

Burman, E. (1991) 'Power, gender and developmental psychology', *Feminism & Psychology,* 1: 141–153.

Burman, E. (1994) *Deconstructing Developmental Psychology*, London: Routledge.

Burrows, L. (2002) 'Constructing the child: developmental discourses in school physical education', *New Zealand Journal of Educational Studies.* 37(2):127–140.

Burrows, L. and Wright, J. (2003) 'The discursive production of childhood, identity and health', in J. Evans, B. Davies and J. Wright (eds) *Body, Knowledge and Control: Studies in the Sociology of Education and Physical Culture*, London: Routledge.

Burt, J.J. (1998) 'The role of kinesiology in elevating modern society', *Quest*, 50: 80–95.

Butler, J. (1997) 'How would Socrates teach games? A constructivist approach', *JOPERD*, 68(9): 42–47.

Byrne, T. (1999) 'Sport: it's a family affair', in M. Lee (ed.), *Coaching Children in Sport: Principles and Practice*, London: Routledge.

Carlson, N. and Buskist, W. (1997) *Psychology. The Science of Behavior*, London: Allyn & Bacon.

Carr, D. (1998) 'What moral educational significance has physical education? A question in need of disambiguation', in M. McNamee and J. Parry (eds) *Ethics and Sport*, London: E & FN Spon.

Carr, W. (ed.) (1989) *Quality in Teaching: Arguments for a Reflective Profession*, London: Falmer Press.

Carter, K. (1993) 'The place of story in the study of teaching and teacher education', *Educational Researcher*, 22: 5–12, 18.

Cassidy, T. (2000) 'Investigating the pedagogical process in physical education teacher education', unpublished doctoral dissertation, Deakin University, Australia.

Cassidy, T. (2002) [Comparative book review] Tinning, R., Macdonald, D., Wright, J. and Hickey, C. (2002) *Becoming A Physical Education Teacher: Contemporary and Enduring Issues*, Frenchs Forest, Australia: Pearson Education, 2001 and Siedentop, D. and Tannehill, D. *Developing Teaching Skills in Physical Education*, 4th edn, Mountain View, CA: Mayfield 2000. *International Sports Studies* 23(1): 90–93.

Cassidy, T. and Tinning, R. (2004) '"Slippage" is not a dirty word: considering the usefulness of Giddens' notion of knowledgeability in understanding the possibilities for teacher education', *Journal of Teaching Education* 15(2): 175–188.

Cazden, C. (1988) *Classroom Discourse: The Language of Teaching and Learning*, Portsmouth, NH: Heinemann.

Chapman, G.E. (1997) 'Making weight: lightweight rowing, technologies of power and technologies of the self', *Sociology of Sport Journal*, 14: 205–223.

Chappell, A. (1992) 'Towards a sociological critique of the normalisation principle', *Disability, Handicap and Society*, 7: 35–50.

Cheffers, J. (1997) 'No man is an island', *AIESEP Conference Proceedings*, Singapore, p. 4.

Chen, W. and Rovegno, I. (2000) 'Examination of expert and novice teachers' constructivist-oriented teaching practices using a movement approach to elementary physical education', *Research Quarterly of Exercise and Sport*, 71(4): 357–372.

Cherryholmes, C. (1988) *Power and Criticism: Post-structural Investigations in Education*, New York: Teachers' College.

Choi, P. (2000) *Femininity and the Physically Active Woman*, London: Routledge.

Christina, R. and Corcos, D. (1988) *Coaches' Guide to Teaching Sport Skills*, Champaign, IL: Human Kinetics.

Chu, D. (1984) 'Teacher/coach orientation and role socialization: a description and explanation', *Journal of Teaching in Physical Education*, 3(2): 308.

Clews, G. and Gross, J. (1995) 'Individual and social motivation in Australian sport', in

T. Morris and J. Summers (eds), *Sport Psychology: Theory, Application and Issues*, Queensland: Jacaranda Wiley.

Coakley, J. (1998) *Sport in Society: Issues and Controversies* 6th edn, Dubuque, IA: McGraw-Hill.

Coakley, J. (2001) *Sport in Society: Issues and Controversies* 7th edn, Dubuque, IA: McGraw-Hill.

Cochran, K.F., DeRuiter, J.A. and King, R.A. (1993) 'Pedagogical content knowing: an integrated model for teacher preparation', *Journal of Teacher Education*, 44(4): 263–272.

Cole, C. (1998) 'Addiction, exercise and cyborgs: technologies of deviant bodies', in G. Rail (ed.) *Sport and Post-Modern Times*, Albany, NY: State University of New York Press.

Collins (1992) *Concise English Dictionary*, London: HarperCollins.

Collins (2003) *Pocket Dictionary and Thesaurus*, London: HarperCollins.

Connell, R. (1985) *Teachers' Work*, London: Allen & Unwin.

Connell, R. (1995) *Masculinities*, Sydney: Allen & Unwin.

Connelly, M. and Clandinin, D. (1990) 'Stories of experience and narrative inquiry', *Educational Researcher*, 19: 2–14.

Côté, J., Salmela, J., Trudel, P., Baria, A. and Russell, S. (1995) 'The coaching model: a grounded assessment of expert gymnastic coaches' knowledge', *Journal of Sport and Exercise Psychology*, 17(1): 1–17.

Côté, J., Yardley, J., Hay, J., Sedgwick, W. and Baker, J. (1999) 'An exploratory examination of the coaching behaviour scale for sport', *Avante*, 5(2): 82–92.

Cross, N. and Lyle, J. (eds) (1999) *The Coaching Process: Principles and Practice for Sport*, Oxford: Butterworth-Heinemann

Crum, B. (1995) 'The urgent need for reflective teaching in Physical Education', in C. Pare (ed.) *Training of Teachers in Reflective Practice of Physical Education*, Trois-Rivieres, Quebec: Université du Quebec a Trois-Rivieres.

Crum, B. (1996) 'In search of the perspectives' paradigmatical identities: general comparison and final commentary', unpublished manuscript, Tilburg University, Netherlands.

Culpan, I. (2000) 'Getting what you got: harnessing the potential', *Journal of Physical Education New Zealand*, 33: 22–36.

Cunningham, G., Keiper, P., Sagas, M. and Ashley, F. (2001) 'Initial reliability of the coaching isomorphism questionnaire for NCCA coaches', *Psychological Reports*, 88(2): 332–334.

Cushion, C. (2001) 'The coaching process in professional youth football: an ethnography of practice', unpublished doctoral thesis, Brunel University, UK.

Cushion, C. and Jones, R. (2001) 'A systematic observation of professional top-level youth soccer coaches', *Journal of Sport Behavior*, 24(4): 354–376.

Cushion, C., Armour, K.M. and Jones, R.L. (2003) 'Coach education and continuing professional development: experience and learning to coach', *Quest*, 55: 215–230.

Davis, L.J. (1995) *Enforcing Normalcy: Disability, Deafness, and the Body*, London: Verso.

Deci, E.L. and Ryan, R.M. (1985) *Intrinsic Motivation and Self Determinism in Human Behaviour*, New Jersey: Plenum.

DeMarco, G., Mancini, V. and West, D. (1993) 'Self-assessment and modification of coaching behaviour', paper presented at the meeting of the International University Sports Federation, Buffalo, NY.

DeMarco, G., Mancini, V. and West, D. (1997) 'Reflections on change: a qualitative analysis of a baseball coach's behaviour', *Journal of Sport Behavior*, 20(2): 135–163.

Denison, J. and Rinehart, R. (2000) 'Introduction: imagining sociological narratives', *Sociology of Sport Journal*, 17: 1–4.

DePauw, K. (2000) 'Social-cultural context of disability: implications for scientific inquiry and professional preparation', *Quest*, 52: 358–368.

DePauw, K. and Doll-Tepper, G. (2000) 'Toward progressive inclusion and acceptance: myth or reality', *Adapted Physical Activity Quarterly*, 17: 135–142.

DePauw, K. and Gavron, S. (1995) *Disability and sport*, Champaign, IL: Human Kinetics.

Dewey, J. (1910) *How We Think*, Boston: Heath.

Dewey, J. (1916) *Democracy and Education: An Introduction to the Philosophy of Education*, New York: Macmillan.

Dewey, J. (1966) *Selected Educational Writings*, London: Heinemann.

Diessner, R. and Simmons, S. (2000) *Notable Selections in Educational Psychology*, Connecticut: McGraw-Hill.

Dodds, P. (1985) 'Are hunters of the functional curriculum seeking quarks or snarks?', *Journal of Teaching in Physical Education*, 4: 91–99.

Dodds, P. (1993) 'Removing the ugly "isms" in your gym: thoughts for teachers on equity', in J. Evans (ed.) *Equality, Education and Physical Education*, London: Falmer Press.

Douge, B. and Hastie, P. (1993) 'Coach effectiveness', *Sport Science Review*, 2: 14–29.

Downs, P. (1995) *Willing and Able: An Introduction to Inclusive Practices*, Canberra: The Australian Sports Commission.

Doyle, W. (1992) 'Curriculum and pedagogy', in P. Jackson (ed.) *Handbook of Research on Curriculum*, New York: Macmillan.

Duda, J. (1993) 'Goals: a study of social-cognitive approaches to the study of achievement motivation in sport', in R. Singer, M. Murphey and L. Tennant (eds), *Handbook of Research on Sport Psychology*, New York: Macmillan.

Duda, J. and Treasure, D. (2001) 'Toward optimal motivation in sport: fostering athletes' competence and sense of control', in J. Williams (ed.), *Applied Sport Psychology: Personal Growth to Peak Performance*, 4th edn, Mountain View, CA: Mayfield.

Durie, M. (1998) *Whaiora: Māori Health Development*, Oxford: Oxford University Press.

Eckert, P. (1989) *Jocks and Burnouts: Social Categories and Identity in the High School*, New York: Teachers College Press.

Eraut, M. (1995) 'Schön shock: a case for reframing reflection-in-action?', *Teachers and Teaching: Theory and Practice*, 1(1): 9–22.

Eskes, T.B., Duncan, C.M. and Miller, M.M. (1998) 'The discourse of empowerment: Foucault, Marcuse and the women's fitness texts', *Journal of Sport and Social Issues*, 18: 48–55.

Evans, J. (1992) 'A short paper about people, power and educational reform. Authority and representation in ethnographic research. Subjectivity, ideology and educational reform: the case of physical education', in A. Sparkes (ed.) *Research in Physical Education and Sport: Exploring Alternative Visions*, London: Falmer.

Evans, J. and Davies, B. (1993) 'Equality, equity and physical education', in J. Evans (ed.) *Equality, Education and Physical Education*, London: Falmer Press.

Evans, J. and Roberts, G. (1987) 'Physical competence and the development of children's peer relationships', *Quest*, 39, 23–35.

Fairs, J. (1987) 'The coaching process: essence of coaching', *Sports Coach*, 1(1): 9.

Fasting, K. (1997) 'Sexual stereotypes in sport: experiences of female soccer players', *Play the Game*. Available at: http://www.play-the-game.org/articles/1997/culture/sexual.html

Faulkener, G. and Finlay, S.J. (2002) 'It's not what you say, it's the way you say it!

Conversation analysis: a discursive methodology for sport, exercise and physical education', *Quest*, 54: 49–66.

Fernandez-Balboa, J.-M. (2000) 'Discrimination: what do we know and what can we do about it?', in R.L. Jones and K.M. Armour (eds) *Sociology of Sport: Theory and Practice*, London: Longman.

Field B. and Field, T. (eds) (1994) *Teachers as Mentors: A Practical Guide*, London: Falmer Press.

Figone, A. (2001) 'The historical evolution of the teacher-coach dual roles: time for a new model, *CAHPER Journal California*, 63(6): 20–22.

Finch, L. (2002) 'Understanding individual motivation in sport', in. J. Silva III and D. Stevens (eds), *Psychological Foundations of Sport*, Boston: Allyn & Bacon.

Fine, M. and Asch, A. (1988) 'Disability beyond stigma: social interaction, discrimination, and activism', *Journal of Social Issues*, 44: 3–21.

First Steps (1996) Issue No. 15, p. 4.

Fleming, N. (1991) 'Sport, schooling and Asian male youth culture', in G. Jarvie (ed.) *Sport, Racism, and Ethnicity*, London: Falmer Press.

Fletcher, S. (2000) *Mentoring in Schools: A Handbook of Good Practice*, London: Kogan Page.

Fortanasce, V., Robinson, L. and Ouellete, J. (2001) *The Official American Youth Soccer Organization Handbook: Rules, Regulations, Skills and Everything Else Kids, Parents and Coaches Need to Participate in Youth Soccer*, American Youth Soccer Organization.

Foucault, M. (1972) *The Archeology of Knowledge*, trans. A. Sheridan, New York: Random House.

Foucault, M. (1977) *Discipline and Punish: The Birth of the Prison*, New York: Pantheon Books.

Franklin, S. (1996) 'Postmodern body techniques: some anthropological considerations in natural and post-natural bodies', *Journal of Sport and Exercise Psychology*, 18: 95–106.

Friedrichsen, F. (1956) *Study of the Effectiveness of Loop Films as Instructional Aids in Teaching Gymnastic Stunts*, Eugene, OR: University of Oregon.

Furlong, J. and Maynard, T. (1995) *Mentoring Student Teachers*, Routledge: London.

Geddis, A. and Wood, E. (1997) 'Transforming subject matter and managing dilemmas: a case study in teacher education', *Teaching and Teacher Education*, 13(6): 611–626.

Geertz, C. (1973) *The Interpretation of Cultures*, New York: Basic Books.

George, L. and Kirk, D. (1988) 'The limits of change in physical education: ideologies, teachers and the experience of physical activity', in J. Evans (ed.) *Teachers, Teaching and Control in Physical Education*, Lewes: Falmer Press.

Giddens, A. (1979) *Central Problems in Social Theory: Action Structure and Contradiction in Social Analysis*, London: Macmillan.

Giddens, A. (1984) *The Constitution of Society: Outline of a Theory of Structuration*, Cambridge: Polity Press.

Giddens, A. (1990) *The Consequences of Modernity*, Cambridge: Polity Press.

Giddens, A. (1997) *Sociology*, 3rd edn, Cambridge: Polity Press.

Gilbert, W. (2002) 'An annotated bibliography and analysis of coaching science', unpublished report sponsored by the Research Consortium of the American Alliance for Health, Physical Education, Recreation and Dance.

Gilbert, W. and Trudel, P. (1999) 'An evaluation strategy for coach education programmes', *Journal of Sport Behavior*, 22: 234–250.

Gilbert, W. and Trudel, P. (2001) 'Learning to coach through experience: reflection in model youth sport coaches', *Journal of Teaching in Physical Education*, 21(1): 16–34.

Gilbert, W., Trudel, P., Gaumond, S. and Larocque, L. (1999) Development and application of an instrument to analyse pedagogical content interventions of ice hockey coaches, *Sociology of Sport Online*, 2(2). Available at: http://physed.otago.ac.nz/sosol/v2i2/v2i2.htm (accessed 27 August 2003).

Goodman, S. (1995) *Coaching Athletes with Disabilities: General Principles*, Canberra, Australia: Australian Sports Commission.

Grace, G. (1998) 'Critical policy scholarship: reflections on the integrity of knowledge and research', in G. Shacklock and J. Smyth (eds) *Being Reflexive in Critical Educational and Social Research*, London: Falmer Press.

Graham, G. (2001) *Teaching Children Physical Education: Becoming a Master Teacher*. Champaign, IL: Human Kinetics.

Green, K. (2000) 'Exploring the everyday "philosophies" of physical education teachers from a sociological perspective', *Sport, Education and Society*, 5: 109–129.

Green, K. (2002) 'Physical education teachers in their figurations: a sociological analysis of everyday philosophies', *Sport, Education and Society*, 7: 65–83.

Griffin, L. (1996) 'Tactical approaches to teaching games: improving net/wall game performance', *JOPERD*, 67(2): 34–37.

Griffin, L., Mitchell, S. and Oslin, J. (1997) *Teaching Sport Concepts and Skills*, Champaign, IL: Human Kinetics.

Griffin, P. (1983) 'Gymnastics is a girl's thing: student participation and interaction patterns in a middle school gymnastics unit', in T. Templin and J. Olson (eds) *Teaching Physical Education*, Champaign, IL: Human Kinetics.

Griffin, P. (1998) *Strong Women, Deep Closets: Lesbians and Homophobia in Sport*, Champaign, IL: Human Kinetics.

Hall, S. (1996) 'Introduction: who needs identity?', in S. Hall and P. DuGay (eds) *Questions of Cultural Identity*, London: Sage.

Hall, S., and DuGay, P. (eds) (1996) *Questions of Cultural Identity*, London: Sage.

Hanks, M. and Poplin, D. (1981) 'The sociology of physical disability: a review of literature and some conceptual perspectives', *Deviant Behaviour: An Interdisciplinary Journal*, 2: 309–328.

Haralambos, M. and Holborn, M. (2000) *Sociology: Themes and Perspectives*, 5th edn, London: HarperCollins.

Hardy, C. and Mawer, M. (1999) *Learning and Teaching in Physical Education*, London: Falmer Press.

Harter, S. (1997) 'Teacher and classmate influences on scholastic motivation, self-esteem, and the level of voice in adolescents', in J. Juvonen and K. Wentzel (eds) *Social Motivation: Understanding Children's School Adjustment*, Cambridge: Cambridge University Press.

Heider, F. (1958) *The Psychology of Interpersonal Relations*, New York: Wiley.

Hellison, D. and Templin, T. (1991) *A Reflective Approach to Teaching Physical Education*, Champaign, IL: Human Kinetics.

Helstad, J. (1987) 'The coach/parent/athlete relationships', *The Sport Psychologist*, 1(2), 151–160.

Heritage, J. (1984) *Garfinkel and Ethnomethodology*. Cambridge, MA: Polity Press.

Heywood, L. (1998) *Bodymakers: A Cultural Anatomy of Women's Bodybuilding*, New Brunswick, NJ: Rutgers University Press.

Hickey, C. and Fitzclarence, L. (1997) 'Masculinity, violence and football', *Changing Education*, 4(2/3): 18–21.

Hoffman, S. (1971) 'Traditional methodology: prospects for change', *Quest*, 15: 51–57.

Horne, J., Tomlinson, A. and Whannel, G. (1999) *Understanding Sport: An Introduction to the Sociological and Cultural Analysis of Sport*, London: E & FN Spon.

Hunter, L., Carlson, T. and Brooker, R. (1999) 'Research in physical and health education: recent trends and future directions', paper presented at the AARE/NZARE joint conference, Melbourne, December.

Hutzler, Y., Fliess, O., Chacham, A. and Van den Auweele, Y. (2002) 'Perspectives of children with physical disabilities on inclusion and empowerment: supporting and limiting factors', *Adapted Physical Activity Quarterly*, 19: 300–317.

Jarvie, G. (1991) 'Introduction: sport, racism and ethnicity', in G. Jarvie (ed.) *Sport, Racism and Ethnicity*, London: Falmer Press.

Jary, D., and Jary, J. (1991) *Collins Dictionary of Sociology*, London: HarperCollins.

Jobson, G. (1998) *Sailing Fundamentals: The Official Learn-to-Sail Manual of the American Sailing Association and the United States Coast Guard Auxillary*, New York: Fireside.

Johns, D.P (1998) 'Fasting and feasting: paradoxes of the sport ethic', *Sociology of Sport Journal*, 15: 41–63.

Johns, D. P. and Johns, J. (2000) 'Surveillance, subjectivism and technologies of power: an analysis of the discursive practice of high-performance sport', *International Review for the Sociology of Sport*, 35: 219–234.

Johnson, D.W. (1996) *Reaching Out: Interpersonal Effectiveness and Self-actualisation*, 6th edn, Needham Heights, MA: Allyn & Bacon.

Jones, R. L. (2000) 'Toward a sociology of coaching', in R.L. Jones and K.M. Armour (eds) *The Sociology of Sport: Theory and Practice*, London: Addison Wesley Longman.

Jones, R.L. (2001) 'Applying empowerment in coaching: some thoughts and considerations', in L. Kidman (ed.) *Innovative Coaching: Empowering your Athletes*, Christchurch, NZ: Innovative Communications.

Jones, R. L. (2002) 'The Black experience in English semi-professional soccer', *Journal of Sport and Social Issues*, 26(1): 47–65.

Jones, R.L. and Armour, K. (2000) *Sociology of Sport: Theory and Practice*, London: Addison Wesley Longman.

Jones, R.L. and Cassidy T. (1999) 'Developing coach education: the case for a more critical approach', paper presented at the Sports Science New Zealand Conference, 27–29 October, Hamilton, New Zealand.

Jones, R.L., Armour, K. and Potrac, P. A. (2002) 'Understanding the coaching process: a framework for social analysis', *Quest*, 54(1): 34–48.

Jones, R.L., Armour, K. and Potrac, P.A. (2003) 'Constructing expert knowledge: a case-study of a top level professional soccer coach', *Sport, Education and Society*, 8(2): 213–229.

Jones, R.L., Armour, K.A. and Potrac, P.A. (2004) *Sports Coaching Cultures: From Practice to Theory*, London: Routledge.

Kemmis, S. and McTaggart, R. (eds) (1992) *The Action Research Planner*, 3rd edn, Geelong, Australia: Deakin University Press.

Kemmis, S. and Stake, R. (1988) *Evaluating Curriculum*, Victoria, Australia: Deakin University Press.

Kenway, J. and Fitzclarence, L. (1997) 'Masculinity, violence and schooling: challenging "poisonous pedagogies"', *Gender and Education*, 9(1): 117–133.

Kew, F. (2000) *Sport: Social Problems and Issues*, Oxford: Butterworth-Heinemann.

Kidd, B. and Donnelly, P. (2000) 'Human rights in sport', *International Review for the Sociology of Sport*, 35: 131–148.

Kidman, L. (2001) *Developing Decision Makers: An Empowerment Approach to Coaching*, Christchurch, NZ: Innovative Press.

Kidman, L. and Hanrahan, S. (1997) *The Coaching Process: A Practical Guide to Improving your Effectiveness*, Palmerston North, NZ: Dunmore Press.

Kirk, D. (1986) 'Beyond the limits of theoretical discourse in teacher education: towards a critical pedagogy', *Teaching and Teacher Education*, 2(2): 155–167.

Kirk, D. (1992) 'Physical education, discourse, and ideology: bringing the hidden curriculum into view', *Quest*, 44: 35–56.

Kirk, D. (1998) *Schooling Bodies: School Practice and Public Discourse, 1880–1950*, London: Leicester University Press.

Kirk, D. (2000) 'A task-based approach to critical pedagogy in sport and physical education', in R.L. Jones and K.M. Armour (eds) *Sociology of Sport: Theory and Practice*, London: Longman.

Kirk, D. and Colquhoun, D. (1989) 'Healthism and physical education', *British Journal of Sociology of Education*, 10: 417–434.

Kirk, D. and Macdonald, D. (1998) 'Situated learning in physical education', *Journal of Teaching in Physical Education*, 17: 376–387.

Kirk, D. and MacPhail, A. (2000) 'Reconsidering the teaching games for understanding model from a situated learning perspective', in M.-K. Chin, L. Hensley and Y.-K. Liu (eds) *Innovation and Application of Physical Education and Sports Science in the New Millennium – An Asia-Pacific Perspective*, Hong Kong: The Hong Kong Institute of Education.

Kirk, D. and Tinning, R. (eds) (1990) *Physical Education, Curriculum and Culture: Critical Issues in the Contemporary Crisis*, London: Falmer Press.

Kirk, D., Nauright, J., Hanrahan, S., Macdonald, D. and Jobling, I. (1996) *The Sociocultural Foundations of Human Movement*, Melbourne: Macmillan.

Knudson, D. and Morrison, C. (2002) *Qualitative Analysis of Human Movement*, 2nd edn, Champaign, IL: Human Kinetics.

Kohen, D. (1994) *The Ground of Professional Ethics*, London: Routledge.

Kretchmar, R.S. (1994) *Practical Philosophy of Sport*, Champaign, IL: Human Kinetics.

Laban, R. (1948) *Modern Educational Dance*, London: Macdonald & Evans.

Langley, D. (1997) 'Exploring student skill learning: a case for investigating the subjective experience', *Quest*, 49: 142–160.

Lave, J. and Wenger, E. (1991) *Situated Learning: Legitimate Peripheral Participation*, Cambridge: Cambridge University Press.

Lawson, H. (1993) 'Dominant discourses, problem setting, and teacher education pedagogies: a critique', *Journal of Teaching in Physical Education*, 12: 149–160.

Lee, M. (ed.) (1999) *Coaching Children in Sport: Principles and Practice*, London: Routledge.

Lefrançois, G. (2000) Theories of learning, 4th edn, Belmont, CA: Wadsworth/Thomson Learning.

Lieberman, J., Houston-Wilson, C. and Kozub, F. (2002) 'Perceived barriers to including students with visual impairments in general physical education', *Adapted Physical Activity Quarterly*, 19: 364–377.

Linton, S. (1998) *Claiming Disability: Knowledge and Identity*, New York: New York University Press.

Locke, L. (1985) 'Research and the improvement in teaching: the professor as the problem', in G. Barette, R. Feingold, R. Rees and M. Pieron (eds) *Myths, Models and Methods in Sport Pedagogy*, Champaign, IL: Human Kinetics.

Lusted, D. (1986) 'Why Pedagogy?' *Screen*, 27(5): 2–14.

Lyle, J (1998) *The Coaching Process*, Leeds: National Coaching Foundation.

Lyle, J. (1999a), 'Coaching philosophy and coaching behaviour' in N. Cross and J. Lyle (eds) *The Coaching Process: Principles and Practice for Sport*, Oxford: Butterworth-Heinemann.

Lyle, J. (1999b) 'The coaching process: an overview', in N. Cross and J. Lyle (eds) *The Coaching Process: Principles and Practice for Sport*, Oxford: Butterworth-Heinemann.

Lyle, J. (2002) *Sports Coaching Concepts. A Framework for Coaches' Behaviour*, London: Routledge.

McCallister, S.G., Blinde, E. and Weiss, W.M. (2000) 'Teaching values and implementing philosophies: dilemmas of the youth sport coach', *Physical Educator*, 57: 33–45.

McCarthy, D., Jones, R. and Potrac, P. (2003). 'Constructing images and interpreting realities: the representation of black footballers in top-level English football', *International Review for the Sociology of Sport*, 38(2): 217–238.

Macdonald, D. and Tinning, R. (1995) 'Physical education teacher education and the trend to proletarianization: a case study', *Journal of Teaching in Physical Education*, 15: 98–118.

McGannon, K.R. and Mauws, M.K. (2000) 'Discursive psychology: an alternative approach for studying adherence to exercise and physical activity', *Quest*, 52: 148–165.

McKay, J., Gore, J. and Kirk, D. (1990) 'Beyond the limits of technocratic physical education,' *Quest*, 42: 52–75.

MacLean, J. and Zakrajsek, D. (1996) 'Factors considered important for evaluating Canadian university athletic coaches', *Journal of Sport Management*, 10(4): 446–462.

McMillan, B. (1991) 'All in the mind: Human learning and development from an ecological perspective', in J. Morrs and T. Linzey (eds) *Growing up: The Politics of Human Learning*, Auckland: Longman Paul.

McNamee, M. (1998) 'Celebrating trust: virtues and rules in the ethical conduct of sport coaches', in M. McNamee and J. Parry (eds) *Ethics and Sport*, London: E & FN Spon.

Markland, R. and Marinek, T. (1988) 'Descriptive analysis of coach augmented feedback given to high school varsity female volleyball players', *Journal of Teaching in Physical Education*, 7: 289–301.

Marsh, C. (1997) *Perspectives: Key Concepts for Understanding Curriculum 1*, London: Falmer Press.

Martens, R. (1988) 'Helping children become independent, responsible adults through sports', in E. Brown and C. Branta (eds) *Competitive Sport for Children and Youth: An Overview of Research and Issues*, Champaign, IL: Human Kinetics.

Martens, R. (1996) *Successful Coaching*, Champaign, IL: Human Kinetics

Martens, R. (1997) *Successful Coaching*, 2nd edn, Champaign, IL: Human Kinetics.

Mayall, B. (ed.) (1994) *Children's Childhoods: Observed and Experienced*, London: Falmer Press.

Merriam, S. (1983) 'Mentors and protégés: a critical review of the literature', *Adult Education Quarterly*, 33: 161–173.

Messner, M. A. (1996) 'Studying up on sex', *Sociology of Sport Journal*, 13(3): 221–237.

Messner, M.A., Duncan, M.C. and Jensen, K. (1993) 'Separating the men from the girls: the gendered language of televised sports', *Gender and Society*, 7: 121–137.

Metzler, M. (1979) 'The measurement of academic learning time in physical education', unpublished doctoral dissertation, Ohio State University, Ann Arbor.

Metzler, M. (1989) 'A review of research on time in sport pedagogy', *Journal of Teaching in Physical Education*, 8: 87–103.

Metzler, M. (2000) *Instructional Models for Physical Education*, Needham Heights, MA: Allyn & Bacon.

Middlethon, A. and Aggleton, P. (2001) 'Reflection and dialogue for HIV prevention among young gay men', *AIDS Care*, 13(4): 515–526.

Miedzian, M. (1991) *Boys Will Be Boys: Breaking the Link Between Masculinity and Violence*, London: Virago Press.

Miller, S. (1994) 'Inclusion of children with disabilities: can we meet the challenge?' *Physical Educator*, 51: 47–52.

Mitchell, S. (1996) 'Tactical approaches to teaching games: improving invasion game performance', *JOPERD*, 67(2): 30–33.

More, K., McGarry, T., Patridge, D. and Franks, I. (1996) 'A computer-assisted analysis of verbal coaching behavior in soccer', *Journal of Sport Behavior*, 19(4): 319–337.

Morss, J. (1991) 'After Piaget: rethinking 'cognitive development', in J. Morrs and T. Linzey, *Growing Up: The Politics of Human Learning*, Auckland: Longman Paul.

Morss, J. (1996) *Growing Critical: Alternatives to Developmental Psychology*, London: Routledge.

Morss, J.R. (2001) 'A rainbow of narratives: childhood after developmentalism', in B. van Oers (ed.) *Proceedings of EECERA Conference 2001*.

Mosston, M. (1966) *Teaching Physical Education*, Columbus, OH: Merrill.

Mosston, M. (1972) *Teaching: From Command to Discovery*, Belmont, CA: Wadsworth Publishing.

Mosston, M. (1992) 'Tug-o-war, no more: meeting teaching-learning objectives using the spectrum of teaching styles', *Journal of Physical Education, Recreation and Dance*, 56: 27–31.

New Zealand Ministry of Education (1999) *Health and Physical Education in the New Zealand Curriculum*, Wellington: Learning Media Limited.

Nicholls, J. (1984) 'Achievement motivation: conceptions of ability, subjective experience, task choice, and performance', *Psychological Review*, 91: 328–346.

Nicholls, J. (1989) *The Competitive Ethos and Democratic Education*, Cambridge, MA: Harvard University Press.

Nicholls, J. (1992) 'The general and the specific in the development and expression of achievement motivation', in G. Roberts (ed.) *Motivation in Sport and Exercise*, Champaign, IL: Human Kinetics.

Nixon, H. (1984) 'The creation of appropriate integration opportunities in sport for disabled and nondisabled people: a guide for research and action', *Sociology of Sport Journal*, 1: 184–192.

Nixon, H. and Frey, J. (1998) *A Sociology of Sport*, Boston: Wadsworth.

Oliver, M. (1990) *The Politics of Disablement*, London: Macmillan.

Oslin, J., Mitchell, S. and Griffin, L. (1998) 'The game performance assessment instrument (GPAI): development and preliminary validation', *Journal of Teaching in Physical Education*, 17: 231–243.

O'Sullivan, M., Siedentop, D. and Locke, L. (1992) 'Toward collegiality: competing viewpoints among teacher educators', *Quest*, 22: 266–280.

Oxford (1991) *Concise Oxford Dictionary*, 8th edn, London: Oxford University Press.

Paraschak, V. (2000) 'Knowing ourselves through the ''other'': indigenous peoples in sport in Canada', in R.L. Jones and K.M. Armour (eds) *Sociology of Sport: Theory and Practice*, London: Longman.

Parker, I. and Shotter, J. (eds) (1990) *Deconstructing Social Psychology*, London: Routledge.

Paul, R.W. (1993) 'Critical thinking and the way we construct the meaning of things', *General Semantics Bulletin*, 55: 24–37.

Payne, G. and Isaacs, L. (1987) *Human Motor Development: A Lifespan Approach*, Mountain View, CA: Mayfield.

Penney, D. (2000) 'Physical education . . . in what and whose interests?', in R.L. Jones and K.M. Armour (eds) *Sociology of Sport: Theory and Practice*, London: Longman.

Pere, R. (1991) *Te Wheke: A celebration of Infinite Wisdom*, Gisborne, NZ: Ao Ako Global Learning.

Placek, J. (1983) 'Conceptions of success in teaching: busy, happy and good?' in T. Templin and J. Olsen (eds.) *Teaching in Physical Education*, Champaign, IL: Human Kinetics.

Potrac, P. (2001) 'A comparative analysis of the working behaviours of top-level English and Norwegian soccer coaches', unpublished doctoral thesis, Brunel University, London.

Potrac, P., Brewer, C., Jones, R.L., Armour, K. and Hoff. J. (2000), 'Towards an holistic understanding of the coaching process', *Quest*, 52(2): 186–199.

Potrac, P., Jones, R.L and Armour, K. (2002) 'It's about getting respect: the coaching behaviours of a top-level English football coach', *Sport, Education and Society*, 7(2): 183–202.

Poynor, R. (1994) 'Building bridges between theory and practice', *ID*, 41: 40–42.

Prain, V. and Hickey, C. (1995) 'Using discourse analysis to change physical education', *Quest*, 47: 76–90.

Pronger, B. (1999) 'Fear and trembling: homophobia in men's sport', in P. White and K. Young (eds) *Sport and Gender in Canada*, Ontario: Oxford University Press.

Raffel, S. (1998) '*Revisiting Role Theory: Roles and the Problem of the Self'*, *Sociological Research Online*, 4(2). Available at: <http://www.socresonline.org.uk/4/2/raffel.html>

Readhead, L. (1997) *Men's Gymnastic Coaching Manual*, British Amateur Gymnastics Association.

Reddiford, G. (1998) 'Cheating and self-deception in sport', in M. McNamee and J. Parry (eds) *Ethics and Sport*, London: E & FN Spon.

Reel, J and Gill, D. (2001) 'Slim enough to swim? Weight pressures for competitive swimmers and coaching implications', *The Sport Journal*, 4(2). Available at: http://www.thesportjournal.org/2001Journal/spring/swimmers-weight.htm

Riemer, H. and Chelladurai, P. (1998) 'Development of the athlete satisfaction questionnaire (ASQ)', *Journal of Sport and Exercise Psychology*, 20: 127–156.

Roberts, C. (2001) 'China, china', *Ceramic Review*, 189: 40–41.

Roberts, G., Spink, K. and Pemberton, C. (1999*) Learning Experiences in Sport Psychology*, 2nd edn, Champaign, IL: Human Kinetics.

Rokeach, M. (1968) *Beliefs, Attitudes and Values*, San Francisco: Jossey-Bass.

Rokeach, M. (1973) *The Nature of Human Values*, New York: Free Press.

Rose, D. (1997) *A Multilevel Approach to the Study of Motor Control and Learning*, Boston: Allyn & Bacon.

Rossi, T. and Cassidy, T. (1999) 'Knowledgeable teachers in physical education: a view of teachers knowledge', in C. Hardy and M. Mawer (eds) *Learning and Teaching in Physical Education*, London: Falmer Press.

Rothig, P. (1985) 'Reflections on researching sport pedagogy', in G. Barette, R. Feingold, R. Rees and M. Pieron (eds) *Myths, Models and Methods in Sport Pedagogy*, Champaign, IL: Human Kinetics.

Rovegno, I. (1995) 'Theoretical perspectives on knowledge and learning and a student teacher's pedagogical content knowledge of dividing and sequencing subject matter', *Journal of Teaching in Physical Education*, 14: 284–304.

Rovegno, I. and Bandhauer, D. (1997) 'Norms of the school culture that facilitated teacher adoption and learning of a constructivist approach to physical education', *Journal of Teaching in Physical Education*, 16: 401–425.

Rovegno, I. and Kirk, D. (1995) 'Articulations and silences in socially critical work on physical education: toward a broader agenda', *Quest*, 47(4): 447–474.

Ryan, J. (1995) *Little Girls in Pretty Boxes: The Making and Breaking of Elite Gymnasts and Figure Skaters*, New York: Doubleday.

Sabo, D and Jensen, S.C. (1994) 'Seen but not heard: images of Black men in sports media', in M.A. Messner and D.F. Sabo (eds) *Sex, Violence and Power in Sports: Rethinking Masculinity*, Freedom, CA: The Crossing Press.

Sage, G. (1998) *Power and Ideology in American Sport*, 2nd edn, Champaign, IL: Human Kinetics.

Salter, G. (2000) 'Deciding between cultural identity or ''success'' in physical education: describing attitudes and values', *Journal of Physical Education New Zealand*, 33(3): 67–83.

Saury, J. and Durand, M. (1998) 'Practical knowledge in expert coaches: on-site study of coaching in sailing', *Research Quarterly in Exercise and Sport*, 69(3): 254–266.

Schempp, P. (1987) 'Research on teaching in physical education: beyond the limits of natural science', *Journal of Teaching in Physical Education*, 6(2): 111–121.

Schempp, P. (1998) 'The dynamics of human diversity in sport pedagogy scholarship', *Sociology of Sport On Line*, 1(1): Available at: http://physed.otago.ac.nz/sosol/v1i1/v1i1.htm

Schempp, P. and Oliver, K. (2000) 'Issues of equity and understanding in sport and physical education: a North American perspective', in R.L. Jones and K.M. Armour (eds) *The Sociology of Sport: Theory and Practice*, London: Addison Wesley Longman.

Schilling, C. (1993) 'The body, class and social inequalities', in J. Evans (ed.) *Equality, Education and Physical Education*, London: Falmer Press.

Schmidt, R. (1982) *Motor Control and Learning: A Behavioral Emphasis*, Champaign, IL: Human Kinetics.

Schön, D. (1983) *The Reflective Practitioner: How Professionals Think in Action*, New York: Basic Books.

Schön, D. (1987) *Educating the Reflective Practitioner: Toward a New Design for Teaching and Learning in the Professions*, San Francisco: Jossey-Bass.

Scraton, S. (1990) *Gender and Physical Education*, Geelong, Victoria: Deakin University Press.

Seaborn, P., Trudel, P. and Gilbert, W. (1998) 'Instructional content provided to female ice hockey players during games', *Applied Research in Coaching and Athletics Annual*, 13: 119–141.

Seedhouse, D. (1997) *Health Promotion. Philosophy, Prejudice and Practice*, Chichester: John Wiley & Sons.

Sheilds, D. and Bredemeier, B. (1995) *Character Development in Physical Activity*, Champaign, IL: Human Kinetics.

Sherrill, C. (1993) *Adapted Physical Activity, Recreation and Sport: Cross-disciplinary and Lifespan*, Dubuque, IA: Wm C. Brown.

Shogan, D. (1999) *The Making of High Performance Athletes: Discipline, Diversity and Ethics*, Toronto: University of Toronto Press.

Shulman, L. (1986) 'Those who understand: knowledge growth in teaching', *Educational Researcher*, 15(2): 4–14.

Siedentop, D. (1987) 'Dialogue or exorcism? A rejoinder to Schempp', *Journal of Teaching in Physical Education*, 6(4): 373–376.

Siedentop, D. and Tannehill, D. (2000) *Developing Teaching Skills in Physical Education*, 4th edn, Mountain View, CA: Mayfield.

Sinclair, D. and Vealey, R. (1989) 'Effects of coaches' expectations and feedback on the self-perceptions of athletes', *Journal of Sport Behavior*, 12(2): 77–91.

Slack, T. (2000) 'Managing voluntary sports organizations: a critique of popular trends', in R.L. Jones and K.M. Armour (eds) *Sociology of Sport: Theory and Practice*, London: Longman.

Smith, S. (1991) 'Where is the child in physical education research?' *Quest*, 43: 37–54.

Smith, A. (1999) 'Perceptions of peer relationships and physical activity participation in early adolescence', *Journal of Sport and Exercise Psychology*, 21: 329–350.

Smith, A. (2003) 'Peer relationships in physical activity contexts: a road less travelled in youth and exercise psychology research', *Psychology of Sport and Exercise*, 4: 25–39.

Smith, R. and Smoll, F. (1996) *Way to Go, Coach: A Scientifically-Proven Approach to Coaching Effectiveness*, Portola Valley, CA: Warde.

Smoll, F. (2001) 'Coach parent relationships in youth sports: increasing harmony and minimising hassle', in J. Williams (ed.), *Applied Sport Psychology: Personal Growth to Peak Performance*, 4th edn, Mountain View, CA: Mayfield.

Smyth, J. (1991) 'Problematising teaching through a ''critical'' approach to clinical supervision', *Curriculum Inquiry*, 21(3): 321–352.

Snow, C. (2001) 'Knowing what we know: children, teachers, researchers', *Educational Researcher*, 30(7): 3–9. Available at: http://www.aera.net/pubs/er/pdf/vol30_07/AERA300702.pdf

Solomon, G. and Kosmitzki, C. (1996) 'Perceptual flexibility and differential feedback among intercollegiate basketball coaches', *Journal of Sport Behaviour*, 19(2): 163–177.

Solomon, G., Striegel, D., Eliot, J., Heon, S. and Maas, J. (1996) 'The self-fulfilling prophecy in college basketball: implications for effective coaching', *Journal of Applied Sport Psychology*, 8(1): 44–59.

Solomon, G., Golden, A., Ciapponi, T. and Matine, A. (1998) 'Coach expectations and differential feedback: perceptual flexibility revisited', *Journal of Sport Behavior*, 21(3): 298–310.

Sparkes, A. and Templin, T (1992) 'Life histories and physical education teachers: exploring the meanings of marginality', in A. Sparkes (ed.) *Research in Physical Education and Sport: Exploring Alternative Visions*, London: Falmer Press.

Squires, G. (1999) *Teaching as a Professional Discipline*, London: Falmer Press.

Squires, N. and Sparkes, A. (1996) 'Circles of silence: sexual identity in physical education and sport', *Sport, Education and Society*, 1(1): 77–101.

Stainton Rogers, R. and Stainton Rogers, W. (1992) *Stories of Childhood: Shifting Agendas of Child Concern*, Buffalo, NY: University of Toronto Press.

Stenhouse, L. (1975) *An Introduction to Curriculum Research and Development*, London: Heinemann.

Stewart, C. (1993) 'Coaching behaviours: ''The way you were, or the way you wished you were'''', *The Physical Educator*, 50: 23–50.

Strean, W. (1998) 'Possibilities for Qualitative Research in Sports Psychology', *The Sport Psychologist*, 12: 333–345.

Tangaere, A. (1997) 'Mäori human development learning theory', in P. Te Whäiti, M. McCarthy and A. Durie (eds), *Mai I Rangiätea: Mäori Wellbeing and Development*, Auckland: Auckland University Press.

Templin, T., Sparkes, A., Grant, B. and Schempp, P. (1994) 'Matching the self: the paradoxical case and life history of a late career teacher/coach', *Journal of Teaching in Physical Education*, 13(3): 274–294.

Thompson, N. (1998) *Promoting Equality: Challenging Discrimination and Oppression in the Human Services*, Basingstoke: Palgrave.

Thorpe, R. (1997) *Game Sense: Developing Thinking Players* (video recording), Belconnen, ACT: Australian Sports Commission.

Tinning, R. (1988) 'Student teaching and the pedagogy of necessity', *Journal of Teaching in Physical Education*, 7(2): 82–89.

Tinning, R. (1990) *Ideology and Physical Education*, Geelong, Australia: Deakin University.

Tinning, R. (1991) 'Teacher education pedagogy: dominant discourses and the process of problem setting', *Journal of Teaching in Physical Education*, 11: 1–20.

Tinning, R. (1995) 'We have ways of making you think, or do we? Reflections on 'training' in reflective teaching', in C. Pare. (ed.) *Training of Teachers in Reflective Practice of Physical Education*, Trois-Rivieres, Quebec: Université du Quebec a Trois-Rivieres.

Tinning, R. (2002) 'Engaging Siedentopian perspectives on content knowledge for physical education', *Quest*, 21: 378–391.

Tinning, R., Kirk, D. and Evans, J. (1993) *Learning to Teach Physical Education*, London: Prentice Hall.

Tinning, R., Macdonald, D., Wright, J. and Hickey, C. (2001) *Becoming a Physical Education Teacher: Contemporary and Enduring Issues*, Frenchs Forest, Australia: Prentice Hall.

Tom, A. (1984) *Teaching as a Moral Craft*, New York: Longman.

Tonkiss, F. (1998) 'Analysing discourse', in C. Seale (ed.) *Researching Society and Culture*, London: Sage.

TV3 (2003) Interview with Daniel Carter, 24 May (video recording).

UK Sports Institute (2002) 'Leadership', paper presented at the World Class Coaching Conference, The Belfry, Birmingham, November 25–27.

Urdan, T. and Maehr, R. (1995) 'Beyond a two-goal theory of motivation and achievement: a case for social goals', *Review of Educational Research*, 65: 213–243.

Vallerand, R.J., Deci, E.L. and Ryan, R.M. (1987) 'Intrinsic motivation in sport', in K.B. Pandolf (ed.) *Exercise and Sport Science Reviews*, New York: Macmillan.

Van Manen, M. (1977) 'Linking ways of knowing with ways of being practical', *Curriculum Inquiry*, 6: 205–228.

Van Manen, M. (1995) 'On the epistemology of reflective practice', *Teachers and Teaching: Theory and Practice*, 1(1): 33–50.

Walkerdine, V. (1984) 'Development psychology and the child-centred pedagogy: the insertion of Piaget into early education', in W. Henriques, C. Hollway, C. Urwin, C. Venn and V. Walkerdine (eds) *Changing the Subject: Psychology, Social Regulation and Subjectivity*, London: Methuen.

Walkerdine, V. (1993) 'Beyond developmentalism?', *Theory and Psychology*, 3: 451–469.

Weeks, J. (1986) *Sexuality*, London: Methuen.

Weinberg, R. and Gould, D. (2003) *Foundations of Sport and Exercise Psychology*, 3rd edn, Champaign, IL: Human Kinetics.

Weiner, B. (1972) *Theories of Motivation: From Mechanics to Cognition*, Chicago: Markham.

Weiner, B. (1979) 'A theory of motivation for some classroom experiences', *Journal of Educational Psychology*, 71: 3–25.

Weiner, B. (1985) 'An attributional theory of achievement motivation and emotion', *Psychological Review*, 92: 548–573.

Weiner, B. (1986) 'An Attributional Theory of Motivation and Emotion', New York: Springer-Verlag.

Weiss M. and Ferrer-Caja, E. (2002) 'Motivational orientations and sport behaviour', in T. Horn (ed.) Advances in Sport Psychology, 2nd edn, Champaign, IL: Human Kinetics.

Weiss, M., Smith, A. and Theeboom, M. (1996) '"That's what friends are for": children's and teenagers' perceptions of peer relationships in the sport domain', Journal of Sport and Exercise Psychology, 18: 347–379.

Wentzel, K. (1999) 'Social motivational processes and interpersonal relationships: implications for understanding motivation at school', Journal of Educational Psychology, 91(1): 76–97.

Werner, P., Thorpe, R. and Bunker, D. (1996) 'Teaching games for understanding: evolution of a model', JOPERD, 67(1): 28–33.

Wheeler, G.D. (1998) 'Challenging our assumptions in the biological area of adapted physical activity: a reaction to Sheppard (1998)', Adapted Physical Activity Quarterly, 15: 236–249.

Wilcox, S. and Trudel, P. (1998) 'Constructing the coaching principles and beliefs of a youth ice hockey coach', Avante, 4: 39–66.

Wilkinson, S. (2000) 'Women with breast cancer talking causes: comparing content, biographical and discursive analyses', Feminism and Psychology, 10: 431–460.

Williams, R. (1977) Marxism and Literature, New York: Oxford University Press.

Wine, S. (2003, 23 September) 'Billy Bean: 'I'm as out as you could be'. Queery.com. Available at: http://www.queery.com/sybfusion.cgi?templ=q-item2.tpl&category=Q-indepth-feature&idx=69252

Winnick, J. (2000) Adapted Physical Education and Sport, 3rd edn, Champaign, IL: Human Kinetics.

Wood, L.A. and Kroger, R.O. (2000) Doing Discourse Analysis: Methods for Studying Action in Talk and Text, Thousand Oaks, CA: Sage.

Woog, D. (1998) Jocks: True Stories of America's Gay Male Athletes, Los Angeles: Alyson Books.

Wright, J. (1997a) 'The construction of gendered contexts in single-sex and co-educational physical education lessons', Sport, Education and Society, 2(1): 55–72.

Wright, J. (1997b) 'Fundamental motor skills testing as problematic practice: a feminist analysis', ACHPER Healthy Lifestyles Journal, 44(4): 18–29.

Wright, J. (2000) 'Bodies, meanings and movement: a comparison of the language of a physical education lesson and a Feldenkrais movement class', Sport, Education and Society, 5: 35–49.

Zakus, D.H. and Malloy, D.C. (1996) 'A critical evaluation of current pedagogical approaches in human movement studies: a suggested alternative', Quest, 48: 501–517.

Ziechner, K. (1980) 'Myths and realities: field-based experiences in preservice teacher education', Journal of Teacher Education, 31: 237–244.

Zeichner, K. (1983) 'Alternative paradigms of teacher education', Journal of Teacher Education, 34(3): 3–9.

Zeichner, K. (1987) 'Preparing reflective teachers: an overview of instructional strategies which have been employed in preservice teacher education', International Journal of Educational Research, 11(5): 565–575.

Zeichner, K. and Liston, P. (1987) 'Teaching student teachers to reflect', Harvard Educational Review, 1: 23–48.

Zeichner, K. and Liston, P. (1996) Reflective Teaching: An Introduction, New Jersey: Lawrence Erlbaum Associates.

▼ INDEX

achievement goal theory, 94–6
action research, 23
age, 87–9
Allen, J., 39–41
altruism, 168
Alvesson, M., 155
apprenticeship, 17–18
  apprentice, 17, 33
assessment, 9, 130–8
  assessing, 9
  authentic forms of assessment, 131,
    134–5
  formative assessment, 133–4
  forms of assessment, 132–3
  learning outcomes, 131, 134, 138
  purposes of assessment, 132
  self-assessment, 137
  summative assessment, 133
athlete adherence, 156
attribution theory, 93–4

Baker, B., 83, 85, 89
Bale, J., 175, 177, 179
Bandura, A., 68, 76, 80
behaviourism, 71, 76, 78–9
  behaviour modification, 73
  Law of Effect, 72
  Law of Exercise, 72
  punishment, 73
  reinforcement, 72–3
beliefs, 35
Bergmann Drewe, S., 28–9
Bill of Rights for Young Athletes, 165
Blasi, A., 169
Bloom, G., 187
body image, 157

body shape, 108, 111–13
Bourdieu, P., 60
Bredemeier, B., 162–5, 168–9
Brettschneider, W., 107
Bridges, E., 186
Brighton Declaration on Women and
  Sport, 165
Bruner, J., 73, 75–6
Burbules, N., 182
Burrows, L., 82
Burt, J., 176
Byrne, T., 101–2

Carr, D., 162–4, 166
Carr, W., 48–9
Cassidy, T., 124, 128
Chapman, G., 157
Cheffers, J., 177
Cherryholmes, C., 154, 159
Clews, G., 91
coach(es)
  effective coach, 47–8
  good coach, 47
  knowledge, 128, *see also* content
    knowledge; tacit knowledge, 6, 7,
    71, 128
  pedagogy, 175
  as a principled actor, 60
  role (of), 61, 161–3, 174–5, 178
coach education, 171, 175, 178–9, 181–9
  inadequacy of, 176, 178–9
coaching
  coach–athlete relationship, 98–101,
    155–6, 159–60, 165, 168, 172,
    175, 178, 184–5
  codes of conduct, 163–70

community of practice, 177
as a complex activity, 175–8, 181
conference, 154
context, importance of, 177–8, 185, 187–8
culture, importance of, 177
discourses of, *see* discourse
ethics, *see* ethics
goals in, 56
holistic, 9, 163, 174–89; definition of, 174–5
honesty, in, 58–9
knowledge(s), 176–8, 181–2, 184–6, 189, *see also* content knowledge
philosophy, *see* philosophy
power, 184–5
professionalization of, *see* professionalism
quality coaching, 9
as a social construction/process, 57, 175, 177
social nature of, 179
styles, 57, *see also* methods
top-level, 59–60, 62, 169, 178
Coakley, J., 108, 110–11, 113–15
cognitive evaluation theory, 96–7
Connell, R., 109–10, 176
constructivism, 71, 73, 76, 79–80
collaborative process, 73
communities of practice, 88
scaffolding, 75
situation learning theory, 88
tuakana/teina, 75–6
zone of proximal development, 74
content knowledge, 9, 123–9
conditional knowledge (CK), 123–5
curriculum content knowledge (CCK), 123–5
declarative knowledge (DK), 123–5
pedagogical content knowledge (PCK), 123–5
procedural knowledge (PK), 123–5
subject matter content knowledge (SMCK), 123–6
Côté, J., 60
Council of Europe, 165
critical tasks, 181, 183–4
Crum, B., 14–15

Culpan, I., 182
curriculum
covert curriculum, 127–8
hidden curriculum, 127–9
null curriculum, 127–8
Cushion, C., 187–8

Davies, B., 182
decision making, 6, 32, 35, 136, 137
Denison, J., 184
DePauw, K., 139–42, 145
development, 9
development, stages of, 188
power relationships, 86
developmentalism, 82–8
cultural constructions, 87
developmental language, 83
developmental norms, 85–6
deviance, 168–9
Dewey, J., 15, 73–4, 78
disability, 9, 139–45
inclusion/integration, 142–5
medical model, 140–1
social model, 141–2
discourses, 9
definition, 151–3
discourse, 151–61
enabling nature, value of, 153
examining discourse, value of, 154
of expertise, 151, 154
influence of, 153
power-laden nature, 152–3, 155–9
rationality-based, 151, 154–8, 175–6, 179
resistance to change, 160
as a social construction, 152–3
Dodds, P., 171–2
domains, 28
affective, 28, 79
cognitive, 28, 32–4, 79
psychomotor, 28, 79
Duda, J., 92–7, 101
Durand, M., 59–60, 169, 176, 178
Durie, M., 177, 180

ethics
coaching, 162–73
definitions, 163, 168
flexibility, 169

unethical behaviour, 165
virtues-based, 164, 166–73
ethnicity, *see* identity
evaluation, 130–1, *see also* assessment
Evans, J., 103, 182

Fasting, K., 114
Faulkener, G., 151–2
feedback, 9, 38–45
  athlete's interpretation, 40–1
  augmented, 39, 44
  coach's perception, 40
  gendered, 42–3
  intrinsic, 39, 44
  knowledge of performance (KP), 38–9
  knowledge of results (KR), 39
  non-verbal, 39–40, 42
  verbal, 38–40, 42–5
Fernandez-Balboa, J-M., 164, 170–3,
  182
Ferrer-Caja, E., 90, 93, 97–8, 102–3
Finch, L., 90–7
Findlay, S., 151–2
First Steps, 84
Fitzclarence, L., 109–11
Fleming, N., 116
Fletcher, S., 187–8
Foucault, M., 153, 156–7
fundamental motor skills (FMS), 83,
  85–7

Game Performance Assessment
  Instrument (GPAI), 135–7
Game Sense, 44, 88
games classification system, 126
Gavron, S., 139, 141
Geertz, C., 179
gender, *see* identity
Giddens, A., 67, 113, 126
Gilbert, W., 16, 27, 38, 67, 123, 130–1,
  179
Goodman, S., 143
Gould, D., 90–5, 104–5
Graham, G., 99–100, 103, 105
Green, K., 54, 57
Griffin, L., 114, 135
Gross, J., 91
guardians, *see* parents
gymnastics, 157

Habermas, J., 168
Hallinger, P., 186
Hanrahan, S., 55–6, 59, 61
Harter, S., 102
Hauora, 180
health, 179–80
hegemony, 108
  hegemonic masculinity, 109–11
Heim, R., 107
Hickey, C., 109–11, 154–5, 160
holistic, *see* coaching

identity, 107–8
  ethnic, 115–16
  gendered, 108–13
  sexualized, 113–15
imitation, *see* observational learning

Johns, D., 111–12, 151–2, 154–60
Johns, J., 151–2, 154–60
Johnson, D., 172
Jones, R., 48, 50–1, 99–101, 103, 106,
  110, 115, 117
journal, 137

Kenway, J., 109
Kidman, L., 5, 7, 13–14, 55–6, 59, 61,
  126
kinesiology, 177
Kirk, D., 17, 27, 29–30, 129, 135,
  152–4, 156–7, 183–4
Kretchmar, S., 54–6, 60, 62, 163–4
Kroger, R., 152–3

Langley, D., 175, 177, 179, 184–5
Lave, J., 88
learning, 68, 81, 177, 183, 186, 189, *see
  also* behaviourism; constructivism
  consequences for the athlete, 78–80
  learning process, 9
  observational learning, 76, 80
Locke, L., 7, 176
Lusted, D., 9, 126
  pedagogical process, *see* pedagogy
Lyle, J., 18–19, 28, 46, 48, 54–60,
  164–5, 178

McCallister, S., 56–7, 162
Macdonald, D., 175–6

McGannon, K., 151–4, 158, 160
McNamee, M., 164, 166–70
Mäori, 175, 177, 180
Martens, R., 178
Mauws, M., 151–4, 158, 160
mentoring, 181, 183, 187–9
  definition of, 187
methods, 9, 26–37
  consequences of, 33–5
  direct, 29–30, 32–6
  guided discovery, 29, 31–5
  hidden meanings of, 36
  problem-solving, 29, 32–6
  reciprocal, 29, 31, 34–5, 75–6,
    see also tuakana/teina
  task, 29–30, 33–5
Metzler, M., 123–5, 129, 135, 137
Miedzian, M., 109–10
modelling, see observational learning
morals, see ethics
Morss, J., 83
Mosston, M., 27, 29, 35
motivation, 9
  direction of effort, 92
  direction of intensity, 92
  extrinsic, 92, 96
  intrinsic, 92, 96

narratives, 181, 183–5
national coaching foundation,
  165
New Zealand, 175, 177, 180
Nixon, H., 139–41, 143–5

Oliver, K., 110, 113, 115
Oresick, R., 169

parents, 101–2
Paul, R., 182
Pavlov, I., 71
pedagogy, 9, 175, 189
  coaches, 175
  craft pedagogies, 17
  critical tasks, see critical tasks
  mentoring, see mentoring
  narratives, see narratives
  of necessity, 78
  pedagogical process, see Lusted, D.
  performance, 154–6, 160

problem-based learning (PBL),
  see problem-based learning
peers, 102–4
Penney, D., 152–4, 160
Pere, R., 180
philosophy (coaching), 9, 53–62
  definition, 55
  functional (flexible) philosophies,
    59–62, 169, 182, 187
  Habermas, see Habermas, J.
  non-relevance, 53, 56–8, 166
  problematizing coaching philosophies,
    56–9
  process of developing one, 60–2
  value of, 54–5, 59, 62
Piaget, J., 73
portfolio, 137
Potrac, P., 99–100, 175, 182
Prain, V., 154–5, 160
problem-based learning (PBL), 181, 183,
  186–7
professionalism, 18–19
Pronger, B., 114

quality coach, 33, 46, 48–52
  instrumental characteristics, 49–50,
    52
  intrinsic characteristics, 50, 52
quality of mind, 182–3

Raffel, S., 59
reasonableness, 182
Reddiford, G., 166–7, 169
reflection, 6–8, 13–25, 171–3,
  186–8
  benefits of reflection, 17–18
  critical level of reflection, 21–2, 24
  practical level of reflection, 21–2, 24
  reflection-in-action, 14, 16–18, 20
  reflection-on-action, 16–17, 20, 24
  reflective, 7, 14, 16, 18–21, 24–5, 44,
    48, 51
  technical level of reflection, 21
  unreflective, 7
Reinhart, R., 184
Roberts, G., 103
Rokeach, M., 168–9
Rossi, T., 126, 128
Rovegno, I., 88

Sage, G., 108–9
Salter, G., 104
Sang, J., 175, 177, 179
Saury, J., 59–60, 169, 176, 178
Schempp, P., 110, 113, 115, 175, 177–8
Schön, D., 14–16, 18–21, 24, 154, 181, 187
sexuality, *see* identity
Sheilds, D., 162–5, 168–9
Sherrill, C., 142
Shogan, D., 160, 176
Shulman, L., 123–6, 129
Siedentop, D., 7, 26, 132–4
Skinner, B., 71–2, 76
Slack, T., 155
Smith, A., 102
Smoll, F., 90, 102
socialization, 171
Sparkes, A., 176
sport
    builds character, 162–4, 171
    culture, influence of, 177
    mirror of society, 164
sportsmanship, 169
stereotyping, 171
style, *see* methods

Templin, T., 176
Thompson, N., 140–1

Thorndike, E., 71
Thorpe, R., 126, *see also Game Sense*
Tinning, R., 7, 18, 26, 33, 35–6, 51, 78, 108–9, 115–16, 126, 128, 132–3, 135, 152, 154, 175–6
Trudel, P., 53, 55, 57–8, 179

UK Sports Institute, 154
unethical behaviour, 165

Van Manen, M., 21–2
Vygotsky, L., 73–4

Walkerdine, V., 84–5
Watson, J., 71
Weinberg, R., 90–5, 104–5
Weiss, M., 90, 93, 97–8, 102–3
Wentzel, K., 98
Wilcox, S., 53, 55, 57–8
Willmott, H., 155
Winnick, J., 143
Wood, L., 152–3
World Health Organisation (WHO), 175, 179–80
Wright, J., 42–3, 154, 159

Zeichner, K., 15, 21–2, 78